28 DAYS
Walking Daily with My Lord

Spend 28 Days Each Month
Being Transformed
As a Follower of Christ

by David E. Sproule, II

28 Days: Walking Daily with My Lord

ISBN: 9781790982905

Preface

The content of this book was first published and used at the Palm Beach Lakes church of Christ in West Palm Beach, Florida. We set as our annual theme one year—**"28 Days: Walking Daily with the Lord."** We wanted a theme that would be very practical and provide something for each member to **personally do** during the month that would draw each of us closer to the Lord and closer to each other. Small booklets were passed out each month for the members to use as their guide to walk daily with the Lord for 28 days.

As the benefit of this endeavor began to manifest itself within the congregation and the lives of the members, it became evident that this material would be beneficial to congregations and brethren in other places, as well. Thus, modifications were made to the material (in an effort to generalize some of the content), so that it could be used by any congregation anywhere. This book can be utilized effectively **by individual Christians** who want to improve and strengthen their daily walk with the Lord. It can also be utilized effectively by **an entire congregation** that wants to work together in being transformed as followers of Christ.

I want to thank my two friends and wonderful coworkers, Dan Jenkins and Josh Blackmer, for their helpful suggestions throughout the process of compiling each month's 28 Days. I love and appreciate you both, and enjoy immensely the opportunity to work alongside each of you in the Lord's kingdom.

For any and every good that comes from this book, to God be the glory!

Introduction

In a warm environment, it takes about 28 days for a monarch butterfly to complete its metamorphosis from an egg laid by the female on a milkweed leaf (4 days), through the caterpillar or larva stage (14 days), into the pupa or chrysalis (for about 10 days), to then emerge as a beautiful butterfly that captures our eyes and our wonder. Each stage along the process is critical, for complete metamorphosis cannot take place if the growth is hindered at any stage.

Coincidentally, many workout regimens and diet programs follow a 28-day cycle and commitment. The promise of many such programs is that following their routine for 28 days will make you a new person. The premise behind such programs is that if you do something for 28 consecutive days then it will become a habit. Isn't it interesting that these kinds of programs are simply following God's design for metamorphosis—28 days to complete transformation?

All of this begs the question—what does this have to do with being a Christian? Children of God are called upon to go through a metamorphosis. The New Testament teaches, "And do not be conformed to this world, but **be transformed** by the renewing of your mind, that you may prove what is that good and acceptable and perfect will of God" (Rom. 12:2). Look carefully at the spelling of the Greek verb for "be transformed" in this verse—*metamorphoo*. God designed a metamorphosis for Christians. Note a few points:

1. True and full transformation is **CHANGE INWARDLY**. The focus in this passage is on an inward transformation of character, which will be manifested in one's outward conduct.

2. True and full transformation is **COMMANDED BY GOD**. The verb in this text is an imperative, emphasizing that this is not optional or merely a heavenly suggestion or wish.

3. True and full transformation is **CULTIVATED BY GOD**. The verb is passive voice, emphasizing that the change is being done TO us and is something with which we need to let God help us.

4. True and full transformation is **CONVERSION INTO THE IMAGE OF CHRIST**. The compound verb consists of *meta* ("change") and *morphe* ("form"), thus a change into another form, whereby one is being "transformed into" the image of Christ (2 Cor. 3:18).

5. True and full transformation is a **CONTINUOUS PROCESS**. The present tense verb emphasizes an ongoing process that never ceases and never finishes. It is continual and repeated effort that creates a habitual walk of life.

The monarch butterfly does not fly away in its beauty until after 28 days of a metamorphosis. Workout programs know that true success (i.e., transformation) will only come after 28 days of dedication. Does this have any application to the metamorphosis/transformation process that God has in mind for His children?

What if you spent 28 days focused on one facet of your walk with the Lord? Would that make a difference? Would that make you stronger, more effective, more enthusiastic and more steadfast in your relationship with Him? What if you then spent another 28 days focused on another facet of your walk with the Lord? God calls upon us to go through a complete transformation! He knows that the longer we engage in an activity, the more it becomes a part of us!

How would you describe your daily walk with the Lord? Would you be interested in taking 28 days each month for one year to engage in a spiritual workout that has the potential to transform your faith and your relationship with your Lord?

This book is designed to do just that! The focus is on practical, tangible things that we can do over a 28-day period each month, in various aspects of our Christian walk, to transform us inwardly into the image of Christ. So take the 28-day challenge! See where you are at the end of each month! See where you are at the end of the year!

One great feature of the twelve 28-Day schedules in this book is that they can actually be done any month of the year, and they can be repeated as many times (over as many years) as a Christian finds to be beneficial in his daily walk. Another feature is that everything in this book can be done by every Christian—there is nothing too hard or too complex, and there is nothing that is applicable to only a certain segment of the Lord's church. Every Christian can do everything in this book, and every Christian can benefit from it in a very personal way.

Let's spend 28 days each month being transformed by our heavenly Father into the image of our Savior, Jesus Christ!

Table of Contents

Walking Daily with My Lord

JANUARY:

28DAYS

To Grow in Praise of God

---

*"I will praise You,
O Lord my God, with all my heart,
And I will glorify Your name
forevermore"
(Psalm 86:12).*

28DAYS To Grow in Praise of God

Start your year off right!

Focus on God!

Focus on the glory of God!

Focus on praising God!

The Book of Psalms was God's devotional book used by those in Old Testament times to worship and praise the Almighty God!

Reading through the book of Psalms:

- Reveals how much **we need God!**

- Draws our hearts into a **deeper reliance upon God!**

- Shows us **how worthy God is** of our praise!

- Prompts us to **honor and praise** our God!

The next 28 days can set the tone for the rest of your year!

- Read a designated psalm each day.

- Meditate on that psalm's relevance to your daily life.

- As a result, grow and grow in your praise of God!

Let's grow in praise by reading 28 psalms in 28 days...

☑ 1. Psalm 1	☑ 8. Psalm 27	☐ 15. Psalm 71	☐ 22. Psalm 111
☑ 2. Psalm 5	☐ 9. Psalm 30	☐ 16. Psalm 84	☐ 23. Psalm 115
☑ 3. Psalm 8	☐ 10. Psalm 34	☐ 17. Psalm 90	☐ 24. Psalm 121
☑ 4. Psalm 18	☐ 11. Psalm 37	☐ 18. Psalm 95	☐ 25. Psalm 139
☑ 5. Psalm 19	☐ 12. Psalm 46	☐ 19. Psalm 100	☐ 26. Psalm 141
☑ 6. Psalm 22	☐ 13. Psalm 51	☐ 20. Psalm 103	☐ 27. Psalm 145
☑ 7. Psalm 23	☐ 14. Psalm 56	☐ 21. Psalm 104	☐ 28. Psalm 148

Day #1 to Grow in Praise of God

"I will praise You, O Lord my God, with all my heart,
And I will glorify Your name forevermore"
(Psalm 86:12).

Read Psalm 1

The Way of the Righteous and
the End of the Ungodly

1. Before you read this psalm, take a moment to clear your mind, devote yourself 100% to the text and ask for God's blessings on your reading. Read the four questions below before reading the psalm.

2. What would you say is the fundamental message of this psalm? (In other words, why did God put it in the Bible for you to read?)

3. What is one thing in this psalm that challenges you and motivates you to want to walk closer to the Lord?

4. What one thing can you take from this psalm today and make immediate application to your life, so that your walk with the Lord is closer and stronger?

5. What one thing can you take from this psalm today and share with others to benefit them in their walk with the Lord?

One more thing: Pray about this today!

Day #2 to Grow in Praise of God

"I will praise You, O Lord my God, with all my heart,
And I will glorify Your name forevermore"
(Psalm 86:12).

Read Psalm 5
A Prayer for Guidance

1. Before you read this psalm, take a moment to clear your mind, devote yourself 100% to the text and ask for God's blessings on your reading. Read the four questions below before reading the psalm.

2. What would you say is the fundamental message of this psalm? (In other words, why did God put it in the Bible for you to read?)

3. What is one thing in this psalm that challenges you and motivates you to want to walk closer to the Lord?

4. What one thing can you take from this psalm today and make immediate application to your life, so that your walk with the Lord is closer and stronger?

5. What one thing can you take from this psalm today and share with others to benefit them in their walk with the Lord?

One more thing: Pray about this today!

Day #3 to Grow in Praise of God

"I will praise You, O Lord my God, with all my heart,
And I will glorify Your name forevermore"
(Psalm 86:12).

Read Psalm 8
The Glory of the Lord
in Creation

1. Before you read this psalm, take a moment to clear your mind, devote yourself 100% to the text and ask for God's blessings on your reading. Read the four questions below before reading the psalm.

2. What would you say is the fundamental message of this psalm? (In other words, why did God put it in the Bible for you to read?)

3. What is one thing in this psalm that challenges you and motivates you to want to walk closer to the Lord?

4. What one thing can you take from this psalm today and make immediate application to your life, so that your walk with the Lord is closer and stronger?

5. What one thing can you take from this psalm today and share with others to benefit them in their walk with the Lord?

One more thing: Pray about this today!

Day #4 to Grow in Praise of God

"I will praise You, O Lord my God, with all my heart,
And I will glorify Your name forevermore"
(Psalm 86:12).

Read Psalm 18
God, the Sovereign Savior

1. Before you read this psalm, take a moment to clear your mind, devote yourself 100% to the text and ask for God's blessings on your reading. Read the four questions below before reading the psalm.

2. What would you say is the fundamental message of this psalm? (In other words, why did God put it in the Bible for you to read?)

3. What is one thing in this psalm that challenges you and motivates you to want to walk closer to the Lord?

4. What one thing can you take from this psalm today and make immediate application to your life, so that your walk with the Lord is closer and stronger?

5. What one thing can you take from this psalm today and share with others to benefit them in their walk with the Lord?

One more thing: Pray about this today!

Day #5 to Grow in Praise of God

*"I will praise You, O Lord my God, with all my heart,
And I will glorify Your name forevermore"
(Psalm 86:12).*

Read Psalm 19
The Perfect Revelation of the Lord

1. Before you read this psalm, take a moment to clear your mind, devote yourself 100% to the text and ask for God's blessings on your reading. Read the four questions below before reading the psalm.

2. What would you say is the fundamental message of this psalm? (In other words, why did God put it in the Bible for you to read?)

3. What is one thing in this psalm that challenges you and motivates you to want to walk closer to the Lord?

4. What one thing can you take from this psalm today and make immediate application to your life, so that your walk with the Lord is closer and stronger?

5. What one thing can you take from this psalm today and share with others to benefit them in their walk with the Lord?

One more thing: Pray about this today!

Day #6 to Grow in Praise of God

"I will praise You, O Lord my God, with all my heart,
And I will glorify Your name forevermore"
(Psalm 86:12).

Read Psalm 22
The Suffering, Praise and
Posterity of the Messiah

1. Before you read this psalm, take a moment to clear your mind, devote yourself 100% to the text and ask for God's blessings on your reading. Read the four questions below before reading the psalm.

2. What would you say is the fundamental message of this psalm? (In other words, why did God put it in the Bible for you to read?)

3. What is one thing in this psalm that challenges you and motivates you to want to walk closer to the Lord?

4. What one thing can you take from this psalm today and make immediate application to your life, so that your walk with the Lord is closer and stronger?

5. What one thing can you take from this psalm today and share with others to benefit them in their walk with the Lord?

One more thing: Pray about this today!

"I will praise You, O Lord my God, with all my heart,
And I will glorify Your name forevermore"
(Psalm 86:12).

Read Psalm 23

The Lord,
the Shepherd of His People

1. Before you read this psalm, take a moment to clear your mind, devote yourself 100% to the text and ask for God's blessings on your reading. Read the four questions below before reading the psalm.

2. What would you say is the fundamental message of this psalm? (In other words, why did God put it in the Bible for you to read?)

3. What is one thing in this psalm that challenges you and motivates you to want to walk closer to the Lord?

4. What one thing can you take from this psalm today and make immediate application to your life, so that your walk with the Lord is closer and stronger?

5. What one thing can you take from this psalm today and share with others to benefit them in their walk with the Lord?

One more thing: Pray about this today!

Day #8 to Grow in Praise of God

*"I will praise You, O Lord my God, with all my heart,
And I will glorify Your name forevermore"
(Psalm 86:12).*

Read Psalm 27
An Exuberant Declaration of Faith

1. Before you read this psalm, take a moment to clear your mind, devote yourself 100% to the text and ask for God's blessings on your reading. Read the four questions below before reading the psalm.

2. What would you say is the fundamental message of this psalm? (In other words, why did God put it in the Bible for you to read?)

3. What is one thing in this psalm that challenges you and motivates you to want to walk closer to the Lord?

4. What one thing can you take from this psalm today and make immediate application to your life, so that your walk with the Lord is closer and stronger?

5. What one thing can you take from this psalm today and share with others to benefit them in their walk with the Lord?

One more thing: Pray about this today!

Day #9 to Grow in Praise of God

"I will praise You, O Lord my God, with all my heart,
And I will glorify Your name forevermore"
(Psalm 86:12).

Read Psalm 30
The Blessedness of
Answered Prayer

1. Before you read this psalm, take a moment to clear your mind, devote yourself 100% to the text and ask for God's blessings on your reading. Read the four questions below before reading the psalm.

2. What would you say is the fundamental message of this psalm? (In other words, why did God put it in the Bible for you to read?)

3. What is one thing in this psalm that challenges you and motivates you to want to walk closer to the Lord?

4. What one thing can you take from this psalm today and make immediate application to your life, so that your walk with the Lord is closer and stronger?

5. What one thing can you take from this psalm today and share with others to benefit them in their walk with the Lord?

One more thing: Pray about this today!

Day #10 to Grow in Praise of God

*"I will praise You, O Lord my God, with all my heart,
And I will glorify Your name forevermore"
(Psalm 86:12).*

Read Psalm 34
The Happiness of Those
Who Trust in God

1. Before you read this psalm, take a moment to clear your mind, devote yourself 100% to the text and ask for God's blessings on your reading. Read the four questions below before reading the psalm.

2. What would you say is the fundamental message of this psalm? (In other words, why did God put it in the Bible for you to read?)

3. What is one thing in this psalm that challenges you and motivates you to want to walk closer to the Lord?

4. What one thing can you take from this psalm today and make immediate application to your life, so that your walk with the Lord is closer and stronger?

5. What one thing can you take from this psalm today and share with others to benefit them in their walk with the Lord?

One more thing: Pray about this today!

Day #11 to Grow in Praise of God

"I will praise You, O Lord my God, with all my heart,
And I will glorify Your name forevermore"
(Psalm 86:12).

Read Psalm 37
The Heritage of the Righteous
and the Calamity of the Wicked

1. Before you read this psalm, take a moment to clear your mind, devote yourself 100% to the text and ask for God's blessings on your reading. Read the four questions below before reading the psalm.

2. What would you say is the fundamental message of this psalm? (In other words, why did God put it in the Bible for you to read?)

3. What is one thing in this psalm that challenges you and motivates you to want to walk closer to the Lord?

4. What one thing can you take from this psalm today and make immediate application to your life, so that your walk with the Lord is closer and stronger?

5. What one thing can you take from this psalm today and share with others to benefit them in their walk with the Lord?

One more thing: Pray about this today!

Day #12 to Grow in Praise of God

"I will praise You, O Lord my God, with all my heart,
And I will glorify Your name forevermore"
(Psalm 86:12).

Read Psalm 46
God, the Refuge of His People
and Conqueror of the Nations

1. Before you read this psalm, take a moment to clear your mind, devote yourself 100% to the text and ask for God's blessings on your reading. Read the four questions below before reading the psalm.

2. What would you say is the fundamental message of this psalm? (In other words, why did God put it in the Bible for you to read?)

3. What is one thing in this psalm that challenges you and motivates you to want to walk closer to the Lord?

4. What one thing can you take from this psalm today and make immediate application to your life, so that your walk with the Lord is closer and stronger?

5. What one thing can you take from this psalm today and share with others to benefit them in their walk with the Lord?

One more thing: Pray about this today!

Day #13 to Grow in Praise of God

"I will praise You, O Lord my God, with all my heart,
And I will glorify Your name forevermore"
(Psalm 86:12).

Read Psalm 51
A Prayer of Repentance

1. Before you read this psalm, take a moment to clear your mind, devote yourself 100% to the text and ask for God's blessings on your reading. Read the four questions below before reading the psalm.

2. What would you say is the fundamental message of this psalm? (In other words, why did God put it in the Bible for you to read?)

3. What is one thing in this psalm that challenges you and motivates you to want to walk closer to the Lord?

4. What one thing can you take from this psalm today and make immediate application to your life, so that your walk with the Lord is closer and stronger?

5. What one thing can you take from this psalm today and share with others to benefit them in their walk with the Lord?

One more thing: Pray about this today!

Day #14 to Grow in Praise of God

"I will praise You, O Lord my God, with all my heart,
And I will glorify Your name forevermore"
(Psalm 86:12).

Read Psalm 56
Prayer for Relief from Tormentors

1. Before you read this psalm, take a moment to clear your mind, devote yourself 100% to the text and ask for God's blessings on your reading. Read the four questions below before reading the psalm.

2. What would you say is the fundamental message of this psalm? (In other words, why did God put it in the Bible for you to read?)

3. What is one thing in this psalm that challenges you and motivates you to want to walk closer to the Lord?

4. What one thing can you take from this psalm today and make immediate application to your life, so that your walk with the Lord is closer and stronger?

5. What one thing can you take from this psalm today and share with others to benefit them in their walk with the Lord?

One more thing: Pray about this today!

Day #15 to Grow in Praise of God

"I will praise You, O Lord my God, with all my heart,
And I will glorify Your name forevermore"
(Psalm 86:12).

Read Psalm 71
God, the Rock of Salvation

1. Before you read this psalm, take a moment to clear your mind, devote yourself 100% to the text and ask for God's blessings on your reading. Read the four questions below before reading the psalm.

2. What would you say is the fundamental message of this psalm? (In other words, why did God put it in the Bible for you to read?)

3. What is one thing in this psalm that challenges you and motivates you to want to walk closer to the Lord?

4. What one thing can you take from this psalm today and make immediate application to your life, so that your walk with the Lord is closer and stronger?

5. What one thing can you take from this psalm today and share with others to benefit them in their walk with the Lord?

One more thing: Pray about this today!

Day #16 to Grow in Praise of God

"I will praise You, O Lord my God, with all my heart,
And I will glorify Your name forevermore"
(Psalm 86:12).

Read Psalm 84
The Blessedness of Dwelling
in the House of God

1. Before you read this psalm, take a moment to clear your mind, devote yourself 100% to the text and ask for God's blessings on your reading. Read the four questions below before reading the psalm.

2. What would you say is the fundamental message of this psalm? (In other words, why did God put it in the Bible for you to read?)

3. What is one thing in this psalm that challenges you and motivates you to want to walk closer to the Lord?

4. What one thing can you take from this psalm today and make immediate application to your life, so that your walk with the Lord is closer and stronger?

5. What one thing can you take from this psalm today and share with others to benefit them in their walk with the Lord?

One more thing: Pray about this today!

Day #17 to Grow in Praise of God

"I will praise You, O Lord my God, with all my heart,
And I will glorify Your name forevermore"
(Psalm 86:12).

Read Psalm 90
The Eternity of God,
and Man's Frailty

1. Before you read this psalm, take a moment to clear your mind, devote yourself 100% to the text and ask for God's blessings on your reading. Read the four questions below before reading the psalm.

2. What would you say is the fundamental message of this psalm? (In other words, why did God put it in the Bible for you to read?)

3. What is one thing in this psalm that challenges you and motivates you to want to walk closer to the Lord?

4. What one thing can you take from this psalm today and make immediate application to your life, so that your walk with the Lord is closer and stronger?

5. What one thing can you take from this psalm today and share with others to benefit them in their walk with the Lord?

One more thing: Pray about this today!

Day #18 to Grow in Praise of God

"I will praise You, O Lord my God, with all my heart,
And I will glorify Your name forevermore"
(Psalm 86:12).

Read Psalm 95
A Call to Worship and Obedience

1. Before you read this psalm, take a moment to clear your mind, devote yourself 100% to the text and ask for God's blessings on your reading. Read the four questions below before reading the psalm.

2. What would you say is the fundamental message of this psalm? (In other words, why did God put it in the Bible for you to read?)

3. What is one thing in this psalm that challenges you and motivates you to want to walk closer to the Lord?

4. What one thing can you take from this psalm today and make immediate application to your life, so that your walk with the Lord is closer and stronger?

5. What one thing can you take from this psalm today and share with others to benefit them in their walk with the Lord?

One more thing: Pray about this today!

Day #19 to Grow in Praise of God

"I will praise You, O Lord my God, with all my heart,
And I will glorify Your name forevermore"
(Psalm 86:12).

Read Psalm 100

A Song of Praise
for the Lord's Faithfulness to His People

1. Before you read this psalm, take a moment to clear your mind, devote yourself 100% to the text and ask for God's blessings on your reading. Read the four questions below before reading the psalm.

2. What would you say is the fundamental message of this psalm? (In other words, why did God put it in the Bible for you to read?)

3. What is one thing in this psalm that challenges you and motivates you to want to walk closer to the Lord?

4. What one thing can you take from this psalm today and make immediate application to your life, so that your walk with the Lord is closer and stronger?

5. What one thing can you take from this psalm today and share with others to benefit them in their walk with the Lord?

One more thing: Pray about this today!

Day #20 to Grow in Praise of God

"I will praise You, O Lord my God, with all my heart,
And I will glorify Your name forevermore"
(Psalm 86:12).

Read Psalm 103
Praise for the Lord's Mercies

1. Before you read this psalm, take a moment to clear your mind, devote yourself 100% to the text and ask for God's blessings on your reading. Read the four questions below before reading the psalm.

2. What would you say is the fundamental message of this psalm? (In other words, why did God put it in the Bible for you to read?)

3. What is one thing in this psalm that challenges you and motivates you to want to walk closer to the Lord?

4. What one thing can you take from this psalm today and make immediate application to your life, so that your walk with the Lord is closer and stronger?

5. What one thing can you take from this psalm today and share with others to benefit them in their walk with the Lord?

One more thing: Pray about this today!

Day #21 to Grow in Praise of God

"I will praise You, O Lord my God, with all my heart,
And I will glorify Your name forevermore"
(Psalm 86:12).

Read Psalm 104

Praise to the Sovereign Lord
for His Creation and Providence

1. Before you read this psalm, take a moment to clear your mind, devote yourself 100% to the text and ask for God's blessings on your reading. Read the four questions below before reading the psalm.

2. What would you say is the fundamental message of this psalm? (In other words, why did God put it in the Bible for you to read?)

3. What is one thing in this psalm that challenges you and motivates you to want to walk closer to the Lord?

4. What one thing can you take from this psalm today and make immediate application to your life, so that your walk with the Lord is closer and stronger?

5. What one thing can you take from this psalm today and share with others to benefit them in their walk with the Lord?

One more thing: Pray about this today!

Day #22 to Grow in Praise of God

"I will praise You, O Lord my God, with all my heart,
And I will glorify Your name forevermore"
(Psalm 86:12).

Read Psalm 111

Praise to God
for His Faithfulness and Justice

1. Before you read this psalm, take a moment to clear your mind, devote yourself 100% to the text and ask for God's blessings on your reading. Read the four questions below before reading the psalm.

2. What would you say is the fundamental message of this psalm? (In other words, why did God put it in the Bible for you to read?)

3. What is one thing in this psalm that challenges you and motivates you to want to walk closer to the Lord?

4. What one thing can you take from this psalm today and make immediate application to your life, so that your walk with the Lord is closer and stronger?

5. What one thing can you take from this psalm today and share with others to benefit them in their walk with the Lord?

One more thing: Pray about this today!

Day #23 to Grow in Praise of God

"I will praise You, O Lord my God, with all my heart,
And I will glorify Your name forevermore"
(Psalm 86:12).

Read Psalm 115
The Futility of Idols
and the Trustworthiness of God

1. Before you read this psalm, take a moment to clear your mind, devote yourself 100% to the text and ask for God's blessings on your reading. Read the four questions below before reading the psalm.

2. What would you say is the fundamental message of this psalm? (In other words, why did God put it in the Bible for you to read?)

3. What is one thing in this psalm that challenges you and motivates you to want to walk closer to the Lord?

4. What one thing can you take from this psalm today and make immediate application to your life, so that your walk with the Lord is closer and stronger?

5. What one thing can you take from this psalm today and share with others to benefit them in their walk with the Lord?

One more thing: Pray about this today!

Day #24 to Grow in Praise of God

"I will praise You, O Lord my God, with all my heart,
And I will glorify Your name forevermore"
(Psalm 86:12).

Read Psalm 121
God, the Help of Those Who Seek Him

1. Before you read this psalm, take a moment to clear your mind, devote yourself 100% to the text and ask for God's blessings on your reading. Read the four questions below before reading the psalm.

2. What would you say is the fundamental message of this psalm? (In other words, why did God put it in the Bible for you to read?)

3. What is one thing in this psalm that challenges you and motivates you to want to walk closer to the Lord?

4. What one thing can you take from this psalm today and make immediate application to your life, so that your walk with the Lord is closer and stronger?

5. What one thing can you take from this psalm today and share with others to benefit them in their walk with the Lord?

One more thing: Pray about this today!

"I will praise You, O Lord my God, with all my heart,
And I will glorify Your name forevermore"
(Psalm 86:12).

Read Psalm 139
God's Perfect Knowledge of Man

1. Before you read this psalm, take a moment to clear your mind, devote yourself 100% to the text and ask for God's blessings on your reading. Read the four questions below before reading the psalm.

2. What would you say is the fundamental message of this psalm? (In other words, why did God put it in the Bible for you to read?)

3. What is one thing in this psalm that challenges you and motivates you to want to walk closer to the Lord?

4. What one thing can you take from this psalm today and make immediate application to your life, so that your walk with the Lord is closer and stronger?

5. What one thing can you take from this psalm today and share with others to benefit them in their walk with the Lord?

One more thing: Pray about this today!

Day #26 to Grow in Praise of God

"I will praise You, O Lord my God, with all my heart,
And I will glorify Your name forevermore"
(Psalm 86:12).

Read Psalm 141
Prayer for Safekeeping from Wickedness

1. Before you read this psalm, take a moment to clear your mind, devote yourself 100% to the text and ask for God's blessings on your reading. Read the four questions below before reading the psalm.

2. What would you say is the fundamental message of this psalm? (In other words, why did God put it in the Bible for you to read?)

3. What is one thing in this psalm that challenges you and motivates you to want to walk closer to the Lord?

4. What one thing can you take from this psalm today and make immediate application to your life, so that your walk with the Lord is closer and stronger?

5. What one thing can you take from this psalm today and share with others to benefit them in their walk with the Lord?

One more thing: Pray about this today!

Day #27 to Grow in Praise of God

"I will praise You, O Lord my God, with all my heart,
And I will glorify Your name forevermore"
(Psalm 86:12).

Read Psalm 145
A Song of God's Majesty and Love

1. Before you read this psalm, take a moment to clear your mind, devote yourself 100% to the text and ask for God's blessings on your reading. Read the four questions below before reading the psalm.

2. What would you say is the fundamental message of this psalm? (In other words, why did God put it in the Bible for you to read?)

3. What is one thing in this psalm that challenges you and motivates you to want to walk closer to the Lord?

4. What one thing can you take from this psalm today and make immediate application to your life, so that your walk with the Lord is closer and stronger?

5. What one thing can you take from this psalm today and share with others to benefit them in their walk with the Lord?

One more thing: Pray about this today!

Day #28 to Grow in Praise of God

"I will praise You, O Lord my God, with all my heart,
And I will glorify Your name forevermore"
(Psalm 86:12).

Read Psalm 148
Praise to the Lord from Creation

1. Before you read this psalm, take a moment to clear your mind, devote yourself 100% to the text and ask for God's blessings on your reading. Read the four questions below before reading the psalm.

2. What would you say is the fundamental message of this psalm? (In other words, why did God put it in the Bible for you to read?)

3. What is one thing in this psalm that challenges you and motivates you to want to walk closer to the Lord?

4. What one thing can you take from this psalm today and make immediate application to your life, so that your walk with the Lord is closer and stronger?

5. What one thing can you take from this psalm today and share with others to benefit them in their walk with the Lord?

One more thing: Pray about this today!

Walking Daily with My Lord

FEBRUARY:

28 DAYS
To Talk to God More Closely

---

*"In everything
by prayer and supplication...
let your requests
be made known to God"
(Philippians 4:6).*

🔲🔲DAYS To Talk to God More Closely

Intimate communication with God requires that we:

- Talk to God **fervently** (Jas. 5:16; Col. 4:12).
- Talk to God **repeatedly** (Luke 18:1; 1 Thess. 5:17).
- Talk to God **reverently** (Psa. 89:7; 111:9; Heb. 12:28).
- Talk to God **confidently** (Jas. 1:6; Heb. 4:16).
- Talk to God **expectantly** (1 John 5:14-15; Matt. 7:7-8).
- Talk to God **sincerely** (Matt. 6:1-8; Phil. 1:10).
- Talk to God **humbly** (Jas. 4:7-10; Luke 18:13-14).

For the next 28 consecutive days, find a quiet time every day when you can pray fervently, repeatedly, reverently, confidently, expectantly, sincerely and humbly to your Father in heaven! Make this a special part of every day.

Spend time earnestly pouring your heart out to God at a set time. You might use the 6-sentence prayer forms on each of the following pages to focus your thoughts.

Heartily and persistently appeal to God for each day's special plea (located at the bottom of each page). Try to focus on that special plea throughout the day, and talk to God about it at least 3-4 times that day.

Talk to God more closely for these 28 days than you ever have before!

Let's enjoy intimate communication with God for 28 days...

☐ Day 1	☐ Day 8	☐ Day 15	☐ Day 22
☐ Day 2	☐ Day 9	☐ Day 16	☐ Day 23
☐ Day 3	☐ Day 10	☐ Day 17	☐ Day 24
☐ Day 4	☐ Day 11	☐ Day 18	☐ Day 25
☐ Day 5	☐ Day 12	☐ Day 19	☐ Day 26
☐ Day 6	☐ Day 13	☐ Day 20	☐ Day 27
☐ Day 7	☐ Day 14	☐ Day 21	☐ Day 28

Day #1 to Talk to God More Closely

"In everything by prayer and supplication...
let your requests be made known to God" (Phil. 4:6).

Take time to fill in this prayer list for today. Then, talk to God.

1. Exaltation: "LORD, YOU ARE…"

2. Supplication: "PLEASE HELP ME…"

3. Intercession: "PLEASE BE WITH…"

4. Appreciation: "THANK YOU FOR…"

5. Confession: "PLEASE FORGIVE ME FOR…"

6. Submission: "NOT MY WILL BUT YOUR WILL BE DONE"

Special Plea for Day #1:
Make a fervent, repeated, confident plea to God today for
God's will to be done on this earth and in my life
(Matt. 6:10; 26:39; Jas. 4:15; John 8:29).

Day #2 to Talk to God More Closely

"In everything by prayer and supplication...
let your requests be made known to God" (Phil. 4:6).

Take time to fill in this prayer list for today. Then, talk to God.

1. Exaltation: "LORD, YOU ARE..."

2. Supplication: "PLEASE HELP ME..."

3. Intercession: "PLEASE BE WITH..."

4. Appreciation: "THANK YOU FOR..."

5. Confession: "PLEASE FORGIVE ME FOR..."

6. Submission: "NOT MY WILL BUT YOUR WILL BE DONE"

Special Plea for Day #2:
Make a fervent, repeated, confident plea to God today for
Open door for the gospel that it may run and triumph
(2 Thess. 3:1; Col. 4:3; Eph. 6:19).

Day #3 to Talk to God More Closely

"In everything by prayer and supplication...
let your requests be made known to God" (Phil. 4:6).

Take time to fill in this prayer list for today. Then, talk to God.

1. Exaltation: "LORD, YOU ARE..."

2. Supplication: "PLEASE HELP ME..."

3. Intercession: "PLEASE BE WITH..."

4. Appreciation: "THANK YOU FOR..."

5. Confession: "PLEASE FORGIVE ME FOR..."

6. Submission: "NOT MY WILL BUT YOUR WILL BE DONE"

Special Plea for Day #3:
Make a fervent, repeated, confident plea to God today for
Unity among believers
(John 17:20-21; Rom. 15:5-6; 12:5, 16; 1 Cor. 1:10; Phil. 2:1-4; Psa. 133:1).

Day #4 to Talk to God More Closely

"In everything by prayer and supplication...
let your requests be made known to God" (Phil. 4:6).

Take time to fill in this prayer list for today. Then, talk to God.

1. Exaltation: "LORD, YOU ARE..."

2. Supplication: "PLEASE HELP ME..."

3. Intercession: "PLEASE BE WITH..."

4. Appreciation: "THANK YOU FOR..."

5. Confession: "PLEASE FORGIVE ME FOR..."

6. Submission: "NOT MY WILL BUT YOUR WILL BE DONE"

Special Plea for Day #4:
Make a fervent, repeated, confident plea to God today for
Deeper love and devotion to God
(Matt. 22:37; Deut. 10:12; 1 Sam. 12:24; 1 John 4:19; 5:2-3; John 14:15).

Day #5 to Talk to God More Closely

"In everything by prayer and supplication...
let your requests be made known to God" (Phil. 4:6).

Take time to fill in this prayer list for today. Then, talk to God.

1. Exaltation: "LORD, YOU ARE..."

2. Supplication: "PLEASE HELP ME..."

3. Intercession: "PLEASE BE WITH..."

4. Appreciation: "THANK YOU FOR..."

5. Confession: "PLEASE FORGIVE ME FOR..."

6. Submission: "NOT MY WILL BUT YOUR WILL BE DONE"

Special Plea for Day #5:
Make a fervent, repeated, confident plea to God today for
Wisdom to make wise decisions
(Jas. 1:5; 1 Kgs. 3:5-9; Prov. 2:3-5).

Day #6 to Talk to God More Closely

"In everything by prayer and supplication...
let your requests be made known to God" (Phil. 4:6).

Take time to fill in this prayer list for today. Then, talk to God.

1. Exaltation: "LORD, YOU ARE..."

2. Supplication: "PLEASE HELP ME..."

3. Intercession: "PLEASE BE WITH..."

4. Appreciation: "THANK YOU FOR..."

5. Confession: "PLEASE FORGIVE ME FOR..."

6. Submission: "NOT MY WILL BUT YOUR WILL BE DONE"

Special Plea for Day #6:
Make a fervent, repeated, confident plea to God today for
Greater faith
(Mark 9:24; Luke 17:5; Rom. 10:17).

Day #7 to Talk to God More Closely

"In everything by prayer and supplication…
let your requests be made known to God" (Phil. 4:6).

Take time to fill in this prayer list for today. Then, talk to God.

1. Exaltation: "LORD, YOU ARE…"

2. Supplication: "PLEASE HELP ME…"

3. Intercession: "PLEASE BE WITH…"

4. Appreciation: "THANK YOU FOR…"

5. Confession: "PLEASE FORGIVE ME FOR…"

6. Submission: "NOT MY WILL BUT YOUR WILL BE DONE"

Special Plea for Day #7:
Make a fervent, repeated, confident plea to God today for
Deliverance from temptation
(Matt. 6:13; 26:41; 1 Cor. 10:13; 1 Pet. 5:8-9; 2 Pet. 2:9).

Day #8 to Talk to God More Closely

"In everything by prayer and supplication...
let your requests be made known to God" (Phil. 4:6).

Take time to fill in this prayer list for today. Then, talk to God.

1. Exaltation: "LORD, YOU ARE..."

2. Supplication: "PLEASE HELP ME..."

3. Intercession: "PLEASE BE WITH..."

4. Appreciation: "THANK YOU FOR..."

5. Confession: "PLEASE FORGIVE ME FOR..."

6. Submission: "NOT MY WILL BUT YOUR WILL BE DONE"

Special Plea for Day #8:
Make a fervent, repeated, confident plea to God today for
Deliverance from evil and the evil one
(Matt. 6:13; 2 Thess. 3:2; John 17:15; Rom. 15:31; 1 John 4:4).

Day #9 to Talk to God More Closely

"In everything by prayer and supplication...
let your requests be made known to God" (Phil. 4:6).

Take time to fill in this prayer list for today. Then, talk to God.

1. Exaltation: "LORD, YOU ARE..."

2. Supplication: "PLEASE HELP ME..."

3. Intercession: "PLEASE BE WITH..."

4. Appreciation: "THANK YOU FOR..."

5. Confession: "PLEASE FORGIVE ME FOR..."

6. Submission: "NOT MY WILL BUT YOUR WILL BE DONE"

Special Plea for Day #9:
Make a fervent, repeated, confident plea to God today for
Mercy and forgiveness for personal sins
(Matt. 6:12, 14-15; Acts 8:22; 1 John 1:9; Psa. 32:5; 51:2; Prov. 28:13).

Day #10 to Talk to God More Closely

"In everything by prayer and supplication...
let your requests be made known to God" (Phil. 4:6).

Take time to fill in this prayer list for today. Then, talk to God.

1. Exaltation: "LORD, YOU ARE..."

2. Supplication: "PLEASE HELP ME..."

3. Intercession: "PLEASE BE WITH..."

4. Appreciation: "THANK YOU FOR..."

5. Confession: "PLEASE FORGIVE ME FOR..."

6. Submission: "NOT MY WILL BUT YOUR WILL BE DONE"

Special Plea for Day #10:
Make a fervent, repeated, confident plea to God today for
Strength and endurance through affliction
(Col. 1:11; Eph. 3:14-16; 6:10; 2 Cor. 12:7-9; Jas. 5:13; Acts 16:25-26).

Day #11 to Talk to God More Closely

"In everything by prayer and supplication...
let your requests be made known to God" (Phil. 4:6).

Take time to fill in this prayer list for today. Then, talk to God.

1. Exaltation: "LORD, YOU ARE..."

2. Supplication: "PLEASE HELP ME..."

3. Intercession: "PLEASE BE WITH..."

4. Appreciation: "THANK YOU FOR..."

5. Confession: "PLEASE FORGIVE ME FOR..."

6. Submission: "NOT MY WILL BUT YOUR WILL BE DONE"

Special Plea for Day #11:
Make a fervent, repeated, confident plea to God today for
Increase in knowledge and discernment
(Phil. 1:9-10; Col. 1:9; Heb. 5:11-6:1; 4:12; 2 Pet. 1:5; 3:18).

Day #12 to Talk to God More Closely

"In everything by prayer and supplication...
let your requests be made known to God" (Phil. 4:6).

Take time to fill in this prayer list for today. Then, talk to God.

1. Exaltation: "LORD, YOU ARE..."

2. Supplication: "PLEASE HELP ME..."

3. Intercession: "PLEASE BE WITH..."

4. Appreciation: "THANK YOU FOR..."

5. Confession: "PLEASE FORGIVE ME FOR..."

6. Submission: "NOT MY WILL BUT YOUR WILL BE DONE"

<u>Special Plea for Day #12</u>:
Make a fervent, repeated, confident plea to God today for
Increase in agape love toward all men
(Phil. 1:9; 1 Thess. 3:12; 4:9-10; John 13:34; 1 Pet. 4:8; 1 John 4:7-21).

Day #13 to Talk to God More Closely

"In everything by prayer and supplication...
let your requests be made known to God" (Phil. 4:6).

Take time to fill in this prayer list for today. Then, talk to God.

1. Exaltation: "LORD, YOU ARE..."

2. Supplication: "PLEASE HELP ME..."

3. Intercession: "PLEASE BE WITH..."

4. Appreciation: "THANK YOU FOR..."

5. Confession: "PLEASE FORGIVE ME FOR..."

6. Submission: "NOT MY WILL BUT YOUR WILL BE DONE"

Special Plea for Day #13:
Make a fervent, repeated, confident plea to God today for
More fruits of righteousness and good works for Christ
(John 15:4-8; Phil. 1:11; Col. 1:10; Eph. 2:10).

Day #14 to Talk to God More Closely

"In everything by prayer and supplication...
let your requests be made known to God" (Phil. 4:6).

Take time to fill in this prayer list for today. Then, talk to God.

1. Exaltation: "LORD, YOU ARE..."

2. Supplication: "PLEASE HELP ME..."

3. Intercession: "PLEASE BE WITH..."

4. Appreciation: "THANK YOU FOR..."

5. Confession: "PLEASE FORGIVE ME FOR..."

6. Submission: "NOT MY WILL BUT YOUR WILL BE DONE"

Special Plea for Day #14:
Make a fervent, repeated, confident plea to God today for
Boldness and courage to spread the gospel
(Acts 4:29; 8:4; Eph. 6:19-20; Phil. 1:20; 1 Pet. 3:15).

Day #15 to Talk to God More Closely

"In everything by prayer and supplication...
let your requests be made known to God" (Phil. 4:6).

Take time to fill in this prayer list for today. Then, talk to God.

1. Exaltation: "LORD, YOU ARE..."

2. Supplication: "PLEASE HELP ME..."

3. Intercession: "PLEASE BE WITH..."

4. Appreciation: "THANK YOU FOR..."

5. Confession: "PLEASE FORGIVE ME FOR..."

6. Submission: "NOT MY WILL BUT YOUR WILL BE DONE"

Special Plea for Day #15:
Make a fervent, repeated, confident plea to God today for
Opportunities to serve and do good to others
(Gal. 6:10; 5:13; 1 Cor. 15:58; Matt. 25:34-46; 1 Tim. 6:18; 1 Thess. 5:15).

Day #16 to Talk to God More Closely

"In everything by prayer and supplication...
let your requests be made known to God" (Phil. 4:6).

Take time to fill in this prayer list for today. Then, talk to God.

1. Exaltation: "LORD, YOU ARE..."

2. Supplication: "PLEASE HELP ME..."

3. Intercession: "PLEASE BE WITH..."

4. Appreciation: "THANK YOU FOR..."

5. Confession: "PLEASE FORGIVE ME FOR..."

6. Submission: "NOT MY WILL BUT YOUR WILL BE DONE"

Special Plea for Day #16:
Make a fervent, repeated, confident plea to God today for
Trust and peace to overcome worries and anxieties
(Phil. 4:6-7; Matt. 6:24-34; Psa. 55:22; Prov. 3:5-6; 1 Pet. 5:7).

Day #17 to Talk to God More Closely

"In everything by prayer and supplication...
let your requests be made known to God" (Phil. 4:6).

Take time to fill in this prayer list for today. Then, talk to God.

1. Exaltation: "LORD, YOU ARE..."

2. Supplication: "PLEASE HELP ME..."

3. Intercession: "PLEASE BE WITH..."

4. Appreciation: "THANK YOU FOR..."

5. Confession: "PLEASE FORGIVE ME FOR..."

6. Submission: "NOT MY WILL BUT YOUR WILL BE DONE"

Special Plea for Day #17:
Make a fervent, repeated, confident plea to God today for
Guidance to faithfully walk the narrow path
(Jer. 10:23; Rev. 2:10; 1 John 1:7; Matt. 7:13-14; 1 Cor. 6:19-20; Psa. 23:3).

Day #18 to Talk to God More Closely

*"In everything by prayer and supplication...
let your requests be made known to God" (Phil. 4:6).*

Take time to fill in this prayer list for today. Then, talk to God.

1. Exaltation: "LORD, YOU ARE..."

2. Supplication: "PLEASE HELP ME..."

3. Intercession: "PLEASE BE WITH..."

4. Appreciation: "THANK YOU FOR..."

5. Confession: "PLEASE FORGIVE ME FOR..."

6. Submission: "NOT MY WILL BUT YOUR WILL BE DONE"

Special Plea for Day #18:
Make a fervent, repeated, confident plea to God today for
Daily provisions, including physical (temporal) needs
(Matt. 6:11, 24-34; 7:7-11; Jas. 1:17).

Day #19 to Talk to God More Closely

"In everything by prayer and supplication...
let your requests be made known to God" (Phil. 4:6).

Take time to fill in this prayer list for today. Then, talk to God.

1. Exaltation: "LORD, YOU ARE..."

2. Supplication: "PLEASE HELP ME..."

3. Intercession: "PLEASE BE WITH..."

4. Appreciation: "THANK YOU FOR..."

5. Confession: "PLEASE FORGIVE ME FOR..."

6. Submission: "NOT MY WILL BUT YOUR WILL BE DONE"

Special Plea for Day #19:
Make a fervent, repeated, confident plea to God today for
Strong personal, family relationships
(Eph. 5:22-33; 6:1-4; 1 Pet. 3:1-7; 1 John 4:7; Matt. 22:39).

Day #20 to Talk to God More Closely

"In everything by prayer and supplication...
let your requests be made known to God" (Phil. 4:6).

Take time to fill in this prayer list for today. Then, talk to God.

1. Exaltation: "LORD, YOU ARE..."

2. Supplication: "PLEASE HELP ME..."

3. Intercession: "PLEASE BE WITH..."

4. Appreciation: "THANK YOU FOR..."

5. Confession: "PLEASE FORGIVE ME FOR..."

6. Submission: "NOT MY WILL BUT YOUR WILL BE DONE"

<u>Special Plea for Day #20:</u>
Make a fervent, repeated, confident plea to God today for
Peaceable life
(1 Tim. 2:2; Phil. 4:6-7; John 14:27; 16:33; 1 Thess. 4:11; Col. 3:15).

Day #21 to Talk to God More Closely

"In everything by prayer and supplication…
let your requests be made known to God" (Phil. 4:6).

Take time to fill in this prayer list for today. Then, talk to God.

1. Exaltation: "LORD, YOU ARE…"

2. Supplication: "PLEASE HELP ME…"

3. Intercession: "PLEASE BE WITH…"

4. Appreciation: "THANK YOU FOR…"

5. Confession: "PLEASE FORGIVE ME FOR…"

6. Submission: "NOT MY WILL BUT YOUR WILL BE DONE"

Special Plea for Day #21:
Make a fervent, repeated, confident plea to God today for
A gracious, merciful and forgiving spirit toward others
(Matt. 5:7; 6:14-15; Mark 11:25-26; Jas. 2:13; Eph. 4:32; Col. 3:12-13).

Day #22 to Talk to God More Closely

"In everything by prayer and supplication...
let your requests be made known to God" (Phil. 4:6).

Take time to fill in this prayer list for today. Then, talk to God.

1. Exaltation: "LORD, YOU ARE..."

2. Supplication: "PLEASE HELP ME..."

3. Intercession: "PLEASE BE WITH..."

4. Appreciation: "THANK YOU FOR..."

5. Confession: "PLEASE FORGIVE ME FOR..."

6. Submission: "NOT MY WILL BUT YOUR WILL BE DONE"

Special Plea for Day #22:
Make a fervent, repeated, confident plea to God today for
Disposition to walk humbly among men
(Phil. 2:3-8; Tit. 3:2; Eph. 4:2; Col. 3:12; Rom. 12:16; Prov. 16:19).

Day #23 to Talk to God More Closely

"In everything by prayer and supplication...
let your requests be made known to God" (Phil. 4:6).

Take time to fill in this prayer list for today. Then, talk to God.

1. Exaltation: "LORD, YOU ARE..."

2. Supplication: "PLEASE HELP ME..."

3. Intercession: "PLEASE BE WITH..."

4. Appreciation: "THANK YOU FOR..."

5. Confession: "PLEASE FORGIVE ME FOR..."

6. Submission: "NOT MY WILL BUT YOUR WILL BE DONE"

Special Plea for Day #23:
Make a fervent, repeated, confident plea to God today for
Contentment with material possessions
(Phil. 4:11-13; Heb. 13:5; 1 Tim. 6:6-8; Psa. 37:16; Prov. 15:16).

Day #24 to Talk to God More Closely

"In everything by prayer and supplication...
let your requests be made known to God" (Phil. 4:6).

Take time to fill in this prayer list for today. Then, talk to God.

1. Exaltation: "LORD, YOU ARE..."

2. Supplication: "PLEASE HELP ME..."

3. Intercession: "PLEASE BE WITH..."

4. Appreciation: "THANK YOU FOR..."

5. Confession: "PLEASE FORGIVE ME FOR..."

6. Submission: "NOT MY WILL BUT YOUR WILL BE DONE"

Special Plea for Day #24:
Make a fervent, repeated, confident plea to God today for
Strength and determination to not conform to the world
(Rom. 12:2; John 15:19; 17:14-16; 1 Pet. 1:13-16; 1 John 2:15-17; Jas. 4:4).

Day #25 to Talk to God More Closely

"In everything by prayer and supplication...
let your requests be made known to God" (Phil. 4:6).

Take time to fill in this prayer list for today. Then, talk to God.

1. Exaltation: "LORD, YOU ARE..."

2. Supplication: "PLEASE HELP ME..."

3. Intercession: "PLEASE BE WITH..."

4. Appreciation: "THANK YOU FOR..."

5. Confession: "PLEASE FORGIVE ME FOR..."

6. Submission: "NOT MY WILL BUT YOUR WILL BE DONE"

Special Plea for Day #25:
Make a fervent, repeated, confident plea to God today for
Greater gratitude and thankfulness for all things
(Col. 3:15-17; 4:2; Eph. 5:20; 1 Thess. 5:18; Phil. 4:6-7).

Day #26 to Talk to God More Closely

"In everything by prayer and supplication...
let your requests be made known to God" (Phil. 4:6).

Take time to fill in this prayer list for today. Then, talk to God.

1. Exaltation: "LORD, YOU ARE..."

2. Supplication: "PLEASE HELP ME..."

3. Intercession: "PLEASE BE WITH..."

4. Appreciation: "THANK YOU FOR..."

5. Confession: "PLEASE FORGIVE ME FOR..."

6. Submission: "NOT MY WILL BUT YOUR WILL BE DONE"

Special Plea for Day #26:
Make a fervent, repeated, confident plea to God today for
Lost souls to have an opportunity to hear the gospel
(Rom. 10:1; Matt. 9:38; 2 Cor. 5:18-20; Acts 7:59-60).

Day #27 to Talk to God More Closely

*"In everything by prayer and supplication...
let your requests be made known to God" (Phil. 4:6).*

Take time to fill in this prayer list for today. Then, talk to God.

1. Exaltation: "LORD, YOU ARE..."

2. Supplication: "PLEASE HELP ME..."

3. Intercession: "PLEASE BE WITH..."

4. Appreciation: "THANK YOU FOR..."

5. Confession: "PLEASE FORGIVE ME FOR..."

6. Submission: "NOT MY WILL BUT YOUR WILL BE DONE"

Special Plea for Day #27:
Make a fervent, repeated, confident plea to God today for
The nation in which you live and those in authority
(1 Tim. 2:1-2; Rom. 13:1-7; 1 Pet. 2:13-17; Ezra 6:10; Prov. 14:34).

Day #28 to Talk to God More Closely

"In everything by prayer and supplication...
let your requests be made known to God" (Phil. 4:6).

Take time to fill in this prayer list for today. Then, talk to God.

1. Exaltation: "LORD, YOU ARE..."

2. Supplication: "PLEASE HELP ME..."

3. Intercession: "PLEASE BE WITH..."

4. Appreciation: "THANK YOU FOR..."

5. Confession: "PLEASE FORGIVE ME FOR..."

6. Submission: "NOT MY WILL BUT YOUR WILL BE DONE"

Special Plea for Day #28:
Make a fervent, repeated, confident plea to God today for
Every congregation of the Lord's church
(Phil. 1:3-4; Rom. 1:8-9; Eph. 1:15-16; 1 Thess. 1:2-4; Jas. 5:16).

Walking Daily with My Lord

MARCH:

28DAYS
To See Souls All Around

*"And He said to them,
'Go into all the world and
preach the gospel
to every creature'"
(Mark 16:15).*

28DAYS To See Souls All Around

Our Savior commands us to "Go" AND "Teach"!

1. **"Going" requires that we open our eyes and see people.**
   - Who do you know who needs to hear and obey the gospel?
   - There is a special category of souls listed on each of the following pages to help you identify those whom you personally know who need the gospel.
   - Some of these categories may have more than one person who fits within them. Some categories for you may have none.

2. **"Teaching" requires creating and opening doors of opportunity.**
   - What can you do or say to open a door for the gospel?
   - There is a special category of opportunities listed on each of the following pages that can be used to perhaps open a door.
   - Some of these ways will work for you, some will not.
   - Most will prove to be an easy way to start the conversation.

3. **28 days of seeing souls can change you when you realize that:**
   - Every Person You See Has a Soul
   - Given By God upon Conception of Life
   - That Is More Valuable Than the Whole World
   - And That Will Abide Forever
   - In Heaven or in Hell
   - And You Can Affect That Soul's Eternal Destiny!

Change your perspective and see souls for 28 days...

☐ Day 1	☐ Day 8	☐ Day 15	☐ Day 22
☐ Day 2	☐ Day 9	☐ Day 16	☐ Day 23
☐ Day 3	☐ Day 10	☐ Day 17	☐ Day 24
☐ Day 4	☐ Day 11	☐ Day 18	☐ Day 25
☐ Day 5	☐ Day 12	☐ Day 19	☐ Day 26
☐ Day 6	☐ Day 13	☐ Day 20	☐ Day 27
☐ Day 7	☐ Day 14	☐ Day 21	☐ Day 28

Day #1 to See Souls All Around

"And He said to them, 'Go into all the world and preach the gospel to every creature'" (Mark 16:15).

Who do you know who needs to hear and obey the gospel?

- Going into the world starts with those we personally know.

- Try to identify specific people within your circle of influence.

Special Category of Souls for Day #1:

Write down the name(s) of any

Close Relative

you have who needs the gospel:

_____

_____

_____

_____

It is critical to see souls and identify those who need the gospel.

Then, one must seek ways to open doors of opportunity for the gospel.

- Not every way to open doors will work with every person.

- Most ways to open doors will work with someone.

Special Category of Opportunities for Day #1:

**Tell at least one person that
you prayed for him/her today.**

Finally, today...
Pray for each prospect of the gospel on your list by name.

Day #2 to See Souls All Around

"And He said to them, 'Go into all the world and preach the gospel to every creature'" (Mark 16:15).

Who do you know who needs to hear and obey the gospel?

- Going into the world starts with those we personally know.

- Try to identify specific people within your circle of influence.

Special Category of Souls for Day #2:

Write down the name(s) of any

Distant Relative

you have who needs the gospel:

_____

_____

_____

_____

It is critical to see souls and identify those who need the gospel.

Then, one must seek ways to open doors of opportunity for the gospel.

- Not every way to open doors will work with every person.

- Most ways to open doors will work with someone.

Special Category of Opportunities for Day #2:

**Tell at least one person that
you asked God to help him/her have a good day.**

Finally, today...
Pray for each prospect of the gospel on your list by name.

Day #3 to See Souls All Around

"And He said to them, 'Go into all the world and preach the gospel to every creature'" (Mark 16:15).

Who do you know who needs to hear and obey the gospel?

- Going into the world starts with those we personally know.

- Try to identify specific people within your circle of influence.

Special Category of Souls for Day #3:

Write down the name(s) of any

Neighbor

you have who needs the gospel:

_____

_____

_____

_____

It is critical to see souls and identify those who need the gospel.

Then, one must seek ways to open doors of opportunity for the gospel.

- Not every way to open doors will work with every person.

- Most ways to open doors will work with someone.

Special Category of Opportunities for Day #3:

**Tell at least one person
"how great" church was on Sunday.**

*Finally, today...
Pray for each prospect of the gospel on your list by name.*

Day #4 to See Souls All Around

*"And He said to them, 'Go into all the world and
preach the gospel to every creature'"* (Mark 16:15).

Who do you know who needs to hear and obey the gospel?

- Going into the world starts with those we personally know.

- Try to identify specific people within your circle of influence.

Special Category of Souls for Day #4:

Write down the name(s) of any

Friend

you have who needs the gospel:

_____

_____

_____

_____

It is critical to see souls and identify those who need the gospel.

Then, one must seek ways to open doors of opportunity for the gospel.

- Not every way to open doors will work with every person.

- Most ways to open doors will work with someone.

Special Category of Opportunities for Day #4:

**Tell at least one person
how God has worked in your life recently.**

---

*Finally, today…
Pray for each prospect of the gospel on your list by name.*

Day #5 to See Souls All Around

"And He said to them, 'Go into all the world and preach the gospel to every creature'" (Mark 16:15).

Who do you know who needs to hear and obey the gospel?

- Going into the world starts with those we personally know.
- Try to identify specific people within your circle of influence.

Special Category of Souls for Day #5:

Write down the name(s) of any

Religious Friend

you have who needs the gospel:

_____

_____

_____

_____

It is critical to see souls and identify those who need the gospel.

Then, one must seek ways to open doors of opportunity for the gospel.

- Not every way to open doors will work with every person.
- Most ways to open doors will work with someone.

Special Category of Opportunities for Day #5:

**Tell at least one person
how thankful you are to be a Christian.**

Finally, today...
Pray for each prospect of the gospel on your list by name.

Day #6 to See Souls All Around

"And He said to them, 'Go into all the world and preach the gospel to every creature'" (Mark 16:15).

Who do you know who needs to hear and obey the gospel?

- Going into the world starts with those we personally know.

- Try to identify specific people within your circle of influence.

Special Category of Souls for Day #6:

Write down the name(s) of any

Workmate/Schoolmate/Teammate

you have who needs the gospel:

_____

_____

_____

_____

It is critical to see souls and identify those who need the gospel.

Then, one must seek ways to open doors of opportunity for the gospel.

- Not every way to open doors will work with every person.

- Most ways to open doors will work with someone.

Special Category of Opportunities for Day #6:

**Tell at least one person
one reason you love "your church."**

---

*Finally, today...
Pray for each prospect of the gospel on your list by name.*

Day #7 to See Souls All Around

"And He said to them, 'Go into all the world and preach the gospel to every creature'" (Mark 16:15).

Who do you know who needs to hear and obey the gospel?

- Going into the world starts with those we personally know.

- Try to identify specific people within your circle of influence.

Special Category of Souls for Day #7:

Write down the name(s) of any

Service/Social Club Member

you know who needs the gospel:

_____

_____

_____

_____

It is critical to see souls and identify those who need the gospel.

Then, one must seek ways to open doors of opportunity for the gospel.

- Not every way to open doors will work with every person.

- Most ways to open doors will work with someone.

Special Category of Opportunities for Day #7:

**Tell at least one person
one reason you're looking forward to heaven.**

Finally, today...
Pray for each prospect of the gospel on your list by name.

Day #8 to See Souls All Around

*"And He said to them, 'Go into all the world and
preach the gospel to every creature'" (Mark 16:15).*

Who do you know who needs to hear and obey the gospel?

- Going into the world starts with those we personally know.

- Try to identify specific people within your circle of influence.

Special Category of Souls for Day #8:

Write down the name(s) of any

Casual Acquaintance

you have who needs the gospel:

_____

_____

_____

_____

It is critical to see souls and identify those who need the gospel.

Then, one must seek ways to open doors of opportunity for the gospel.

- Not every way to open doors will work with every person.

- Most ways to open doors will work with someone.

Special Category of Opportunities for Day #8:

**<u>Give</u> at least one person
a church business card or information about your church.**

---

*Finally, today...
Pray for each prospect of the gospel on your list by name.*

Day #9 to See Souls All Around

"And He said to them, 'Go into all the world and preach the gospel to every creature'" (Mark 16:15).

Who do you know who needs to hear and obey the gospel?

- Going into the world starts with those we personally know.
- Try to identify specific people within your circle of influence.

Special Category of Souls for Day #9:

Write down the name(s) of any

Worker at a Restaurant

you know who needs the gospel:

_____

_____

_____

_____

It is critical to see souls and identify those who need the gospel.

Then, one must seek ways to open doors of opportunity for the gospel.

- Not every way to open doors will work with every person.
- Most ways to open doors will work with someone.

Special Category of Opportunities for Day #9:

**<u>Give</u> at least one person
a Bible tract.**

Finally, today...
Pray for each prospect of the gospel on your list by name.

Day #10 to See Souls All Around

"And He said to them, 'Go into all the world and preach the gospel to every creature'" (Mark 16:15).

Who do you know who needs to hear and obey the gospel?

- Going into the world starts with those we personally know.

- Try to identify specific people within your circle of influence.

Special Category of Souls for Day #10:

Write down the name(s) of any

Worker at a Retail Store

you know who needs the gospel:

_____

_____

_____

_____

It is critical to see souls and identify those who need the gospel.

Then, one must seek ways to open doors of opportunity for the gospel.

- Not every way to open doors will work with every person.

- Most ways to open doors will work with someone.

Special Category of Opportunities for Day #10:

**Give at least one person
a printout of some Bible article.**

---

*Finally, today...
Pray for each prospect of the gospel on your list by name.*

Day #11 to See Souls All Around

"And He said to them, 'Go into all the world and preach the gospel to every creature'" (Mark 16:15).

Who do you know who needs to hear and obey the gospel?

- Going into the world starts with those we personally know.

- Try to identify specific people within your circle of influence.

Special Category of Souls for Day #11:

Write down the name(s) of any

Worker at a Grocery/Pharmacy

you know who needs the gospel:

_____

_____

_____

_____

It is critical to see souls and identify those who need the gospel.

Then, one must seek ways to open doors of opportunity for the gospel.

- Not every way to open doors will work with every person.

- Most ways to open doors will work with someone.

Special Category of Opportunities for Day #11:

Give at least one person
a list of Bible verses that you have found helpful.

Finally, today...
Pray for each prospect of the gospel on your list by name.

Day #12 to See Souls All Around

"And He said to them, 'Go into all the world and preach the gospel to every creature'" (Mark 16:15).

Who do you know who needs to hear and obey the gospel?

- Going into the world starts with those we personally know.

- Try to identify specific people within your circle of influence.

Special Category of Souls for Day #12:

Write down the name(s) of any

Repair Man/Service Man

you know who needs the gospel:

_____

_____

_____

_____

It is critical to see souls and identify those who need the gospel.

Then, one must seek ways to open doors of opportunity for the gospel.

- Not every way to open doors will work with every person.

- Most ways to open doors will work with someone.

Special Category of Opportunities for Day #12:

**Give at least one person
a copy of the church bulletin.**

Finally, today...
Pray for each prospect of the gospel on your list by name.

Day #13 to See Souls All Around

"And He said to them, 'Go into all the world and preach the gospel to every creature'" (Mark 16:15).

Who do you know who needs to hear and obey the gospel?

- Going into the world starts with those we personally know.

- Try to identify specific people within your circle of influence.

Special Category of Souls for Day #13:

Write down the name(s) of any

Worker Seen Often

you know who needs the gospel:

_____

_____

_____

_____

It is critical to see souls and identify those who need the gospel.

Then, one must seek ways to open doors of opportunity for the gospel.

- Not every way to open doors will work with every person.

- Most ways to open doors will work with someone.

Special Category of Opportunities for Day #13:

**Send at least one person
a link to your church's website or other helpful site.**

Finally, today...
Pray for each prospect of the gospel on your list by name.

Day #14 to See Souls All Around

"And He said to them, 'Go into all the world and preach the gospel to every creature'" (Mark 16:15).

Who do you know who needs to hear and obey the gospel?

- Going into the world starts with those we personally know.

- Try to identify specific people within your circle of influence.

Special Category of Souls for Day #14:

Write down the name(s) of any

Visitor to Worship Services

you know who needs the gospel:

_____

_____

_____

_____

It is critical to see souls and identify those who need the gospel.

Then, one must seek ways to open doors of opportunity for the gospel.

- Not every way to open doors will work with every person.

- Most ways to open doors will work with someone.

Special Category of Opportunities for Day #14:

Send at least one person
a link to a specific article or sermon on a church website.

Finally, today...
Pray for each prospect of the gospel on your list by name.

Day #15 to See Souls All Around

*"And He said to them, 'Go into all the world and
preach the gospel to every creature'" (Mark 16:15).*

Who do you know who needs to hear and obey the gospel?

- Going into the world starts with those we personally know.

- Try to identify specific people within your circle of influence.

Special Category of Souls for Day #15:

Write down the name(s) of any

Relative of a Church Member

you know who needs the gospel:

_____

_____

_____

_____

It is critical to see souls and identify those who need the gospel.

Then, one must seek ways to open doors of opportunity for the gospel.

- Not every way to open doors will work with every person.

- Most ways to open doors will work with someone.

Special Category of Opportunities for Day #15:

Send at least one person a link to
an article on ApologeticsPress.org or ChristianCourier.com
or a link to an article or video on HouseToHouse.com.

---

*Finally, today...
Pray for each prospect of the gospel on your list by name.*

Day #16 to See Souls All Around

"And He said to them, 'Go into all the world and preach the gospel to every creature'" (Mark 16:15).

Who do you know who needs to hear and obey the gospel?

- Going into the world starts with those we personally know.

- Try to identify specific people within your circle of influence.

Special Category of Souls for Day #16:

Write down the name(s) of any

Friend of a Church Member

you know who needs the gospel:

_____

_____

_____

_____

It is critical to see souls and identify those who need the gospel.

Then, one must seek ways to open doors of opportunity for the gospel.

- Not every way to open doors will work with every person.

- Most ways to open doors will work with someone.

Special Category of Opportunities for Day #16:

**<u>Send</u> at least one person
an encouraging Bible verse to read and contemplate.**

*Finally, today...
Pray for each prospect of the gospel on your list by name.*

Day #17 to See Souls All Around

"And He said to them, 'Go into all the world and preach the gospel to every creature'" (Mark 16:15).

Who do you know who needs to hear and obey the gospel?

- Going into the world starts with those we personally know.
- Try to identify specific people within your circle of influence.

Special Category of Souls for Day #17:

Write down the name(s) of anyone who is

Experiencing Life Changes

and you know needs the gospel:

_____

_____

_____

_____

It is critical to see souls and identify those who need the gospel.

Then, one must seek ways to open doors of opportunity for the gospel.

- Not every way to open doors will work with every person.
- Most ways to open doors will work with someone.

Special Category of Opportunities for Day #17:

**Invite at least one person
to church this Sunday.**

Finally, today...
Pray for each prospect of the gospel on your list by name.

Day #18 to See Souls All Around

"And He said to them, 'Go into all the world and
preach the gospel to every creature'" (Mark 16:15).

Who do you know who needs to hear and obey the gospel?

- Going into the world starts with those we personally know.

- Try to identify specific people within your circle of influence.

Special Category of Souls for Day #18:

Write down the name(s) of anyone who

Recently Got Engaged or Married

and you know needs the gospel:

_____

_____

_____

_____

It is critical to see souls and identify those who need the gospel.

Then, one must seek ways to open doors of opportunity for the gospel.

- Not every way to open doors will work with every person.

- Most ways to open doors will work with someone.

Special Category of Opportunities for Day #18:

**Invite at least one person
to a church event.**

Finally, today...
Pray for each prospect of the gospel on your list by name.

Day #19 to See Souls All Around

"And He said to them, 'Go into all the world and
preach the gospel to every creature'" (Mark 16:15).

Who do you know who needs to hear and obey the gospel?

- Going into the world starts with those we personally know.

- Try to identify specific people within your circle of influence.

Special Category of Souls for Day #19:

Write down the name(s) of anyone who

Recently Had a Baby

and you know needs the gospel:

_____

_____

_____

_____

It is critical to see souls and identify those who need the gospel.

Then, one must seek ways to open doors of opportunity for the gospel.

- Not every way to open doors will work with every person.

- Most ways to open doors will work with someone.

Special Category of Opportunities for Day #19:

Invite at least one person
to have coffee or come to your place for dinner (just for a visit).

Finally, today...
Pray for each prospect of the gospel on your list by name.

Day #20 to See Souls All Around

"And He said to them, 'Go into all the world and preach the gospel to every creature'" (Mark 16:15).

Who do you know who needs to hear and obey the gospel?

- Going into the world starts with those we personally know.

- Try to identify specific people within your circle of influence.

Special Category of Souls for Day #20:

Write down the name(s) of anyone who

Recently Retired or Now Has an Empty Nest

and you know needs the gospel:

_____

_____

_____

_____

It is critical to see souls and identify those who need the gospel.

Then, one must seek ways to open doors of opportunity for the gospel.

- Not every way to open doors will work with every person.

- Most ways to open doors will work with someone.

Special Category of Opportunities for Day #20:

**Say to at least one person,
"I sure am ready for Jesus to come back. How about you?"**

---

*Finally, today...
Pray for each prospect of the gospel on your list by name.*

Day #21 to See Souls All Around

*"And He said to them, 'Go into all the world and
preach the gospel to every creature'"* (Mark 16:15).

Who do you know who needs to hear and obey the gospel?

- Going into the world starts with those we personally know.

- Try to identify specific people within your circle of influence.

Special Category of Souls for Day #21:

Write down the name(s) of anyone who

Recently Had a Change in Job Situation

and you know needs the gospel:

_____

_____

_____

_____

It is critical to see souls and identify those who need the gospel.

Then, one must seek ways to open doors of opportunity for the gospel.

- Not every way to open doors will work with every person.

- Most ways to open doors will work with someone.

Special Category of Opportunities for Day #21:

**Say to at least one person,
"I've been reading my Bible a lot recently.
It's such a great book."**

Finally, today...
Pray for each prospect of the gospel on your list by name.

Day #22 to See Souls All Around

"And He said to them, 'Go into all the world and preach the gospel to every creature'" (Mark 16:15).

Who do you know who needs to hear and obey the gospel?

- Going into the world starts with those we personally know.

- Try to identify specific people within your circle of influence.

Special Category of Souls for Day #22:

Write down the name(s) of anyone who is

Experiencing Financial Hardships

and you know needs the gospel:

_____

_____

_____

_____

It is critical to see souls and identify those who need the gospel.

Then, one must seek ways to open doors of opportunity for the gospel.

- Not every way to open doors will work with every person.

- Most ways to open doors will work with someone.

Special Category of Opportunities for Day #22:

**Say to at least one person,
"God has made a huge difference in my life.
I'd like to tell you how some time."**

---

*Finally, today...
Pray for each prospect of the gospel on your list by name.*

Day #23 to See Souls All Around

"And He said to them, 'Go into all the world and preach the gospel to every creature'" (Mark 16:15).

Who do you know who needs to hear and obey the gospel?

- Going into the world starts with those we personally know.

- Try to identify specific people within your circle of influence.

Special Category of Souls for Day #23:

Write down the name(s) of anyone who

Recently Suffered the Death of Someone Very Close

and you know needs the gospel:

_____

_____

_____

_____

It is critical to see souls and identify those who need the gospel.

Then, one must seek ways to open doors of opportunity for the gospel.

- Not every way to open doors will work with every person.

- Most ways to open doors will work with someone.

Special Category of Opportunities for Day #23:

<u>Ask</u> at least one person
if he/she goes to church anywhere
and invite them to come with you.

Finally, today...
Pray for each prospect of the gospel on your list by name.

Day #24 to See Souls All Around

"And He said to them, 'Go into all the world and preach the gospel to every creature'" (Mark 16:15).

Who do you know who needs to hear and obey the gospel?

- Going into the world starts with those we personally know.

- Try to identify specific people within your circle of influence.

Special Category of Souls for Day #24:

Write down the name(s) of anyone who

Recently Suffered a Personal Injury or Illness

and you know needs the gospel:

_____

_____

_____

_____

It is critical to see souls and identify those who need the gospel.

Then, one must seek ways to open doors of opportunity for the gospel.

- Not every way to open doors will work with every person.

- Most ways to open doors will work with someone.

Special Category of Opportunities for Day #24:

**Ask at least one person
if they know about the church of Christ
and if you can share it with them.**

Finally, today...
Pray for each prospect of the gospel on your list by name.

Day #25 to See Souls All Around

"And He said to them, 'Go into all the world and preach the gospel to every creature'" (Mark 16:15).

Who do you know who needs to hear and obey the gospel?

- Going into the world starts with those we personally know.

- Try to identify specific people within your circle of influence.

Special Category of Souls for Day #25:

Write down the name(s) of anyone who is

Experiencing Marital or Parental Problems

and you know needs the gospel:

_____

_____

_____

_____

It is critical to see souls and identify those who need the gospel.

Then, one must seek ways to open doors of opportunity for the gospel.

- Not every way to open doors will work with every person.

- Most ways to open doors will work with someone.

Special Category of Opportunities for Day #25:

Ask at least one person,
"Is there anything I can include for you in my prayers today?"

Finally, today...
Pray for each prospect of the gospel on your list by name.

Day #26 to See Souls All Around

*"And He said to them, 'Go into all the world and
preach the gospel to every creature'" (Mark 16:15).*

Who do you know who needs to hear and obey the gospel?

- Going into the world starts with those we personally know.

- Try to identify specific people within your circle of influence.

Special Category of Souls for Day #26:

Write down the name(s) of anyone who is

Stressed About Life

and you know needs the gospel:

_____

_____

_____

_____

It is critical to see souls and identify those who need the gospel.

Then, one must seek ways to open doors of opportunity for the gospel.

- Not every way to open doors will work with every person.

- Most ways to open doors will work with someone.

Special Category of Opportunities for Day #26:

**<u>Ask</u> at least one person,
"Is there anything I can do to help you today?"**

Finally, today...
Pray for each prospect of the gospel on your list by name.

Day #27 to See Souls All Around

"And He said to them, 'Go into all the world and preach the gospel to every creature'" (Mark 16:15).

Who do you know who needs to hear and obey the gospel?

- Going into the world starts with those we personally know.

- Try to identify specific people within your circle of influence.

Special Category of Souls for Day #27:

Write down the name(s) of anyone who is

Dissatisfied with the Moral Trends of Our Society

and you know needs the gospel:

_____

_____

_____

_____

It is critical to see souls and identify those who need the gospel.

Then, one must seek ways to open doors of opportunity for the gospel.

- Not every way to open doors will work with every person.

- Most ways to open doors will work with someone.

Special Category of Opportunities for Day #27:

<u>Ask</u> at least one person,
"Can I tell you why I go to church so much?"

Finally, today...
Pray for each prospect of the gospel on your list by name.

Day #28 to See Souls All Around

"And He said to them, 'Go into all the world and preach the gospel to every creature'" (Mark 16:15).

Who do you know who needs to hear and obey the gospel?

- Going into the world starts with those we personally know.

- Try to identify specific people within your circle of influence.

Special Category of Souls for Day #28:

Write down the name(s) of anyone who

Does Not Fit in the Previous 27 Categories

and you know needs the gospel:

_____

_____

_____

_____

It is critical to see souls and identify those who need the gospel.

Then, one must seek ways to open doors of opportunity for the gospel.

- Not every way to open doors will work with every person.

- Most ways to open doors will work with someone.

Special Category of Opportunities for Day #28:

Ask at least one person
**if he or she would be interested in a personal Bible study
(either with you or someone from church).**

Finally, today...
Pray for each prospect of the gospel on your list by name.

Walking Daily with My Lord

APRIL:

28 DAYS

To Worship God More Fully

"Give to the Lord, O families of the peoples,
Give to the Lord glory and strength.
Give to the Lord the glory due His name;
Bring an offering, and come before Him.
Oh, worship the Lord in the beauty of holiness!"
(1 Chronicles 16:28-29).

28DAYS To Worship God More Fully

Worshiping God is a tremendous privilege, because...

- We get to enter into the presence of God (Heb. 4:16).

- We get to obey the commands of God (Matt. 4:10; 7:21).

- We get to honor our Creator and Savior (1 Chron. 16:28-29).

- We get to please God as He desires (John 4:23-24).

Worshiping God ought to bring us tremendous joy, because...

- We get to enter into the presence of God (Heb. 4:16).

- We get to obey the commands of God (Matt. 4:10; 7:21).

- We get to honor our Creator and Savior (1 Chron. 16:28-29).

- We get to please God as He desires (John 4:23-24).

The following pages will help each of us to spend 28 days:

- Being refreshed by the great privilege and joy of worship.

- Preparing for worship throughout the week.

- Devoting our hearts more fully to worshiping God.

Let's focus on worshiping God more fully for 28 days...

☐ Day 1	☐ Day 8	☐ Day 15	☐ Day 22
☐ Day 2	☐ Day 9	☐ Day 16	☐ Day 23
☐ Day 3	☐ Day 10	☐ Day 17	☐ Day 24
☐ Day 4	☐ Day 11	☐ Day 18	☐ Day 25
☐ Day 5	☐ Day 12	☐ Day 19	☐ Day 26
☐ Day 6	☐ Day 13	☐ Day 20	☐ Day 27
☐ Day 7	☐ Day 14	☐ Day 21	☐ Day 28

Day #1 to Worship God More Fully

"Give to the Lord the glory due His name...
Oh, worship the Lord in the beauty of holiness!"
(1 Chron. 16:28-29).

A worshiper of God ought to be able to say:

"I will call upon the Lord,
who is worthy to be praised"
(Psalm 18:3)!

As you think about worshiping God
on the Lord's Day,
why (to you) is He WORTHY?

Day #2 to Worship God More Fully

"Give to the Lord the glory due His name...
Oh, worship the Lord in the beauty of holiness!"
(1 Chron. 16:28-29).

Magnify how worthy and great God is by singing (silently or out loud) **"To God Be the Glory"** today.

To God be the glory, great things He hath done,
So loved He the world that He gave us His Son,
Who yielded His life an atonement for sin,
And opened the life gate that all may go in.

Praise the Lord, praise the Lord,
Let the earth hear His voice!
Praise the Lord, praise the Lord,
Let the people rejoice!
O come to the Father, through Jesus the Son,
And give Him the glory, great things He hath done.

Great things He hath taught us, great things He hath done,
And great our rejoicing through Jesus the Son;
But purer, and higher, and greater will be
Our wonder, our transport, when Jesus we see.

Praise the Lord, praise the Lord,
Let the earth hear His voice!
Praise the Lord, praise the Lord,
Let the people rejoice!
O come to the Father, through Jesus the Son,
And give Him the glory, great things He hath done.

(Fanny J. Crosby, 1875)

Day #3 to Worship God More Fully

"Give to the Lord the glory due His name...
Oh, worship the Lord in the beauty of holiness!"
(1 Chron. 16:28-29).

Deepen your heart of worship by reading today of those who worshiped God in 1 Chronicles 16:8-13, 23-34.

Oh, give thanks to the Lord! Call upon His name; Make known His deeds among the peoples! Sing to Him, sing psalms to Him; Talk of all His wondrous works! Glory in His holy name; Let the hearts of those rejoice who seek the Lord! Seek the Lord and His strength; Seek His face evermore! Remember His marvelous works which He has done, His wonders, and the judgments of His mouth, O seed of Israel His serv-ant, You children of Jacob, His chosen ones!...

Sing to the Lord, all the earth; Proclaim the good news of His salvation from day to day. Declare His glory among the nations, His wonders among all peoples. For the Lord is great and greatly to be praised; He is also to be feared above all gods. For all the gods of the peoples are idols, But the Lord made the heavens. Honor and majesty are before Him; Strength and gladness are in His place. Give to the Lord, O fami-lies of the peoples, Give to the Lord glory and strength. Give to the Lord the glory due His name; Bring an offering, and come before Him. Oh, worship the Lord in the beauty of holiness! Tremble before Him, all the earth. The world also is firmly established, It shall not be moved. Let the heavens rejoice, and let the earth be glad; And let them say among the nations, 'The Lord reigns.' Let the sea roar, and all its full-ness; Let the field rejoice, and all that is in it. Then the trees of the woods shall rejoice before the Lord, For He is coming to judge the earth. Oh, give thanks to the Lord, for He is good! For His mercy en-dures forever.

Day #4 to Worship God More Fully

"Give to the Lord the glory due His name...
Oh, worship the Lord in the beauty of holiness!"
(1 Chron. 16:28-29).

Express your heart-felt awe for God by praying with **Mary in Luke 1:46-55** today.

And Mary said:
"My soul magnifies the Lord,
And my spirit has rejoiced in God my Savior.
For He has regarded the lowly state of His maidservant;
For behold, henceforth all generations will call me blessed.
For He who is mighty has done great things for me,
And holy is His name.
And His mercy is on those who fear Him
From generation to generation.
He has shown strength with His arm;
He has scattered the proud
In the imagination of their hearts.
He has put down the mighty from their thrones,
And exalted the lowly.
He has filled the hungry with good things,
And the rich He has sent away empty.
He has helped His servant Israel,
In remembrance of His mercy,
As He spoke to our fathers,
To Abraham and to his seed forever."

Day #5 to Worship God More Fully

"Give to the Lord the glory due His name...
Oh, worship the Lord in the beauty of holiness!"
(1 Chron. 16:28-29).

Anticipate worshiping God by imagining Jesus singing **"This Is My Father's World"** with you in worship.

This is my Father's world,
And to my list'ning ears
All nature sings, and round me rings
The music of the spheres.
This is my Father's world:
I rest me in the thought
Of rocks and trees, of skies and seas;
His hand the wonders wrought.

This is my Father's world:
The birds their carols raise,
The morning light, the lily white,
Declare their Maker's praise.
This is my Father's world:
He shines in all that's fair;
In the rustling grass I hear Him pass,
He speaks to me everywhere.

This is my Father's world:
Oh, let me ne'er forget
That though the wrong seems oft so strong,
God is the ruler yet.
This is my Father's world:
Why should my heart be sad?
The Lord is King: Let heaven ring!
God reigns: Let earth be glad!

(Maltbie D. Babcock, 1901)

Day #6 to Worship God More Fully

"Give to the Lord the glory due His name...
Oh, worship the Lord in the beauty of holiness!"
(1 Chron. 16:28-29).

Prepare for the Lord's Supper on Sunday by meditating on **Psalm 22:1-31** today.

My God, My God, why have You forsaken Me? Why are You so far from help-ing Me, And from the words of My groaning? O My God, I cry in the daytime, but You do not hear; And in the night season, and am not silent. But You are holy, Enthroned in the praises of Israel....But I am a worm, and no man; A re-proach of men, and despised by the people. All those who see Me ridicule Me; They shoot out the lip, they shake the head, saying, "He trusted in the Lord, let Him rescue Him; Let Him deliver Him, since He delights in Him!" But You are He who took Me out of the womb; You made Me trust while on My mother's breasts. I was cast upon You from birth. From My mother's womb You have been My God. Be not far from Me, For trouble is near; For there is none to help. Many bulls have surrounded Me; Strong bulls of Bashan have encircled Me. They gape at Me with their mouths, Like a raging and roaring lion. I am poured out like water, And all My bones are out of joint; My heart is like wax; It has melted within Me. My strength is dried up like a potsherd, And My tongue clings to My jaws; You have brought Me to the dust of death. For dogs have surrounded Me; The congregation of the wicked has enclosed Me. They pierced My hands and My feet; I can count all My bones. They look and stare at Me. They divide My garments among them, And for My clothing they cast lots. But You, O Lord, do not be far from Me; O My Strength, hasten to help Me! Deliver Me from the sword, My precious life from the power of the dog. Save Me from the lion's mouth And from the horns of the wild oxen! You have answered Me. I will declare Your name to My brethren; In the midst of the assembly I will praise You. You who fear the Lord, praise Him! All you descend-ants of Jacob, glorify Him, And fear Him, all you offspring of Israel! For He has not despised nor abhorred the affliction of the afflicted; Nor has He hidden His face from Him; But when He cried to Him, He heard...It will be recounted of the Lord to the next generation, They will come and declare His righteousness to a people who will be born, That He has done this.

[Passage condensed to fit on this page]

Day #7 to Worship God More Fully

"Give to the Lord the glory due His name...
Oh, worship the Lord in the beauty of holiness!"
(1 Chron. 16:28-29).

Prepare for the privilege
of giving to God on Sunday by reading
2 Corinthians 8:1-5, 9, 12 today.

Moreover, brethren, we make known to you the grace of God
bestowed on the churches of Macedonia:
that in a great trial of affliction
the abundance of their joy and their deep poverty
abounded in the riches of their liberality.
For I bear witness that according to their ability,
yes, and beyond their ability, they were freely willing,
imploring us with much urgency that we would receive the gift
and the fellowship of the ministering to the saints.
And not only as we had hoped,
but they first gave themselves to the Lord,
and then to us by the will of God...
For you know the grace of our Lord Jesus Christ,
that though He was rich, yet for your sakes He became poor,
that you through His poverty might become rich...
For if there is first a willing mind,
it is accepted according to what one has,
and not according to what he does not have.

Day #8 to Worship God More Fully

"Give to the Lord the glory due His name...
Oh, worship the Lord in the beauty of holiness!"
(1 Chron. 16:28-29).

A worshiper of God ought to be able to say:

"This is the day which the Lord has made;
Let us rejoice and be glad in it"
(Psalm 118:24)!

As you think about worshiping God
on the Lord's Day,
why are you GLAD?

_____

_____

_____

_____

_____

_____

_____

_____

Day #9 to Worship God More Fully

"Give to the Lord the glory due His name...
Oh, worship the Lord in the beauty of holiness!"
(1 Chron. 16:28-29).

Magnify how worthy and great God is by singing (silently or out loud) **"As the Deer"** today.

As the deer panteth for the water,
So my soul longeth after Thee;
You alone are my heart's desire,
And I long to worship Thee.

[Chorus]
You alone are my strength, my shield,
To You alone may my spirit yield;
You alone are my heart's desire,
And I long to worship Thee.

You're my friend and You are my brother
Even though You are a King.
I love You more than any other,
So much more than anything. [Chorus]

I want You more than gold or silver,
Only You can satisfy.
You alone are the real joy giver
And the apple of my eye. [Chorus]

(Martin Nystrom, 1984)

Day #10 to Worship God More Fully

"Give to the Lord the glory due His name...
Oh, worship the Lord in the beauty of holiness!"
(1 Chron. 16:28-29).

Deepen your heart of worship by reading today of those who worshiped God in **Psalm 95:1-7**.

Oh come, let us sing to the Lord!
Let us shout joyfully to the Rock of our salvation.
Let us come before His presence with thanksgiving;
Let us shout joyfully to Him with psalms.
For the Lord is the great God,
And the great King above all gods.
In His hand are the deep places of the earth;
The heights of the hills are His also.
The sea is His, for He made it;
And His hands formed the dry land.
Oh come, let us worship and bow down;
Let us kneel before the Lord our Maker.
For He is our God,
And we are the people of His pasture,
And the sheep of His hand.

Day #11 to Worship God More Fully

"Give to the Lord the glory due His name...
Oh, worship the Lord in the beauty of holiness!"
(1 Chron. 16:28-29).

Express your heart-felt awe for God by praying with Hannah in 1 Samuel 2:1-10 today.

And Hannah prayed and said:
"My heart rejoices in the Lord; My horn is exalted in the Lord.
I smile at my enemies, Because I rejoice in Your salvation.
No one is holy like the Lord, For there is none besides You,
Nor is there any rock like our God.
Talk no more so very proudly; Let no arrogance come from your mouth,
For the Lord is the God of knowledge;
And by Him actions are weighed.
The bows of the mighty men are broken,
And those who stumbled are girded with strength.
Those who were full have hired themselves out for bread,
And the hungry have ceased to hunger.
Even the barren has borne seven,
And she who has many children has become feeble.
The Lord kills and makes alive;
He brings down to the grave and brings up.
The Lord makes poor and makes rich; He brings low and lifts up.
He raises the poor from the dust And lifts the beggar from the ash heap,
To set them among princes And make them inherit the throne of glory.
For the pillars of the earth are the Lord's,
And He has set the world upon them.
He will guard the feet of His saints,
But the wicked shall be silent in darkness.
For by strength no man shall prevail.
The adversaries of the Lord shall be broken in pieces;
From heaven He will thunder against them.
The Lord will judge the ends of the earth.
He will give strength to His king, And exalt the horn of His anointed."

Day #12 to Worship God More Fully

"Give to the Lord the glory due His name...
Oh, worship the Lord in the beauty of holiness!"
(1 Chron. 16:28-29).

Anticipate worshiping God by imagining Jesus singing **"Hold to God's Unchanging Hand"** with you in worship.

Time is filled with swift transition,
Naught of earth unmoved can stand,
Build your hopes on things eternal,
Hold to God's unchanging hand.

[Chorus]
Hold to God's unchanging hand,
Hold to God's unchanging hand;
Build your hopes on things eternal,
Hold to God's unchanging hand.

Trust in Him who will not leave you,
Whatsoever years may bring,
If by earthly friends forsaken,
Still more closely to Him cling. [Chorus]

Covet not this world's vain riches,
That so rapidly decay,
Seek to gain the heav'nly treasures,
They will never pass away. [Chorus]

When your journey is completed,
If to God you have been true,
Fair and bright the home in glory
Your enraptured soul will view. [Chorus]

(Jennie Wilson, 1904)

Day #13 to Worship God More Fully

"Give to the Lord the glory due His name...
Oh, worship the Lord in the beauty of holiness!"
(1 Chron. 16:28-29).

Prepare for the Lord's Supper on Sunday by meditating on **Isaiah 53:1-12** today.

Who has believed our report?
And to whom has the arm of the Lord been revealed?
For He shall grow up before Him as a tender plant,
And as a root out of dry ground. He has no form or comeliness;
And when we see Him, There is no beauty that we should desire Him.
He is despised and rejected by men, A Man of sorrows and acquainted with grief.
And we hid, as it were, our faces from Him;
He was despised, and we did not esteem Him.
Surely He has borne our griefs And carried our sorrows;
Yet we esteemed Him stricken, Smitten by God, and afflicted.
But He was wounded for our transgressions, He was bruised for our iniquities;
The chastisement for our peace was upon Him, And by His stripes we are healed.
All we like sheep have gone astray; We have turned, every one, to his own way;
And the Lord has laid on Him the iniquity of us all.
He was oppressed and He was afflicted, Yet He opened not His mouth;
He was led as a lamb to the slaughter,
And as a sheep before its shearers is silent, So He opened not His mouth.
...For He was cut off from the land of the living;
For the transgressions of My people He was stricken.
And they made His grave with the wicked—But with the rich at His death,
Because He had done no violence, Nor was any deceit in His mouth.
Yet it pleased the Lord to bruise Him; He has put Him to grief.
When You make His soul an offering for sin, He shall see His seed,
He shall prolong His days, And the pleasure of the Lord shall prosper in His hand.
He shall see the labor of His soul, and be satisfied.
By His knowledge My righteous Servant shall justify many,
For He shall bear their iniquities....Because He poured out His soul unto death,
And He was numbered with the transgressors,
And He bore the sin of many, And made intercession for the transgressors.

[Passage condensed to fit on this page]

Day #14 to Worship God More Fully

"Give to the Lord the glory due His name...
Oh, worship the Lord in the beauty of holiness!"
(1 Chron. 16:28-29).

Prepare for the privilege
of giving to God on Sunday by reading
2 Corinthians 9:6-11 today.

But this I say:
He who sows sparingly will also reap sparingly,
and he who sows bountifully will also reap bountifully.
So let each one give as he purposes in his heart,
not grudgingly or of necessity;
for God loves a cheerful giver.
And God is able to make all grace abound toward you,
that you, always having all sufficiency in all things,
may have an abundance for every good work.
As it is written:
"He has dispersed abroad, He has given to the poor;
His righteousness endures forever."
Now may He who supplies seed to the sower, and bread for food,
supply and multiply the seed you have sown
and increase the fruits of your righteousness,
while you are enriched in everything for all liberality,
which causes thanksgiving through us to God.

Day #15 to Worship God More Fully

"Give to the Lord the glory due His name...
Oh, worship the Lord in the beauty of holiness!"
(1 Chron. 16:28-29).

A worshiper of God ought to be able to say:

"Enter into His gates with thanksgiving,
And into His courts with praise.
Be thankful to Him, and bless His name"
(Psalm 100:4)!

As you think about worshiping God
on the Lord's Day,
for what are you THANKFUL?

Day #16 to Worship God More Fully

"Give to the Lord the glory due His name...
Oh, worship the Lord in the beauty of holiness!"
(1 Chron. 16:28-29).

Magnify how worthy and great God is by singing (silently or out loud) **"How Great Thou Art"** today.

O Lord my God! When I in awesome wonder
Consider all the worlds Thy Hands have made,
I see the stars, I hear the rolling thunder,
Thy power throughout the universe displayed,

[Chorus]
Then sings my soul, My Savior God to Thee;
How great Thou art, How great Thou art!
Then sings my soul, My Savior God to Thee;
How great Thou art, How great Thou art!

When through the woods and forest glades I wander
And hear the birds sing sweetly in the trees;
When I look down from lofty mountain grandeur
And hear the brook and feel the gentle breeze; [Chorus]

And when I think that God, His Son not sparing,
Sent Him to die, I scarce can take it in;
That on the cross, my burden gladly bearing,
He bled and died to take away my sin: [Chorus]

When Christ shall come with shout of acclamation
And take me home, what joy shall fill my heart!
Then I shall bow in humble adoration
And there proclaim, "My God, how great Thou art!" [Chorus]

(Carl Boberg, 1886)

Day #17 to Worship God More Fully

"Give to the Lord the glory due His name...
Oh, worship the Lord in the beauty of holiness!"
(1 Chron. 16:28-29).

Deepen your heart of worship by reading today of those who worshiped God in **Revelation 4:8-11**.

The four living creatures, each having six wings,
were full of eyes around and within.
And they do not rest day or night, saying:
"Holy, holy, holy, Lord God Almighty,
Who was and is and is to come!"
Whenever the living creatures give
glory and honor and thanks to Him
who sits on the throne, who lives forever and ever,
the twenty-four elders fall down before Him
who sits on the throne
and worship Him who lives forever and ever,
and cast their crowns before the throne, saying:
"You are worthy, O Lord,
To receive glory and honor and power;
For You created all things,
And by Your will they exist and were created."

Day #18 to Worship God More Fully

"Give to the Lord the glory due His name...
Oh, worship the Lord in the beauty of holiness!"
(1 Chron. 16:28-29).

Express your heart-felt awe for God by praying with
Daniel in Daniel 2:20-23a today.

Daniel answered and said:
"Blessed be the name of God forever and ever,
For wisdom and might are His.
And He changes the times and the seasons;
He removes kings and raises up kings;
He gives wisdom to the wise
And knowledge to those who have understanding.
He reveals deep and secret things;
He knows what is in the darkness,
And light dwells with Him.
I thank You and praise You,
O God of my fathers;
You have given me wisdom and might..."

Day #19 to Worship God More Fully

"Give to the Lord the glory due His name...
Oh, worship the Lord in the beauty of holiness!"
(1 Chron. 16:28-29).

Anticipate worshiping God by imagining Jesus singing **"When We All Get to Heaven"** with you in worship.

Sing the wondrous love of Jesus,
Sing His mercy and His grace;
In the mansions bright and blessed,
He'll prepare for us a place.

[Chorus]
When we all get to heaven,
What a day of rejoicing that will be!
When we all see Jesus,
We'll sing and shout the victory!

While we walk the pilgrim pathway,
Clouds will overspread the sky;
But when trav'ling days are over,
Not a shadow, not a sigh. [Chorus]

Let us then be true and faithful,
Trusting, serving every day;
Just one glimpse of Him in glory
Will the toils of life repay. [Chorus]

Onward to the prize before us!
Soon His beauty we'll behold;
Soon the pearly gates will open,
We shall tread the streets of gold. [Chorus]

(Eliza E. Hewitt, 1898)

Day #20 to Worship God More Fully

"Give to the Lord the glory due His name...
Oh, worship the Lord in the beauty of holiness!"
(1 Chron. 16:28-29).

Prepare for the Lord's Supper on Sunday by meditating on **Luke 22:39-23:49** today.

Coming out, He went to the Mount of Olives...He knelt down and prayed, saying, "Father, if it is Your will, take this cup away from Me; nevertheless not My will, but Yours, be done."...And being in agony, He prayed more earnestly. Then His sweat became like great drops of blood falling down to the ground... Judas, one of the twelve, went before them and drew near to Jesus to kiss Him...Having arrested Him, they led Him and brought Him into the high priest's house... Now the men who held Jesus mocked Him and beat Him. And having blindfolded Him, they struck Him on the face and asked Him, saying, "Prophesy! Who is the one who struck You?" And many other things they blasphemously spoke against Him...Then Herod, with his men of war, treated Him with contempt and mocked Him, arrayed Him in a gorgeous robe...Then Pilate, when he had called together the chief priests, the rulers, and the people, said to them, "...I have found no fault in this Man...and indeed nothing deserving of death has been done by Him. I will therefore chastise Him and release Him"...They shouted, saying, "Crucify Him, crucify Him!"...they were insistent, demanding with loud voices that He be crucified. And the voices of these men and of the chief priests prevailed. So Pilate gave sentence that it should be as they requested...Now as they led Him away, they laid hold of a certain man, Simon a Cyrenian, who was coming from the country, and on him they laid the cross that he might bear it after Jesus...There were also two others, criminals, led with Him to be put to death. And when they had come to the place called Calvary, there they crucified Him, and the criminals, one on the right hand and the other on the left. Then Jesus said, "Father, forgive them, for they do not know what they do." And they divided His garments and cast lots. And the people stood looking on...Now it was about the sixth hour, and there was darkness over all the earth until the ninth hour. Then the sun was darkened, and the veil of the temple was torn in two. And when Jesus had cried out with a loud voice, He said, "Father, 'into Your hands I commit My spirit.'" Having said this, He breathed His last...

[Passage condensed to fit on this page]

Day #21 to Worship God More Fully

"Give to the Lord the glory due His name...
Oh, worship the Lord in the beauty of holiness!"
(1 Chron. 16:28-29).

Prepare for the privilege of giving to God on Sunday by reading **Luke 21:1-4** today.

And He looked up
and saw the rich putting their gifts into the treasury,
and He saw also a certain poor widow
putting in two mites.
So He said,
"Truly I say to you that this poor widow
has put in more than all;
for all these out of their abundance
have put in offerings for God
but she out of her poverty
put in all the livelihood that she had."

Day #22 to Worship God More Fully

"Give to the Lord the glory due His name...
Oh, worship the Lord in the beauty of holiness!"
(1 Chron. 16:28-29).

A worshiper of God ought to be able to say:

"I was glad when they said to me,
'Let us go into the house of the Lord'"
(Psalm 122:1)!

As you think about worshiping God
on the Lord's Day,
what do you look forward to THE MOST?

Day #23 to Worship God More Fully

"Give to the Lord the glory due His name...
Oh, worship the Lord in the beauty of holiness!"
(1 Chron. 16:28-29).

Magnify how worthy and great God is by singing (silently or out loud) **"I Stand in Awe"** today.

You are beautiful beyond description,
Too marvelous for words,
Too wonderful for comprehension,
Like nothing ever seen or heard.

Who can grasp Your infinite wisdom,
Who can fathom the depth of Your love?

You are beautiful beyond description,
Majesty enthroned above.

And I stand, I stand in awe of You,
I stand, I stand in awe of You;
Holy God, to whom all praise is due,
I stand in awe of You!

(Mark Altrogge, 1987)

Day #24 to Worship God More Fully

"Give to the Lord the glory due His name...
Oh, worship the Lord in the beauty of holiness!"
(1 Chron. 16:28-29).

Deepen your heart of worship by reading today of those who worshiped God in **Revelation 5:9-14**.

And they sang a new song, saying:
"You are worthy to take the scroll,
And to open its seals;
For You were slain,
And have redeemed us to God by Your blood
Out of every tribe and tongue and people and nation,
And have made us kings and priests to our God;
And we shall reign on the earth."
Then I looked, and I heard the voice of many angels around the throne,
the living creatures, and the elders;
and the number of them was ten thousand times ten thousand,
and thousands of thousands, saying with a loud voice:
"Worthy is the Lamb who was slain
To receive power and riches and wisdom,
And strength and honor and glory and blessing!"
And every creature which is in heaven and on the earth
and under the earth and such as are in the sea,
and all that are in them, I heard saying:
"Blessing and honor and glory and power
Be to Him who sits on the throne,
And to the Lamb, forever and ever!"
Then the four living creatures said, "Amen!"
And the twenty-four elders fell down and worshiped Him
who lives forever and ever.

Day #25 to Worship God More Fully

"Give to the Lord the glory due His name...
Oh, worship the Lord in the beauty of holiness!"
(1 Chron. 16:28-29).

Express your heart-felt awe for God by praying with David in 1 Chronicles 29:10-13 today.

Therefore David blessed the Lord before all the assembly;
and David said:
"Blessed are You,
Lord God of Israel, our Father, forever and ever.
Yours, O Lord, is the greatness,
The power and the glory,
The victory and the majesty;
For all that is in heaven and in earth is Yours;
Yours is the kingdom, O Lord,
And You are exalted as head over all.
Both riches and honor come from You,
And You reign over all.
In Your hand is power and might;
In Your hand it is to make great
And to give strength to all.
Now therefore, our God,
We thank You
And praise Your glorious name."

Day #26 to Worship God More Fully

"Give to the Lord the glory due His name...
Oh, worship the Lord in the beauty of holiness!"
(1 Chron. 16:28-29).

Anticipate worshiping God by imagining Jesus singing **"Our God, He Is Alive"** with you in worship.

There is, beyond the azure blue,
A God, concealed from human sight.
He tinted skies with heav'nly hue
And framed the worlds with His great might.

[Chorus]
There is a God, He is alive,
In Him we live and we survive;
From dust our God created man,
He is our God, the great I AM.

There was a long, long time ago,
A God whose voice the prophets heard.
He is the God that we should know,
Who speaks from His inspired word. [Chorus]

Secure, is life from mortal mind,
God holds the germ within His hand,
Though men may search, they cannot find,
For God alone does understand. [Chorus]

Our God, whose Son upon a tree,
A life was willing there to give,
That He from sin might set man free,
And evermore with Him could live. [Chorus]

(Aaron W. Dicus, 1966)

Day #27 to Worship God More Fully

"Give to the Lord the glory due His name...
Oh, worship the Lord in the beauty of holiness!"
(1 Chron. 16:28-29).

Prepare for the Lord's Supper on Sunday by meditating on **John 18:12-19:37** today.

Then the detachment of troops and the captain and the officers of the Jews ar-rested Jesus and bound Him...Then they led Jesus from Caiaphas to the Praetori-um, and it was early morning...Pilate then went out to them and said, "What accusation do you bring against this Man?" They answered and said to him, "If He were not an evildoer, we would not have delivered Him up to you."...So then Pilate took Jesus and scourged Him. And the soldiers twisted a crown of thorns and put it on His head, and they put on Him a purple robe. Then they said, "Hail, King of the Jews!" And they struck Him with their hands. Pilate then went out again, and said to them, "Behold, I am bringing Him out to you, that you may know that I find no fault in Him." Then Jesus came out, wearing the crown of thorns and the purple robe. And Pilate said to them, "Behold the Man!" There-fore, when the chief priests and officers saw Him, they cried out, saying, "Crucify Him, crucify Him!"...From then on Pilate sought to release Him...Now it was the Preparation Day of the Passover, and about the sixth hour. And he said to the Jews, "Behold your King!" But they cried out, "Away with Him, away with Him! Crucify Him!" Pilate said to them, "Shall I crucify your King?" The chief priests answered, "We have no king but Caesar!" Then he delivered Him to them to be crucified. So they took Jesus and led Him away. And He, bearing His cross, went out to a place called the Place of a Skull, which is called in Hebrew, Golgotha, where they crucified Him, and two others with Him, one on either side, and Jesus in the center...So when Jesus had received the sour wine, He said, "It is finished!" And bowing His head, He gave up His spirit. Therefore, because it was the Prepa-ration Day, that the bodies should not remain on the cross on the Sabbath...the Jews asked Pilate that their legs might be broken, and that they might be taken away. Then the soldiers came and broke the legs of the first and of the other who was crucified with Him. But when they came to Jesus and saw that He was al-ready dead, they did not break His legs. But one of the soldiers pierced His side with a spear, and immediately blood and water came out.

[Passage condensed to fit on this page]

Day #28 to Worship God More Fully

"Give to the Lord the glory due His name...
Oh, worship the Lord in the beauty of holiness!"
(1 Chron. 16:28-29).

Prepare for the privilege
of giving to God on Sunday by reading
Romans 8:31-39 today.

What then shall we say to these things?
If God is for us, who can be against us?
He who did not spare His own Son, but delivered Him up for us all,
how shall He not with Him also freely give us all things?
Who shall bring a charge against God's elect?
It is God who justifies.
Who is he who condemns?
It is Christ who died, and furthermore is also risen,
who is even at the right hand of God,
who also makes intercession for us.
Who shall separate us from the love of Christ?
Shall tribulation, or distress, or persecution, or famine,
or nakedness, or peril, or sword?
As it is written:
"For Your sake we are killed all day long;
We are accounted as sheep for the slaughter."
Yet in all these things
we are more than conquerors through Him who loved us.
For I am persuaded that neither death nor life,
nor angels nor principalities nor powers,
nor things present nor things to come,
nor height nor depth, nor any other created thing,
shall be able to separate us
from the love of God which is in Christ Jesus our Lord.

Walking Daily with My Lord

MAY:

28 DAYS
To Strengthen My Family

"Now therefore, fear the Lord,
serve Him in sincerity and in truth...
Choose for yourselves this day
whom you will serve...
But as for me and my house,
we will serve the Lord"
(Joshua 24:14-15).

28DAYS To Strengthen My Family

True and enduring strength can only come from God's Word!

- King David asked of God,
  "Strengthen me according to Your word" (Psa. 119:28).

- The apostle John linked three Christian essentials together:
  " ...you are strong, and the word of God abides in you,
  and you have overcome the evil one" (1 John 2:14).

Christian families grow stronger when they:

- Fear God together (Acts 10:2, 22, 35; Heb. 11:7).
- Hear God together (Acts 10:22, 24, 27, 33; 2 Tim. 3:14-15).
- Believe God together (2 Tim. 1:5; Acts 18:8).
- Obey God together (Acts 16:30-34, 14-15; 10:47-48).
- Serve God together (1 Cor. 16:15).

Three steps that will strengthen your family over the next 28 days:

Step 1: PONDER Together a Bible Passage!

- *Read it together as a family.*

Step 2: PRAY Together About That Passage!

- *Talk to God about it together as a family.*

Step 3: PACT Together to Practice That Passage!

- *Make a commitment together as a family to live it.*

Let's strengthen our family for 28 days...

☐	Day 1	☐	Day 8	☐	Day 15	☐	Day 22
☐	Day 2	☐	Day 9	☐	Day 16	☐	Day 23
☐	Day 3	☐	Day 10	☐	Day 17	☐	Day 24
☐	Day 4	☐	Day 11	☐	Day 18	☐	Day 25
☐	Day 5	☐	Day 12	☐	Day 19	☐	Day 26
☐	Day 6	☐	Day 13	☐	Day 20	☐	Day 27
☐	Day 7	☐	Day 14	☐	Day 21	☐	Day 28

Day #1 to Strengthen My Family

"Now therefore, fear the Lord,
serve Him in sincerity and in truth...
Choose for yourselves this day whom you will serve...
*But as for me and my house, **we will serve the Lord**"*
(Joshua 24:14-15).

Read Deuteronomy 6:4-9

"Hear, O Israel: The LORD our God, the LORD is one! You shall love the LORD your God with all your heart, with all your soul, and with all your strength. And these words which I command you today shall be in your heart. You shall teach them diligently to your children, and shall talk of them when you sit in your house, when you walk by the way, when you lie down, and when you rise up. You shall bind them as a sign on your hand, and they shall be as frontlets between your eyes. You shall write them on the doorposts of your house and on your gates."

Special Family Prayer for Day #1:

Pray for God to help each one
to truly love God every day with our entire being.

Day #2 to Strengthen My Family

"Now therefore, fear the Lord,
serve Him in sincerity and in truth...
Choose for yourselves this day whom you will serve...
*But as for me and my house, **we will serve the Lord***"
(Joshua 24:14-15).

Read Philippians 2:3-8

"Let nothing be done through selfish ambition or conceit, but in lowliness of mind let each esteem others better than himself. Let each of you look out not only for his own interests, but also for the interests of others. Let this mind be in you which was also in Christ Jesus, who, being in the form of God, did not consider it robbery to be equal with God, but made Himself of no reputation, taking the form of a bondservant, and coming in the likeness of men. And being found in appearance as a man, He humbled Himself and became obedient to the point of death, even the death of the cross."

Special Family Prayer for Day #2:

Pray for God to help each one
to (like Jesus) humbly look out for the needs of others.

Day #3 to Strengthen My Family

*"Now therefore, fear the Lord,
serve Him in sincerity and in truth...
Choose for yourselves this day whom you will serve...
But as for me and my house, **we will serve the Lord**"
(Joshua 24:14-15).*

Read Proverbs 4:14-19

"Do not enter the path of the wicked, And do not walk in the way of evil. Avoid it, do not travel on it; Turn away from it and pass on. For they do not sleep unless they have done evil; And their sleep is taken away unless they make someone fall. For they eat the bread of wickedness, And drink the wine of violence. But the path of the just is like the shining sun, That shines ever brighter unto the perfect day. The way of the wicked is like darkness; They do not know what makes them stumble."

Special Family Prayer for Day #3:

**Pray for God to help each one
to avoid the path and influence of ungodly people.**

Day #4 to Strengthen My Family

"Now therefore, fear the Lord,
serve Him in sincerity and in truth...
Choose for yourselves this day whom you will serve...
*But as for me and my house, **we will serve the Lord***"
(Joshua 24:14-15).

Read Romans 1:14-17

"I am a debtor both to Greeks and to barbarians, both to wise and to unwise. So, as much as is in me, I am ready to preach the gospel to you who are in Rome also. For I am not ashamed of the gospel of Christ, for it is the power of God to salvation for everyone who believes, for the Jew first and also for the Greek. For in it the righteousness of God is revealed from faith to faith; as it is written, 'The just shall live by faith.'"

Special Family Prayer for Day #4:

**Pray for God to help each one
to be unashamed to teach, stand for and defend the gospel.**

Day #5 to Strengthen My Family

*"Now therefore, fear the Lord,
serve Him in sincerity and in truth...
Choose for yourselves this day whom you will serve...
But as for me and my house, **we will serve the Lord**"*
(Joshua 24:14-15).

Read Ephesians 5:22-6:4

"Wives, submit to your own husbands, as to the Lord. For the husband is head of the wife, as also Christ is head of the church; and He is the Savior of the body. Therefore, just as the church is subject to Christ, so let the wives be to their own husbands in everything. Husbands, love your wives, just as Christ also loved the church and gave Himself for her, that He might sanctify and cleanse her with the washing of water by the word, that He might present her to Himself a glorious church, not having spot or wrinkle or any such thing, but that she should be holy and without blemish. So husbands ought to love their own wives as their own bodies; he who loves his wife loves himself. For no one ever hated his own flesh, but nourishes and cherishes it, just as the Lord does the church. For we are members of His body, of His flesh and of His bones. 'For this reason a man shall leave his father and mother and be joined to his wife, and the two shall become one flesh.' This is a great mystery, but I speak concerning Christ and the church. Nevertheless let each one of you in particular so love his own wife as himself, and let the wife see that she respects her husband. Children, obey your parents in the Lord, for this is right. 'Honor your father and mother,' which is the first commandment with promise: 'that it may be well with you and you may live long on the earth.' And you, fathers, do not provoke your children to wrath, but bring them up in the training and admonition of the Lord."

Special Family Prayer for Day #5:

**Pray for God to help each one
to fulfill God's place and purposes for them in the family.**

Day #6 to Strengthen My Family

"Now therefore, fear the Lord,
serve Him in sincerity and in truth...
Choose for yourselves this day whom you will serve...
*But as for me and my house, **we will serve the Lord***"
(Joshua 24:14-15).

Read 1 Corinthians 13:1-7

"Though I speak with the tongues of men and of angels, but have not love, I have become sounding brass or a clanging cymbal. And though I have the gift of prophecy, and understand all mysteries and all knowledge, and though I have all faith, so that I could remove mountains, but have not love, I am nothing. And though I bestow all my goods to feed the poor, and though I give my body to be burned, but have not love, it profits me nothing. Love suffers long and is kind; love does not envy; love does not parade itself, is not puffed up; does not behave rudely, does not seek its own, is not provoked, thinks no evil; does not rejoice in iniquity, but rejoices in the truth; bears all things, believes all things, hopes all things, endures all things."

Special Family Prayer for Day #6:

Pray for God to help each one
to truly practice agape love toward all people.

Day #7 to Strengthen My Family

"Now therefore, fear the Lord,
serve Him in sincerity and in truth...
Choose for yourselves this day whom you will serve...
*But as for me and my house, **we will serve the Lord***"
(Joshua 24:14-15).

Read James 3:1-12

"My brethren, let not many of you become teachers, knowing that we shall receive a stricter judgment. For we all stumble in many things. If anyone does not stumble in word, he is a perfect man, able also to bridle the whole body. Indeed, we put bits in horses' mouths that they may obey us, and we turn their whole body. Look also at ships: although they are so large and are driven by fierce winds, they are turned by a very small rudder wherever the pilot desires. Even so the tongue is a little member and boasts great things. See how great a forest a little fire kindles! And the tongue is a fire, a world of iniquity. The tongue is so set among our members that it defiles the whole body, and sets on fire the course of nature; and it is set on fire by hell. For every kind of beast and bird, of reptile and creature of the sea, is tamed and has been tamed by mankind. But no man can tame the tongue. It is an unruly evil, full of deadly poison. With it we bless our God and Father, and with it we curse men, who have been made in the similitude of God. Out of the same mouth proceed blessing and cursing. My brethren, these things ought not to be so. Does a spring send forth fresh water and bitter from the same opening? Can a fig tree, my brethren, bear olives, or a grapevine bear figs? Thus no spring yields both salt water and fresh."

Special Family Prayer for Day #7:

**Pray for God to help each one
to control his words and his tone when speaking to others.**

Day #8 to Strengthen My Family

"Now therefore, fear the Lord,
serve Him in sincerity and in truth...
Choose for yourselves this day whom you will serve...
*But as for me and my house, **we will serve the Lord***"
(Joshua 24:14-15).

Read Matthew 5:13-16

"You are the salt of the earth; but if the salt loses its flavor, how shall it be seasoned? It is then good for nothing but to be thrown out and trampled underfoot by men. You are the light of the world. A city that is set on a hill cannot be hidden. Nor do they light a lamp and put it under a basket, but on a lampstand, and it gives light to all who are in the house. Let your light so shine before men, that they may see your good works and glorify your Father in heaven."

Special Family Prayer for Day #8:

Pray for God to help each one
to be a good example and influence for others to follow.

Day #9 to Strengthen My Family

"Now therefore, fear the Lord,
serve Him in sincerity and in truth...
Choose for yourselves this day whom you will serve...
*But as for me and my house, **we will serve the Lord**"*
(Joshua 24:14-15).

Read Matthew 5:38-42

"You have heard that it was said, 'An eye for an eye and a tooth for a tooth.' But I tell you not to resist an evil person. But whoever slaps you on your right cheek, turn the other to him also. If anyone wants to sue you and take away your tunic, let him have your cloak also. And whoever compels you to go one mile, go with him two. Give to him who asks you, and from him who wants to borrow from you do not turn away."

Special Family Prayer for Day #9:

**Pray for God to help each one
to go over and above in showing kindness to all people.**

Day #10 to Strengthen My Family

"Now therefore, fear the Lord,
serve Him in sincerity and in truth...
Choose for yourselves this day whom you will serve...
*But as for me and my house, **we will serve the Lord***"
(Joshua 24:14-15).

Read 1 Thessalonians 4:1-8

"Finally then, brethren, we urge and exhort in the Lord Jesus that you should abound more and more, just as you received from us how you ought to walk and to please God; for you know what commandments we gave you through the Lord Jesus. For this is the will of God, your sanctification: that you should abstain from sexual immorality; that each of you should know how to possess his own vessel in sanctification and honor, not in passion of lust, like the Gentiles who do not know God; that no one should take advantage of and defraud his brother in this matter, because the Lord is the avenger of all such, as we also forewarned you and testified. For God did not call us to uncleanness, but in holiness. Therefore he who rejects this does not reject man, but God, who has also given us His Holy Spirit."

Special Family Prayer for Day #10:

Pray for God to help each one
to stay pure in heart and in actions as God desires.

Day #11 to Strengthen My Family

"Now therefore, fear the Lord,
serve Him in sincerity and in truth...
Choose for yourselves this day whom you will serve...
*But as for me and my house, **we will serve the Lord***"
(Joshua 24:14-15).

Read Luke 9:57-62

"Now it happened as they journeyed on the road, that some-
one said to Him, 'Lord, I will follow You wherever You go.' And
Jesus said to him, 'Foxes have holes and birds of the air have
nests, but the Son of Man has nowhere to lay His head.' Then
He said to another, 'Follow Me.' But he said, 'Lord, let me first
go and bury my father.' Jesus said to him, 'Let the dead bury
their own dead, but you go and preach the kingdom of God.'
And another also said, 'Lord, I will follow You, but let me first
go and bid them farewell who are at my house.' But Jesus said
to him, 'No one, having put his hand to the plow, and looking
back, is fit for the kingdom of God.'"

Special Family Prayer for Day #11:

Pray for God to help each one
to not make excuses in following and serving the Lord.

Day #12 to Strengthen My Family

"Now therefore, fear the Lord,
serve Him in sincerity and in truth...
Choose for yourselves this day whom you will serve...
*But as for me and my house, **we will serve the Lord**"*
(Joshua 24:14-15).

Read Ephesians 4:12-16

"...For the equipping of the saints for the work of ministry, for the edifying of the body of Christ, till we all come to the unity of the faith and of the knowledge of the Son of God, to a perfect man, to the measure of the stature of the fullness of Christ; that we should no longer be children, tossed to and fro and carried about with every wind of doctrine, by the trickery of men, in the cunning craftiness of deceitful plotting, but, speaking the truth in love, may grow up in all things into Him who is the head—Christ—from whom the whole body, joined and knit together by what every joint supplies, according to the effective working by which every part does its share, causes growth of the body for the edifying of itself in love."

Special Family Prayer for Day #12:

Pray for God to help each one
to grow stronger as a result of working hard in the church.

Day #13 to Strengthen My Family

"Now therefore, fear the Lord,
serve Him in sincerity and in truth...
Choose for yourselves this day whom you will serve...
*But as for me and my house, **we will serve the Lord***"
(Joshua 24:14-15).

Read 2 Corinthians 7:6-11

"Nevertheless God, who comforts the downcast, comforted us by the coming of Titus, and not only by his coming, but also by the consolation with which he was comforted in you, when he told us of your earnest desire, your mourning, your zeal for me, so that I rejoiced even more. For even if I made you sorry with my letter, I do not regret it; though I did regret it. For I perceive that the same epistle made you sorry, though only for a while. Now I rejoice, not that you were made sorry, but that your sorrow led to repentance. For you were made sorry in a godly manner, that you might suffer loss from us in nothing. For godly sorrow produces repentance leading to salvation, not to be regretted; but the sorrow of the world produces death. For observe this very thing, that you sorrowed in a godly manner: What diligence it produced in you, what clearing of yourselves, what indignation, what fear, what vehement desire, what zeal, what vindication! In all things you proved yourselves to be clear in this matter."

Special Family Prayer for Day #13:

**Pray for God to help each one
to be truly sorrowful and repentant when we do wrong.**

Day #14 to Strengthen My Family

"Now therefore, fear the Lord,
serve Him in sincerity and in truth...
Choose for yourselves this day whom you will serve...
*But as for me and my house, **we will serve the Lord**"*
(Joshua 24:14-15).

Read Joshua 24:13-18

*"'"I have given you a land for which you did not labor, and
cities which you did not build, and you dwell in them; you eat
of the vineyards and olive groves which you did not plant."
'Now therefore, fear the LORD, serve Him in sincerity and in
truth, and put away the gods which your fathers served on the
other side of the River and in Egypt. Serve the LORD! And if it
seems evil to you to serve the LORD, choose for yourselves this
day whom you will serve, whether the gods which your fathers
served that were on the other side of the River, or the gods of
the Amorites, in whose land you dwell. But as for me and my
house, we will serve the LORD.' So the people answered and
said: 'Far be it from us that we should forsake the LORD to
serve other gods; for the LORD our God is He who brought us
and our fathers up out of the land of Egypt, from the house of
bondage, who did those great signs in our sight, and preserved
us in all the way that we went and among all the people
through whom we passed. And the LORD drove out from before us all the people, including the Amorites who dwelt in the
land. We also will serve the LORD, for He is our God.'"*

Special Family Prayer for Day #14:

**Pray for God to help each one
to worship and serve the Lord no matter what others are doing.**

Day #15 to Strengthen My Family

"Now therefore, fear the Lord,
serve Him in sincerity and in truth...
Choose for yourselves this day whom you will serve...
*But as for me and my house, **we will serve the Lord**"*
(Joshua 24:14-15).

Read Philippians 2:12-17

"Therefore, my beloved, as you have always obeyed, not as in my presence only, but now much more in my absence, work out your own salvation with fear and trembling; for it is God who works in you both to will and to do for His good pleasure. Do all things without complaining and disputing, that you may become blameless and harmless, children of God without fault in the midst of a crooked and perverse generation, among whom you shine as lights in the world, holding fast the word of life, so that I may rejoice in the day of Christ that I have not run in vain or labored in vain. Yes, and if I am being poured out as a drink offering on the sacrifice and service of your faith, I am glad and rejoice with you all."

Special Family Prayer for Day #15:

**Pray for God to help each one
to stop complaining and to rejoice in serving others.**

Day #16 to Strengthen My Family

"Now therefore, fear the Lord,
serve Him in sincerity and in truth...
Choose for yourselves this day whom you will serve...
*But as for me and my house, **we will serve the Lord***
(Joshua 24:14-15).

Read Acts 4:1-12

"Now as they spoke to the people, the priests, the captain of the temple, and the Sadducees came upon them, being greatly disturbed that they taught the people and preached in Jesus the resurrection from the dead. And they laid hands on them, and put them in custody until the next day, for it was already evening. However, many of those who heard the word believed; and the number of the men came to be about five thousand. And it came to pass, on the next day, that their rulers, elders, and scribes, as well as Annas the high priest, Caiaphas, John, and Alexander, and as many as were of the family of the high priest, were gathered together at Jerusalem. And when they had set them in the midst, they asked, 'By what power or by what name have you done this?' Then Peter, filled with the Holy Spirit, said to them, 'Rulers of the people and elders of Israel: If we this day are judged for a good deed done to a helpless man, by what means he has been made well, let it be known to you all, and to all the people of Israel, that by the name of Jesus Christ of Nazareth, whom you crucified, whom God raised from the dead, by Him this man stands here before you whole. This is the "stone which was rejected by you builders, which has become the chief cornerstone." Nor is there salvation in any other, for there is no other name under heaven given among men by which we must be saved.'"

Special Family Prayer for Day #16:

Pray for God to help each one
to never be ashamed of following and serving Jesus.

Day #17 to Strengthen My Family

"Now therefore, fear the Lord,
serve Him in sincerity and in truth...
Choose for yourselves this day whom you will serve...
*But as for me and my house, **we will serve the Lord***"
(Joshua 24:14-15).

Read James 4:7-10

"Therefore submit to God. Resist the devil and he will flee from you. Draw near to God and He will draw near to you. Cleanse your hands, you sinners; and purify your hearts, you double-minded. Lament and mourn and weep! Let your laughter be turned to mourning and your joy to gloom. Humble yourselves in the sight of the Lord, and He will lift you up."

Special Family Prayer for Day #17:

**Pray for God to help each one
to draw closer to Him individually and as a family.**

Day #18 to Strengthen My Family

"Now therefore, fear the Lord,
serve Him in sincerity and in truth...
Choose for yourselves this day whom you will serve...
*But as for me and my house, **we will serve the Lord***"
(Joshua 24:14-15).

Read Philippians 4:4-7

"Rejoice in the Lord always. Again I will say, rejoice! Let your gentleness be known to all men. The Lord is at hand. Be anxious for nothing, but in everything by prayer and supplication, with thanksgiving, let your requests be made known to God; and the peace of God, which surpasses all understanding, will guard your hearts and minds through Christ Jesus."

Special Family Prayer for Day #18:

**Pray for God to help each one
to quit worrying and to trust God to take care of us.**

Day #19 to Strengthen My Family

"Now therefore, fear the Lord,
serve Him in sincerity and in truth...
Choose for yourselves this day whom you will serve...
*But as for me and my house, **we will serve the Lord***"
(Joshua 24:14-15).

Read James 2:1-9

"My brethren, do not hold the faith of our Lord Jesus Christ, the Lord of glory, with partiality. For if there should come into your assembly a man with gold rings, in fine apparel, and there should also come in a poor man in filthy clothes, and you pay attention to the one wearing the fine clothes and say to him, 'You sit here in a good place,' and say to the poor man, 'You stand there,' or, 'Sit here at my footstool,' have you not shown partiality among yourselves, and become judges with evil thoughts? Listen, my beloved brethren: Has God not chosen the poor of this world to be rich in faith and heirs of the kingdom which He promised to those who love Him? But you have dishonored the poor man. Do not the rich oppress you and drag you into the courts? Do they not blaspheme that noble name by which you are called? If you really fulfill the royal law according to the Scripture, 'You shall love your neighbor as yourself,' you do well; but if you show partiality, you commit sin, and are convicted by the law as transgressors."

Special Family Prayer for Day #19:

Pray for God to help each one
to treat all people fairly and without showing favoritism.

Day #20 to Strengthen My Family

"Now therefore, fear the Lord,
serve Him in sincerity and in truth...
Choose for yourselves this day whom you will serve...
*But as for me and my house, **we will serve the Lord***"
(Joshua 24:14-15).

Read 1 Timothy 6:6-10

"Now godliness with contentment is great gain. For we brought nothing into this world, and it is certain we can carry nothing out. And having food and clothing, with these we shall be content. But those who desire to be rich fall into temptation and a snare, and into many foolish and harmful lusts which drown men in destruction and perdition. For the love of money is a root of all kinds of evil, for which some have strayed from the faith in their greediness, and pierced themselves through with many sorrows."

Special Family Prayer for Day #20:

**Pray for God to help each one
to be content with the money and material things we have.**

Day #21 to Strengthen My Family

"Now therefore, fear the Lord,
serve Him in sincerity and in truth...
Choose for yourselves this day whom you will serve...
*But as for me and my house, **we will serve the Lord***"
(Joshua 24:14-15).

Read Philippians 4:8-13

"Finally, brethren, whatever things are true, whatever things
are noble, whatever things are just, whatever things are pure,
whatever things are lovely, whatever things are of good report,
if there is any virtue and if there is anything praiseworthy—
meditate on these things. The things which you learned and
received and heard and saw in me, these do, and the God of
peace will be with you. But I rejoiced in the Lord greatly that
now at last your care for me has flourished again; though you
surely did care, but you lacked opportunity. Not that I speak in
regard to need, for I have learned in whatever state I am, to be
content: I know how to be abased, and I know how to abound.
Everywhere and in all things I have learned both to be full and
to be hungry, both to abound and to suffer need. I can do all
things through Christ who strengthens me."

Special Family Prayer for Day #21:

Pray for God to help each one
to control our thoughts and keep them focused on right things.

Day #22 to Strengthen My Family

"Now therefore, fear the Lord,
serve Him in sincerity and in truth...
Choose for yourselves this day whom you will serve...
*But as for me and my house, **we will serve the Lord***"
(Joshua 24:14-15).

Read Romans 12:10-16

"Be kindly affectionate to one another with brotherly love, in honor giving preference to one another; not lagging in diligence, fervent in spirit, serving the Lord; rejoicing in hope, patient in tribulation, continuing steadfastly in prayer; distributing to the needs of the saints, given to hospitality. Bless those who persecute you; bless and do not curse. Rejoice with those who rejoice, and weep with those who weep. Be of the same mind toward one another. Do not set your mind on high things, but associate with the humble. Do not be wise in your own opinion."

Special Family Prayer for Day #22:

**Pray for God to help each one
to be respectful and generous toward others.**

Day #23 to Strengthen My Family

"Now therefore, fear the Lord,
serve Him in sincerity and in truth...
Choose for yourselves this day whom you will serve...
*But as for me and my house, **we will serve the Lord**"*
(Joshua 24:14-15).

Read Titus 2:11-14

"For the grace of God that brings salvation has appeared to all
men, teaching us that, denying ungodliness and worldly lusts,
we should live soberly, righteously, and godly in the present
age, looking for the blessed hope and glorious appearing of our
great God and Savior Jesus Christ, who gave Himself for us,
that He might redeem us from every lawless deed and purify
for Himself His own special people, zealous for good works."

Special Family Prayer for Day #23:

Pray for God to help each one
to live a life thankful for Jesus and what He's done for us.

Day #24 to Strengthen My Family

"Now therefore, fear the Lord,
serve Him in sincerity and in truth...
Choose for yourselves this day whom you will serve...
*But as for me and my house, **we will serve the Lord***"
(Joshua 24:14-15).

Read Psalm 119:97-104

"Oh, how I love Your law! It is my meditation all the day. You, through Your commandments, make me wiser than my enemies; For they are ever with me. I have more understanding than all my teachers, For Your testimonies are my meditation. I understand more than the ancients, Because I keep Your precepts. I have restrained my feet from every evil way, That I may keep Your word. I have not departed from Your judgments, For You Yourself have taught me. How sweet are Your words to my taste, Sweeter than honey to my mouth! Through Your precepts I get understanding; Therefore I hate every false way."

Special Family Prayer for Day #24:

**Pray for God to help each one
to grow in knowledge, love and appreciation for God's Word.**

Day #25 to Strengthen My Family

"Now therefore, fear the Lord,
serve Him in sincerity and in truth...
Choose for yourselves this day whom you will serve...
*But as for me and my house, **we will serve the Lord**"*
(Joshua 24:14-15).

Read Romans 12:17-21

"Repay no one evil for evil. Have regard for good things in the sight of all men. If it is possible, as much as depends on you, live peaceably with all men. Beloved, do not avenge yourselves, but rather give place to wrath; for it is written, 'Vengeance is Mine, I will repay,' says the Lord. Therefore 'If your enemy is hungry, feed him; If he is thirsty, give him a drink; For in so doing you will heap coals of fire on his head.' Do not be overcome by evil, but overcome evil with good."

Special Family Prayer for Day #25:

**Pray for God to help each one
to respond properly when mistreated by others.**

Day #26 to Strengthen My Family

"Now therefore, fear the Lord,
serve Him in sincerity and in truth...
Choose for yourselves this day whom you will serve...
But as for me and my house, we will serve the Lord"
(Joshua 24:14-15).

Read Ephesians 5:25-27

"Husbands, love your wives, just as Christ also loved the church and gave Himself for her, that He might sanctify and cleanse her with the washing of water by the word, that He might present her to Himself a glorious church, not having spot or wrinkle or any such thing, but that she should be holy and without blemish."

Special Family Prayer for Day #26:

**Pray for God to help each one
to love the church (and everything about it) like Jesus loved it.**

Day #27 to Strengthen My Family

"Now therefore, fear the Lord,
serve Him in sincerity and in truth...
Choose for yourselves this day whom you will serve...
*But as for me and my house, **we will serve the Lord**"*
(Joshua 24:14-15).

Read 1 Peter 5:5-11

"Likewise you younger people, submit yourselves to your elders. Yes, all of you be submissive to one another, and be clothed with humility, for 'God resists the proud, But gives grace to the humble.' Therefore humble yourselves under the mighty hand of God, that He may exalt you in due time, casting all your care upon Him, for He cares for you. Be sober, be vigilant; because your adversary the devil walks about like a roaring lion, seeking whom he may devour. Resist him, steadfast in the faith, knowing that the same sufferings are experienced by your brotherhood in the world. But may the God of all grace, who called us to His eternal glory by Christ Jesus, after you have suffered a while, perfect, establish, strengthen, and settle you. To Him be the glory and the dominion forever and ever. Amen."

Special Family Prayer for Day #27:

Pray for God to help each one
to resist the devil and all of his temptations.

Day #28 to Strengthen My Family

*"Now therefore, fear the Lord,
serve Him in sincerity and in truth...
Choose for yourselves this day whom you will serve...
But as for me and my house, **we will serve the Lord**"*
(Joshua 24:14-15).

Read Matthew 25:1-13

*"Then the kingdom of heaven shall be likened to ten virgins
who took their lamps and went out to meet the bridegroom.
Now five of them were wise, and five were foolish. Those who
were foolish took their lamps and took no oil with them, but
the wise took oil in their vessels with their lamps. But while the
bridegroom was delayed, they all slumbered and slept. And at
midnight a cry was heard: 'Behold, the bridegroom is coming;
go out to meet him!' Then all those virgins arose and trimmed
their lamps. And the foolish said to the wise, 'Give us some of
your oil, for our lamps are going out.' But the wise answered,
saying, 'No, lest there should not be enough for us and you; but
go rather to those who sell, and buy for yourselves.' And while
they went to buy, the bridegroom came, and those who were
ready went in with him to the wedding; and the door was shut.
Afterward the other virgins came also, saying, 'Lord, Lord, open
to us!' But he answered and said, 'Assuredly, I say to you, I do
not know you.' Watch therefore, for you know neither the day
nor the hour in which the Son of Man is coming."*

Special Family Prayer for Day #28:

**Pray for God to help each one
to make sure we are ready at all times for Jesus to come back.**

Walking Daily with My Lord

JUNE:

28 DAYS
To Grow Closer to Jesus

---

*"We all, with unveiled face,
beholding as in a mirror the glory of the Lord,
are being transformed into the same image
from glory to glory,
just as by the Spirit of the Lord"
(2 Corinthians 3:18).*

28DAYS To Grow Closer to Jesus

Growing Closer in Our Relationships with Others Requires:
- **Time** with them.
- **Trust** in them.
- **Tenacity** for them.

Growing Closer in Our Relationship with Jesus Requires:
- **Time** with Him.
- **Trust** in Him.
- **Tenacity** for Him.

The BEST way to spend time with Jesus, build our trust in Jesus, show our tenacity for Jesus and GROW CLOSER to Him is to:

- Get into His Word and WALK with Him.

- Get into His Word and CONNECT with Him.

For the next 28 days, let's take these steps to walk and connect:

Step 1: READ a Chapter in the Book of Matthew.

Step 2: REFLECT on the Passage and a Few Questions.

Step 3: RECONNECT with Jesus By Making Application.

Let's grow closer to Jesus for 28 days...

☐ Matthew 1	☐ Matthew 8	☐ Matthew 15	☐ Matthew 22
☐ Matthew 2	☐ Matthew 9	☐ Matthew 16	☐ Matthew 23
☐ Matthew 3	☐ Matthew 10	☐ Matthew 17	☐ Matthew 24
☐ Matthew 4	☐ Matthew 11	☐ Matthew 18	☐ Matthew 25
☐ Matthew 5	☐ Matthew 12	☐ Matthew 19	☐ Matthew 26
☐ Matthew 6	☐ Matthew 13	☐ Matthew 20	☐ Matthew 27
☐ Matthew 7	☐ Matthew 14	☐ Matthew 21	☐ Matthew 28

Day #1 to Grow Closer to Jesus

"We all, with unveiled face,
beholding as in a mirror the glory of the Lord,
are being transformed into the same image
from glory to glory, just as by the Spirit of the Lord"
(2 Cor. 3:18).

Read Matthew 1

The Royal Lineage and Birth
of Jesus, My King

1. Why do you think it was important to the Jews for Jesus to be traced all the way back to Abraham?

2. What kind of man was Jesus' foster-father, Joseph? Why do you think that he was the right man to be the earthly father of Jesus?

3. Why is it so significant that the king of heaven had to fulfill Isaiah's prophecy and be born of a virgin?

4. **What can I draw from this chapter to help me grow closer to Jesus, my King?**

Answering the questions from this chapter is GOOD.

Applying the message of this chapter is BETTER.

Today's purpose: Read. Reflect. Reconnect with Jesus.

One more thing: Pray about this today!

Day #2 to Grow Closer to Jesus

"We all, with unveiled face,
beholding as in a mirror the glory of the Lord,
are being transformed into the same image
from glory to glory, just as by the Spirit of the Lord"
(2 Cor. 3:18).

Read Matthew 2

The Early Responses to the Birth of Jesus, My King

1. For what purpose had wise men come to find Jesus when He was a young child? Think about how significant this is.

2. Why did Herod have a very different response to the news of Jesus' birth from the response of the wise men?

3. How do we see the Father's hand involved throughout this chapter in the veneration and protection of Jesus?

4. **What can I draw from this chapter to help me grow closer to Jesus, my King?**

Answering the questions from this chapter is GOOD.

Applying the message of this chapter is BETTER.

Today's purpose: Read. Reflect. Reconnect with Jesus.

One more thing: Pray about this today!

"We all, with unveiled face,
beholding as in a mirror the glory of the Lord,
are being transformed into the same image
from glory to glory, just as by the Spirit of the Lord"
(2 Cor. 3:18).

Read Matthew 3

The Righteous Obedience
of Jesus, My King

1. What was the significance of the simple message that John was preaching about repentance and the kingdom?

2. What warning did John issue about the nature of Jesus' ensuing work?

3. What correlation is there between Jesus' words in verse 15 and the Father's words in verse 17?

4. **What can I draw from this chapter to help me grow closer to Jesus, my King?**

Answering the questions from this chapter is GOOD.

Applying the message of this chapter is BETTER.

Today's purpose: Read. Reflect. Reconnect with Jesus.

One more thing: Pray about this today!

*"We all, with unveiled face,
beholding as in a mirror the glory of the Lord,
are being transformed into the same image
from glory to glory, just as by the Spirit of the Lord"*
(2 Cor. 3:18).

Read Matthew 4

The Sinless Life and Early Preaching of Jesus, My King

1. What three words did Jesus use in each response to the devil's temptations that show the surefire way to overcome every temptation?

2. While Jesus refused to follow the devil's calling, what would have prompted the fishermen to immediately follow Jesus' calling?

3. Although people don't like to be told that they need to change the way they're living to please God, what do you think made this a successful plea for Jesus?

4. **What can I draw from this chapter to help me grow closer to Jesus, my King?**

Answering the questions from this chapter is GOOD.

Applying the message of this chapter is BETTER.

Today's purpose: Read. Reflect. Reconnect with Jesus.

One more thing: Pray about this today!

"We all, with unveiled face,
beholding as in a mirror the glory of the Lord,
are being transformed into the same image
from glory to glory, just as by the Spirit of the Lord"
(2 Cor. 3:18).

Read Matthew 5

The Heavenly Authority
of Jesus, My King

1. Which of the beatitudes stands out the most to you as the one that needs the most attention in your life right now?

2. What are the different areas of daily living that Jesus addresses each time He says, "I say to you," in this chapter?

3. Why do you think Jesus placed such a strong emphasis on the influence that we have on others?

4. **What can I draw from this chapter to help me grow closer to Jesus, my King?**

Answering the questions from this chapter is GOOD.

Applying the message of this chapter is BETTER.

Today's purpose: Read. Reflect. Reconnect with Jesus.

One more thing: Pray about this today!

Day #6 to Grow Closer to Jesus

"We all, with unveiled face,
beholding as in a mirror the glory of the Lord,
are being transformed into the same image
from glory to glory, just as by the Spirit of the Lord"
(2 Cor. 3:18).

Read Matthew 6

The Heavenly Focus
of Jesus, My King

1. What sorts of things will we do differently if we want "to be seen of God" rather than "to be seen of man"?

2. What does Jesus tell us about prayer and our Father that ought to give us great comfort and assurance every time we pray?

3. How does Jesus tell us that we can remove worry from our lives and live a truly rewarding life?

4. **What can I draw from this chapter to help me grow closer to Jesus, my King?**

Answering the questions from this chapter is GOOD.

Applying the message of this chapter is BETTER.

Today's purpose: Read. Reflect. Reconnect with Jesus.

One more thing: Pray about this today!

Day #7 to Grow Closer to Jesus

*"We all, with unveiled face,
beholding as in a mirror the glory of the Lord,
are being transformed into the same image
from glory to glory, just as by the Spirit of the Lord"*
(2 Cor. 3:18).

Read Matthew 7

*The Heavenly Way
of Jesus, My King*

1. While Jesus does not teach that it is wrong to judge another, what must we do first before evaluating or seeking to change someone else?

2. How is the God of heaven described by Jesus as our Father and what does He long to do for us as His children?

3. While there are many who believe that many paths and doctrines will lead to heaven, what does Jesus make very clear about the path to heaven?

4. **What can I draw from this chapter to help me grow closer to Jesus, my King?**

Answering the questions from this chapter is GOOD.

Applying the message of this chapter is BETTER.

Today's purpose: Read. Reflect. Reconnect with Jesus.

One more thing: Pray about this today!

Day #8 to Grow Closer to Jesus

"We all, with unveiled face,
beholding as in a mirror the glory of the Lord,
are being transformed into the same image
from glory to glory, just as by the Spirit of the Lord"
(2 Cor. 3:18).

Read Matthew 8

The Power of Jesus, My King,
Over Disease, Nature and Demons

1. In the variety of miracles in this chapter, what do you notice about the personal nature and the immediate efficacy of the miracles of Jesus?

2. In the middle of all of these miracles, what was Jesus' point for us when He talked about foxes, birds and the dead?

3. What kind of reactions were people having to these early miracles of Jesus?

4. **What can I draw from this chapter to help me grow closer to Jesus, my King?**

Answering the questions from this chapter is GOOD.

Applying the message of this chapter is BETTER.

Today's purpose: Read. Reflect. Reconnect with Jesus.

One more thing: Pray about this today!

Day #9 to Grow Closer to Jesus

"We all, with unveiled face,
beholding as in a mirror the glory of the Lord,
are being transformed into the same image
from glory to glory, just as by the Spirit of the Lord"
(2 Cor. 3:18).

Read Matthew 9

The Power of Jesus, My King,
Over Sin and Death

1. Among all the miracles that Jesus did, why would it be such a big deal for Him to (1) forgive a man of his sins and (2) raise someone from the dead?

2. Why was it such a big deal that Jesus selected a tax collector to be one of His apostles? How would something like that be viewed today?

3. While Jesus had responded to many health conditions of people's physical well-being, what was He most concerned about at the end of the chapter?

4. **What can I draw from this chapter to help me grow closer to Jesus, my King?**

Answering the questions from this chapter is GOOD.

Applying the message of this chapter is BETTER.

Today's purpose: Read. Reflect. Reconnect with Jesus.

One more thing: Pray about this today!

---

*"We all, with unveiled face,
beholding as in a mirror the glory of the Lord,
are being transformed into the same image
from glory to glory, just as by the Spirit of the Lord"*
(2 Cor. 3:18).

Read Matthew 10

The Inspired Ambassadors
of Jesus, My King

1. From the hundreds of disciples that Jesus had, why do you think He selected a small handful (i.e., twelve) to be His closest workers (i.e., His apostles)?

2. If you were to summarize all that Jesus told His twelve apostles, what would you say was their primary task on this limited commission?

3. What did Jesus tell His disciples (with the message for us, too) to convey to them the value that they had in the eyes of God?

4. **What can I draw from this chapter to help me grow closer to Jesus, my King?**

Answering the questions from this chapter is GOOD.

Applying the message of this chapter is BETTER.

Today's purpose: Read. Reflect. Reconnect with Jesus.

One more thing: Pray about this today!

*"We all, with unveiled face,
beholding as in a mirror the glory of the Lord,
are being transformed into the same image
from glory to glory, just as by the Spirit of the Lord"*
(2 Cor. 3:18).

Read Matthew 11

The Identification and Invitation of Jesus, My King

1. By quoting from Isaiah to answer John's inquiry, how did Jesus answer for everyone's benefit (including ours) the clear evidence that proved He was "the Coming One"?

2. While Jesus says that there was no one greater than John, what did He then say to explain how anyone can become greater than John?

3. What is it about Jesus' invitation at the end of the chapter that is the most appealing to you?

4. **What can I draw from this chapter to help me grow closer to Jesus, my King?**

Answering the questions from this chapter is GOOD.

Applying the message of this chapter is BETTER.

Today's purpose: Read. Reflect. Reconnect with Jesus.

One more thing: Pray about this today!

"We all, with unveiled face,
beholding as in a mirror the glory of the Lord,
are being transformed into the same image
from glory to glory, just as by the Spirit of the Lord"
(2 Cor. 3:18).

Read Matthew 12

The Authoritative Rebukes
of Jesus, My King

1. How would you characterize the manner in which Jesus responded to those who had ill intentions toward Him in their thoughts and questions?

2. What warning does Jesus give about the origin of our words and the grave consequences that our words can bring upon us?

3. What message was Jesus trying to impress upon His hearers as He talked about His mother and brothers at the end of the chapter?

4. **What can I draw from this chapter to help me grow closer to Jesus, my King?**

Answering the questions from this chapter is GOOD.

Applying the message of this chapter is BETTER.

Today's purpose: Read. Reflect. Reconnect with Jesus.

One more thing: Pray about this today!

"We all, with unveiled face,
beholding as in a mirror the glory of the Lord,
are being transformed into the same image
from glory to glory, just as by the Spirit of the Lord"
(2 Cor. 3:18).

Read Matthew 13

The Beautiful and Valuable Kingdom of Jesus, My King

1. While some might incorrectly look at parables as childish stories, what was Jesus' stated reason for teaching the people in parables?

2. Knowing that the "kingdom" of which Jesus spoke is another word for His "church," how did Jesus depict how valuable His church should be to us?

3. While some might disparage the need to be in Jesus' church, how essential does Jesus make His kingdom to be in this chapter? Could one be outside of it and be ok?

4. **What can I draw from this chapter to help me grow closer to Jesus, my King?**

Answering the questions from this chapter is GOOD.

Applying the message of this chapter is BETTER.

Today's purpose: Read. Reflect. Reconnect with Jesus.

One more thing: Pray about this today!

"We all, with unveiled face,
beholding as in a mirror the glory of the Lord,
are being transformed into the same image
from glory to glory, just as by the Spirit of the Lord"
(2 Cor. 3:18).

Read Matthew 14

The Faith-Building Marvels of Jesus, My King

1. What do we learn about faithfulness to the Lord and His message from John the Baptist?

2. While Jesus was deeply saddened by the news of the murder of His dear friend, John the Baptist, why did He still take time to feed the multitude?

3. What can we learn about the presence, the pity and the power of Jesus from the account of His walking on the Sea of Galilee to His disciples?

4. **What can I draw from this chapter to help me grow closer to Jesus, my King?**

Answering the questions from this chapter is GOOD.

Applying the message of this chapter is BETTER.

Today's purpose: Read. Reflect. Reconnect with Jesus.

One more thing: Pray about this today!

"We all, with unveiled face,
beholding as in a mirror the glory of the Lord,
are being transformed into the same image
from glory to glory, just as by the Spirit of the Lord"
(2 Cor. 3:18).

Read Matthew 15

The Response of Jesus, My King,
to the Faithless & the Faith-Filled

1. What were the Pharisees doing that caused Jesus to call them out as "Hypocrites"?

2. Since Jesus teaches us that evil thoughts, words and deeds proceed from our hearts, what should we do to protect our hearts from such?

3. While the Jewish leadership (who should have been the first to believe in Jesus) was rejecting Jesus, what was astounding about the woman from Tyre?

4. **What can I draw from this chapter to help me grow closer to Jesus, my King?**

Answering the questions from this chapter is GOOD.

Applying the message of this chapter is BETTER.

Today's purpose: Read. Reflect. Reconnect with Jesus.

One more thing: Pray about this today!

"We all, with unveiled face,
beholding as in a mirror the glory of the Lord,
are being transformed into the same image
from glory to glory, just as by the Spirit of the Lord"
(2 Cor. 3:18).

Read Matthew 16

The Certain Death and Promised Church of Jesus, My King

1. What is the bedrock truth (stated by Peter) upon which Jesus said that His church would be built and would forever prevail?

2. While it was still a year away, why was it so significant for Jesus to already be predicting His death and His resurrection?

3. As Jesus was explaining the steep costs of following Him, why do you think that He did not moderate the sacrifices that would be necessary?

4. **What can I draw from this chapter to help me grow closer to Jesus, my King?**

Answering the questions from this chapter is GOOD.

Applying the message of this chapter is BETTER.

Today's purpose: Read. Reflect. Reconnect with Jesus.

One more thing: Pray about this today!

"We all, with unveiled face,
beholding as in a mirror the glory of the Lord,
are being transformed into the same image
from glory to glory, just as by the Spirit of the Lord"
(2 Cor. 3:18).

Read Matthew 17

The Glory and Majesty
of Jesus, My King

1. What benefit would you say the transfiguration of Jesus had for Jesus Himself, and then what benefit for His disciples?

2. Why do you think that Jesus' disciples continued to struggle with a feeble faith, even after more than two years of following Jesus every day?

3. Why would it have been so critical for the people to see Jesus exercising supreme and decisive power over all demons?

4. **What can I draw from this chapter to help me grow closer to Jesus, my King?**

Answering the questions from this chapter is GOOD.

Applying the message of this chapter is BETTER.

Today's purpose: Read. Reflect. Reconnect with Jesus.

One more thing: Pray about this today!

"We all, with unveiled face,
beholding as in a mirror the glory of the Lord,
are being transformed into the same image
from glory to glory, just as by the Spirit of the Lord"
(2 Cor. 3:18).

Read Matthew 18

The Humble and Merciful Servants of Jesus, My King

1. In a practical way today, what can we do to be considered (by Jesus) to be great in the kingdom of God?

2. When there is conflict between brethren in the church, what would you say is the major key that Jesus gives for proper resolution?

3. While forgiving someone who has done us wrong is one of the hardest things to do, what are some things that Jesus gave us to remember in this regard?

4. **What can I draw from this chapter to help me grow closer to Jesus, my King?**

Answering the questions from this chapter is GOOD.

Applying the message of this chapter is BETTER.

Today's purpose: Read. Reflect. Reconnect with Jesus.

One more thing: Pray about this today!

Day #19 to Grow Closer to Jesus

"We all, with unveiled face,
beholding as in a mirror the glory of the Lord,
are being transformed into the same image
from glory to glory, just as by the Spirit of the Lord"
(2 Cor. 3:18).

Read Matthew 19

The Seriousness of Following Jesus, My King, and His Will

1. While modern society mocks God's design for marriage, how can we know that Jesus' teachings on marriage and divorce still apply to us today?

2. If God was open to accepting any marriages comprised of any two people, how would you explain such restrictive teaching from Jesus on this subject?

3. The Bible never says that it is wrong to be rich, but what warnings does Jesus give to (and about) those who have riches?

4. **What can I draw from this chapter to help me grow closer to Jesus, my King?**

Answering the questions from this chapter is GOOD.

Applying the message of this chapter is BETTER.

Today's purpose: Read. Reflect. Reconnect with Jesus.

One more thing: Pray about this today!

"We all, with unveiled face,
beholding as in a mirror the glory of the Lord,
are being transformed into the same image
from glory to glory, just as by the Spirit of the Lord"
(2 Cor. 3:18).

Read Matthew 20

The True Laborers and Servants in the Kingdom of Jesus, My King

1. Even though the Gentiles came into the Lord's kingdom after the Jews, what was the promise that Jesus made to them?

2. Knowing that there is no one greater than Jesus who has ever lived, what did He teach (in word and example) is the only path to greatness in His kingdom?

3. How did Jesus' response to the beggarly blind men contrast with the response of the multitude to these men? What can we learn from that?

4. **What can I draw from this chapter to help me grow closer to Jesus, my King?**

Answering the questions from this chapter is GOOD.

Applying the message of this chapter is BETTER.

Today's purpose: Read. Reflect. Reconnect with Jesus.

One more thing: Pray about this today!

*"We all, with unveiled face,
beloding as in a mirror the glory of the Lord,*
are being transformed into the same image
from glory to glory, just as by the Spirit of the Lord"
(2 Cor. 3:18).

Read Matthew 21

The Reverence for and the Rejection of Jesus, My King

1. Why do you think it was necessary for the King of kings to ride triumphantly into the capital city on a lowly donkey, instead of in a royal carriage?

2. By cleansing the temple for now the second time in His ministry, what was the primary message that Jesus was trying to get across to the people?

3. By specifying that a doctrine or practice is either "from heaven or from men," how should those words from Jesus help us in our observations and evaluations today?

4. **What can I draw from this chapter to help me grow closer to Jesus, my King?**

Answering the questions from this chapter is GOOD.

Applying the message of this chapter is BETTER.

Today's purpose: Read. Reflect. Reconnect with Jesus.

One more thing: Pray about this today!

"We all, with unveiled face,
beholding as in a mirror the glory of the Lord,
are being transformed into the same image
from glory to glory, just as by the Spirit of the Lord"
(2 Cor. 3:18).

Read Matthew 22

The Repeated Plots and Challenges
Against Jesus, My King

1. While all were invited to the wedding and marriage feast, what was the difference between those who rejected the invitation and those who accepted it?

2. What did Jesus teach about the state of the dead, when He used the present tense to talk about God's relationship with Abraham, Isaac and Jacob?

3. Why do you think Jesus chose the two command- ments that He did as "the greatest" ones and upon which all the Law hangs?

4. **What can I draw from this chapter to help me grow closer to Jesus, my King?**

Answering the questions from this chapter is GOOD.

Applying the message of this chapter is BETTER.

Today's purpose: Read. Reflect. Reconnect with Jesus.

One more thing: Pray about this today!

"We all, with unveiled face,
beholding as in a mirror the glory of the Lord,
are being transformed into the same image
from glory to glory, just as by the Spirit of the Lord"
(2 Cor. 3:18).

Read Matthew 23

The Woe-Filled Rebukes
of Jesus, My King

1. How did Jesus describe the hypocrisy of the scribes and Pharisees in the first seven verses of the chapter? What can we learn from this?

2. Although some people today have tried to depict Jesus as soft and weak, what do we learn about Jesus' character from the pronouncement of woes in this chapter?

3. Even though the Jews had repeatedly and vehemently been denying Him, what did Jesus long for them in verse 37?

4. **What can I draw from this chapter to help me grow closer to Jesus, my King?**

Answering the questions from this chapter is GOOD.

Applying the message of this chapter is BETTER.

Today's purpose: Read. Reflect. Reconnect with Jesus.

One more thing: Pray about this today!

Day #24 to Grow Closer to Jesus

"We all, with unveiled face,
beholding as in a mirror the glory of the Lord,
are being transformed into the same image
from glory to glory, just as by the Spirit of the Lord"
(2 Cor. 3:18).

Read Matthew 24

The Comings of Jesus, My King,
in Judgments

1. Knowing the context (i.e., Jesus went into the temple in 21:23), what event is Jesus specifically addressing in the first 34 verses of this chapter (read verses 1-2)?

2. In warning these Jews that He would be coming (figuratively) in judgment upon Jerusalem, when did Jesus say that everything before verse 34 would take place?

3. When Jesus changed subjects in verse 36 to discuss His literal coming at the end of the world, what did He say about being able to know and predict that date?

4. **What can I draw from this chapter to help me grow closer to Jesus, my King?**

Answering the questions from this chapter is GOOD.

Applying the message of this chapter is BETTER.

Today's purpose: Read. Reflect. Reconnect with Jesus.

One more thing: Pray about this today!

---

*"We all, with unveiled face,
beholding as in a mirror the glory of the Lord,
are being transformed into the same image
from glory to glory, just as by the Spirit of the Lord"
(2 Cor. 3:18).*

Read Matthew 25

The Second Coming of Jesus, My King

1. From the parable of the virgins, what do we learn about proper preparedness for the coming of Jesus in regard to its timing?

2. From the parable of the talents, what do we learn about proper preparedness for the coming of Jesus in regard to our faithful work as His stewards?

3. From the depiction of the judgment scene in the closing verses, what we do learn about proper preparedness for the coming of Jesus in regard to serving others?

4. **What can I draw from this chapter to help me grow closer to Jesus, my King?**

Answering the questions from this chapter is GOOD.

Applying the message of this chapter is BETTER.

Today's purpose: Read. Reflect. Reconnect with Jesus.

One more thing: Pray about this today!

---

*"We all, with unveiled face,
beholding as in a mirror the glory of the Lord,
are being transformed into the same image
from glory to glory, just as by the Spirit of the Lord"
(2 Cor. 3:18).*

Read Matthew 26

The Closing Hours of the Life of Jesus, My King

1. While Jesus could have left the memorializing of His death up to His disciples, why do you think it was so critical for Him to specify the details of the Lord's Supper?

2. What insights do we receive into the heart of Jesus as Matthew describes for us how Jesus was praying in the Garden of Gethsemane?

3. How could Jesus possibly endure being betrayed by a friend, denied by a friend, abandoned by friends, put on trial, lied about, mocked, blasphemed, spit upon, beaten and slapped?

4. **What can I draw from this chapter to help me grow closer to Jesus, my King?**

Answering the questions from this chapter is GOOD.

Applying the message of this chapter is BETTER.

Today's purpose: Read. Reflect. Reconnect with Jesus.

One more thing: Pray about this today!

"We all, with unveiled face,
beholding as in a mirror the glory of the Lord,
are being transformed into the same image
from glory to glory, just as by the Spirit of the Lord"
(2 Cor. 3:18).

Read Matthew 27

The Suffering and Death
of Jesus, My King

1. What would cause a people to become so recklessly blind to reality that they would demand the release of a murderer into their midst rather than Jesus?

2. While the startling events of nature that accompanied and followed the death of Jesus should have captured everyone's attention, why do you think only the centurion noticed?

3. How do the facts of a hewn-out rock tomb, a large stone, a governor's seal and a military guard add iron-clad evidence to the actual resurrection of Jesus?

4. **What can I draw from this chapter to help me grow closer to Jesus, my King?**

Answering the questions from this chapter is GOOD.

Applying the message of this chapter is BETTER.

Today's purpose: Read. Reflect. Reconnect with Jesus.

One more thing: Pray about this today!

"We all, with unveiled face,
beholding as in a mirror the glory of the Lord,
are being transformed into the same image
from glory to glory, just as by the Spirit of the Lord"
(2 Cor. 3:18).

Read Matthew 28

The Resurrection and Commission of Jesus, My King

1. What was the common, natural and immediate reaction of the women when they saw the resurrected Jesus, and also of the disciples when they saw Him?

2. What would have been the purpose for the soldiers to tell others that Jesus' disciples had stolen His body away? Do you think that such a claim worked?

3. In the Great Commission that Jesus gave us, what are the four "all's" of which we need to be constantly reminded? (The fourth "all" is "always.")

4. **What can I draw from this chapter to help me grow closer to Jesus, my King?**

Answering the questions from this chapter is GOOD.

Applying the message of this chapter is BETTER.

Today's purpose: Read. Reflect. Reconnect with Jesus.

One more thing: Pray about this today!

Walking Daily with My Lord

JULY:

28DAYS

To Pray for One Another

"Pray for one another...
The effective, fervent prayer
of a righteous man
avails much"
(James 5:16).

28DAYS To Pray for One Another

The Greatest Thing You Can Do for a Person Is to Pray for Him!

Christians have a responsibility to:

- Serve one another (Gal. 5:13; 6:10)!

- Put each other's needs above our own (Phil. 2:3-4)!

- Be impartial in our treatment of each other (Jas. 2:9)!

We will find it much easier to fulfill our responsibilities toward each other as Christians when we devote ourselves to pray for each other!

Use the following pages over the next 28 days to:

1. Make a list of those for whom you need to pray.

2. Include the special category of specific members in your prayers.

3. Include members from your church directory in your prayers.

4. Pray for each person on your list (by name, if possible).

5. Then, let some folks know that you prayed for them.

Let's pray for one another for 28 days...

☐	Day 1	☐	Day 8	☐	Day 15	☐	Day 22
☐	Day 2	☐	Day 9	☐	Day 16	☐	Day 23
☐	Day 3	☐	Day 10	☐	Day 17	☐	Day 24
☐	Day 4	☐	Day 11	☐	Day 18	☐	Day 25
☐	Day 5	☐	Day 12	☐	Day 19	☐	Day 26
☐	Day 6	☐	Day 13	☐	Day 20	☐	Day 27
☐	Day 7	☐	Day 14	☐	Day 21	☐	Day 28

Day #1 to Pray for One Another

*"Pray for one another...The effective, fervent prayer of
a righteous man avails much" (James 5:16).*

Take time to fill in this prayer list for today. Then, pray for one another.

"Heavenly Father, please be with your church, and bless our every effort as we strive to glorify and honor your name. Please be with my brothers and sisters in Christ today. Strengthen us and draw each of us closer to you. Give us greater faith, love, courage and peace. Today, please be especially with:

First Special Category of Intercession for Day #1:
Make a special plea to God today (by name, if possible) for
Elders, Along with Their Wives and Families.

Second Special Category of Intercession for Day #1:
Make a special plea to God today (by name) for
Specific brethren in your Church Directory.

Let some folks know that you are praying for them today.

Day #2 to Pray for One Another

*"Pray for one another...The effective, fervent prayer of
a righteous man avails much" (James 5:16).*

Take time to fill in this prayer list for today. Then, pray for one another.

"Heavenly Father, please be with your church, and bless our every
effort as we strive to glorify and honor your name. Please be with my
brothers and sisters in Christ today. Strengthen us and draw each of
us closer to you. Give us greater faith, love, courage and peace.
Today, please be especially with:

_____

_____

_____

_____

_____

_____

_____

_____

_____

_____

First Special Category of Intercession for Day #2:
Make a special plea to God today (by name, if possible) for
Deacons, Along with Their Wives and Families.

Second Special Category of Intercession for Day #2:
Make a special plea to God today (by name) for
Specific brethren in your Church Directory.

Let some folks know that you are praying for them today.

Day #3 to Pray for One Another

*"Pray for one another...The effective, fervent prayer of
a righteous man avails much" (James 5:16).*

Take time to fill in this prayer list for today. Then, pray for one another.

"Heavenly Father, please be with your church, and bless our every effort as we strive to glorify and honor your name. Please be with my brothers and sisters in Christ today. Strengthen us and draw each of us closer to you. Give us greater faith, love, courage and peace. Today, please be especially with:

First Special Category of Intercession for Day #3:
Make a special plea to God today (by name, if possible) for
Preachers, Along with Their Wives and Families.

Second Special Category of Intercession for Day #3:
Make a special plea to God today (by name) for
Specific brethren in your Church Directory.

Let some folks know that you are praying for them today.

Day #4 to Pray for One Another

"Pray for one another...The effective, fervent prayer of
a righteous man avails much" (James 5:16).

Take time to fill in this prayer list for today. Then, pray for one another.

"Heavenly Father, please be with your church, and bless our every effort as we strive to glorify and honor your name. Please be with my brothers and sisters in Christ today. Strengthen us and draw each of us closer to you. Give us greater faith, love, courage and peace. Today, please be especially with:

First Special Category of Intercession for Day #4:
Make a special plea to God today for
Future Elders & Deacons (and the Wives of These Men).

Second Special Category of Intercession for Day #4:
Make a special plea to God today (by name) for
Specific brethren in your Church Directory.

Let some folks know that you are praying for them today.

Day #5 to Pray for One Another

"Pray for one another...The effective, fervent prayer of a righteous man avails much" (James 5:16).

Take time to fill in this prayer list for today. Then, pray for one another.

"Heavenly Father, please be with your church, and bless our every effort as we strive to glorify and honor your name. Please be with my brothers and sisters in Christ today. Strengthen us and draw each of us closer to you. Give us greater faith, love, courage and peace. Today, please be especially with:

First Special Category of Intercession for Day #5:
Make a special plea to God today (by name, if possible) for
Bible Class Teachers.

Second Special Category of Intercession for Day #5:
Make a special plea to God today (by name) for
Specific brethren in your Church Directory.

Let some folks know that you are praying for them today.

Day #6 to Pray for One Another

*"Pray for one another...The effective, fervent prayer of
a righteous man avails much" (James 5:16).*

Take time to fill in this prayer list for today. Then, pray for one another.

"Heavenly Father, please be with your church, and bless our every
effort as we strive to glorify and honor your name. Please be with my
brothers and sisters in Christ today. Strengthen us and draw each of
us closer to you. Give us greater faith, love, courage and peace.
Today, please be especially with:

_____

_____

_____

_____

_____

_____

_____

_____

First Special Category of Intercession for Day #6:
Make a special plea to God today (by name, if possible) for
Married Couples (Young & Old) in the Church.

Second Special Category of Intercession for Day #6:
Make a special plea to God today (by name) for
Specific brethren in your Church Directory.

Let some folks know that you are praying for them today.

Day #7 to Pray for One Another

"Pray for one another...The effective, fervent prayer of
a righteous man avails much" (James 5:16).

Take time to fill in this prayer list for today. Then, pray for one another.

"Heavenly Father, please be with your church, and bless our every effort as we strive to glorify and honor your name. Please be with my brothers and sisters in Christ today. Strengthen us and draw each of us closer to you. Give us greater faith, love, courage and peace. Today, please be especially with:

First Special Category of Intercession for Day #7:
Make a special plea to God today (by name, if possible) for
Those Who Are Married to Non-Christians.

Second Special Category of Intercession for Day #7:
Make a special plea to God today (by name) for
Specific brethren in your Church Directory.

Let some folks know that you are praying for them today.

Day #8 to Pray for One Another

*"Pray for one another...The effective, fervent prayer of
a righteous man avails much" (James 5:16).*

Take time to fill in this prayer list for today. Then, pray for one another.

"Heavenly Father, please be with your church, and bless our every effort as we strive to glorify and honor your name. Please be with my brothers and sisters in Christ today. Strengthen us and draw each of us closer to you. Give us greater faith, love, courage and peace. Today, please be especially with:

First Special Category of Intercession for Day #8:
Make a special plea to God today (by name, if possible) for
Those Whose Adult Children Are Not Faithful Christians.

Second Special Category of Intercession for Day #8:
Make a special plea to God today (by name) for
Specific brethren in your Church Directory.

Let some folks know that you are praying for them today.

Day #9 to Pray for One Another

"Pray for one another...The effective, fervent prayer of
a righteous man avails much" (James 5:16).

Take time to fill in this prayer list for today. Then, pray for one another.

"Heavenly Father, please be with your church, and bless our every effort as we strive to glorify and honor your name. Please be with my brothers and sisters in Christ today. Strengthen us and draw each of us closer to you. Give us greater faith, love, courage and peace. Today, please be especially with:

_____

_____

_____

_____

_____

_____

_____

_____

_____

First Special Category of Intercession for Day #9:
Make a special plea to God today (by name, if possible) for
Those Who Are Divorced and for the Children of Divorce.

Second Special Category of Intercession for Day #9:
Make a special plea to God today (by name) for
Specific brethren in your Church Directory.

Let some folks know that you are praying for them today.

Day #10 to Pray for One Another

"Pray for one another...The effective, fervent prayer of
a righteous man avails much" (James 5:16).

Take time to fill in this prayer list for today. Then, pray for one another.

"Heavenly Father, please be with your church, and bless our every effort as we strive to glorify and honor your name. Please be with my brothers and sisters in Christ today. Strengthen us and draw each of us closer to you. Give us greater faith, love, courage and peace. Today, please be especially with:

First Special Category of Intercession for Day #10:
Make a special plea to God today (by name, if possible) for
Single Men & Single Women in the Church.

Second Special Category of Intercession for Day #10:
Make a special plea to God today (by name) for
Specific brethren in your Church Directory.

Let some folks know that you are praying for them today.

Day #11 to Pray for One Another

*"Pray for one another...The effective, fervent prayer of
a righteous man avails much" (James 5:16).*

Take time to fill in this prayer list for today. Then, pray for one another.

"Heavenly Father, please be with your church, and bless our every effort as we strive to glorify and honor your name. Please be with my brothers and sisters in Christ today. Strengthen us and draw each of us closer to you. Give us greater faith, love, courage and peace. Today, please be especially with:

First Special Category of Intercession for Day #11:
Make a special plea to God today (by name, if possible) for
Young Adults in the Church.

Second Special Category of Intercession for Day #11:
Make a special plea to God today (by name) for
Specific brethren in your Church Directory.

Let some folks know that you are praying for them today.

Day #12 to Pray for One Another

*"Pray for one another...The effective, fervent prayer of
a righteous man avails much" (James 5:16).*

Take time to fill in this prayer list for today. Then, pray for one another.

"Heavenly Father, please be with your church, and bless our every
effort as we strive to glorify and honor your name. Please be with my
brothers and sisters in Christ today. Strengthen us and draw each of
us closer to you. Give us greater faith, love, courage and peace.
Today, please be especially with:

_____

_____

_____

_____

_____

_____

_____

_____

_____

First Special Category of Intercession for Day #12:
Make a special plea to God today (by name, if possible) for
All Parents in the Church Who Still Have Children at Home.

Second Special Category of Intercession for Day #12:
Make a special plea to God today (by name) for
Specific brethren in your Church Directory.

Let some folks know that you are praying for them today.

Day #13 to Pray for One Another

"Pray for one another...The effective, fervent prayer of
a righteous man avails much" (James 5:16).

Take time to fill in this prayer list for today. Then, pray for one another.

"Heavenly Father, please be with your church, and bless our every effort as we strive to glorify and honor your name. Please be with my brothers and sisters in Christ today. Strengthen us and draw each of us closer to you. Give us greater faith, love, courage and peace. Today, please be especially with:

First Special Category of Intercession for Day #13:
Make a special plea to God today (by name, if possible) for
Single Moms and Single Dads in the Church.

Second Special Category of Intercession for Day #13:
Make a special plea to God today (by name) for
Specific brethren in your Church Directory.

Let some folks know that you are praying for them today.

Day #14 to Pray for One Another

"Pray for one another...The effective, fervent prayer of a righteous man avails much" (James 5:16).

Take time to fill in this prayer list for today. Then, pray for one another.

"Heavenly Father, please be with your church, and bless our every effort as we strive to glorify and honor your name. Please be with my brothers and sisters in Christ today. Strengthen us and draw each of us closer to you. Give us greater faith, love, courage and peace. Today, please be especially with:

First Special Category of Intercession for Day #14:
Make a special plea to God today (by name, if possible) for
All Children in the Church.

Second Special Category of Intercession for Day #14:
Make a special plea to God today (by name) for
Specific brethren in your Church Directory.

Let some folks know that you are praying for them today.

Day #15 to Pray for One Another

"Pray for one another...The effective, fervent prayer of
a righteous man avails much" (James 5:16).

Take time to fill in this prayer list for today. Then, pray for one another.

"Heavenly Father, please be with your church, and bless our every effort as we strive to glorify and honor your name. Please be with my brothers and sisters in Christ today. Strengthen us and draw each of us closer to you. Give us greater faith, love, courage and peace. Today, please be especially with:

First Special Category of Intercession for Day #15:
Make a special plea to God today for
Middle School and High School Youth Groups in the Church.

Second Special Category of Intercession for Day #15:
Make a special plea to God today (by name) for
Specific brethren in your Church Directory.

Let some folks know that you are praying for them today.

Day #16 to Pray for One Another

*"Pray for one another...The effective, fervent prayer of
a righteous man avails much" (James 5:16).*

Take time to fill in this prayer list for today. Then, pray for one another.

"Heavenly Father, please be with your church, and bless our every
effort as we strive to glorify and honor your name. Please be with my
brothers and sisters in Christ today. Strengthen us and draw each of
us closer to you. Give us greater faith, love, courage and peace.
Today, please be especially with:

_____

_____

_____

_____

_____

_____

_____

_____

First Special Category of Intercession for Day #16:
Make a special plea to God today (by name, if possible) for
Widows and Widowers in the Church.

Second Special Category of Intercession for Day #16:
Make a special plea to God today (by name) for
Specific brethren in your Church Directory.

Let some folks know that you are praying for them today.

Day #17 to Pray for One Another

*"Pray for one another...The effective, fervent prayer of
a righteous man avails much" (James 5:16).*

Take time to fill in this prayer list for today. Then, pray for one another.

"Heavenly Father, please be with your church, and bless our every
effort as we strive to glorify and honor your name. Please be with my
brothers and sisters in Christ today. Strengthen us and draw each of
us closer to you. Give us greater faith, love, courage and peace.
Today, please be especially with:

First Special Category of Intercession for Day #17:
Make a special plea to God today (by name, if possible) for
Shut-Ins in the Church.

Second Special Category of Intercession for Day #17:
Make a special plea to God today (by name) for
Specific brethren in your Church Directory.

Let some folks know that you are praying for them today.

Day #18 to Pray for One Another

*"Pray for one another...The effective, fervent prayer of
a righteous man avails much" (James 5:16).*

Take time to fill in this prayer list for today. Then, pray for one another.

"Heavenly Father, please be with your church, and bless our every
effort as we strive to glorify and honor your name. Please be with my
brothers and sisters in Christ today. Strengthen us and draw each of
us closer to you. Give us greater faith, love, courage and peace.
Today, please be especially with:

_____

_____

_____

_____

_____

_____

_____

_____

_____

First Special Category of Intercession for Day #18:
Make a special plea to God today (by name, if possible) for
The Elderly in the Church.

Second Special Category of Intercession for Day #18:
Make a special plea to God today (by name) for
Specific brethren in your Church Directory.

Let some folks know that you are praying for them today.

Day #19 to Pray for One Another

"Pray for one another...The effective, fervent prayer of
a righteous man avails much" (James 5:16).

Take time to fill in this prayer list for today. Then, pray for one another.

"Heavenly Father, please be with your church, and bless our every effort as we strive to glorify and honor your name. Please be with my brothers and sisters in Christ today. Strengthen us and draw each of us closer to you. Give us greater faith, love, courage and peace. Today, please be especially with:

First Special Category of Intercession for Day #19:
Make a special plea to God today (by name, if possible) for
Those Who Are Dealing with Health Problems.

Second Special Category of Intercession for Day #19:
Make a special plea to God today (by name) for
Specific brethren in your Church Directory.

Let some folks know that you are praying for them today.

Day #20 to Pray for One Another

*"Pray for one another...The effective, fervent prayer of
a righteous man avails much" (James 5:16).*

Take time to fill in this prayer list for today. Then, pray for one another.

"Heavenly Father, please be with your church, and bless our every effort as we strive to glorify and honor your name. Please be with my brothers and sisters in Christ today. Strengthen us and draw each of us closer to you. Give us greater faith, love, courage and peace. Today, please be especially with:

First Special Category of Intercession for Day #20:
Make a special plea to God today (by name, if possible) for
All New Converts in the Church.

Second Special Category of Intercession for Day #20:
Make a special plea to God today (by name) for
Specific brethren in your Church Directory.

Let some folks know that you are praying for them today.

Day #21 to Pray for One Another

*"Pray for one another...The effective, fervent prayer of
a righteous man avails much" (James 5:16).*

Take time to fill in this prayer list for today. Then, pray for one another.

"Heavenly Father, please be with your church, and bless our every effort as we strive to glorify and honor your name. Please be with my brothers and sisters in Christ today. Strengthen us and draw each of us closer to you. Give us greater faith, love, courage and peace. Today, please be especially with:

First Special Category of Intercession for Day #21:
Make a special plea to God today for
Those Who Often Attend But Have Not Obeyed the Gospel Yet.

Second Special Category of Intercession for Day #21:
Make a special plea to God today (by name) for
Specific brethren in your Church Directory.

Let some folks know that you are praying for them today.

Day #22 to Pray for One Another

*"Pray for one another...The effective, fervent prayer of
a righteous man avails much" (James 5:16).*

Take time to fill in this prayer list for today. Then, pray for one another.

"Heavenly Father, please be with your church, and bless our every effort as we strive to glorify and honor your name. Please be with my brothers and sisters in Christ today. Strengthen us and draw each of us closer to you. Give us greater faith, love, courage and peace. Today, please be especially with:

First Special Category of Intercession for Day #22:
Make a special plea to God today (by name, if possible) for
College Students in the Church.

Second Special Category of Intercession for Day #22:
Make a special plea to God today (by name) for
Specific brethren in your Church Directory.

Let some folks know that you are praying for them today.

Day #23 to Pray for One Another

*"Pray for one another...The effective, fervent prayer of
a righteous man avails much" (James 5:16).*

Take time to fill in this prayer list for today. Then, pray for one another.

"Heavenly Father, please be with your church, and bless our every effort as we strive to glorify and honor your name. Please be with my brothers and sisters in Christ today. Strengthen us and draw each of us closer to you. Give us greater faith, love, courage and peace. Today, please be especially with:

First Special Category of Intercession for Day #23:
Make a special plea to God today (by name, if possible) for
All Missionaries of the Lord's Church.

Second Special Category of Intercession for Day #23:
Make a special plea to God today (by name) for
Specific brethren in your Church Directory.

Let some folks know that you are praying for them today.

Day #24 to Pray for One Another

*"Pray for one another...The effective, fervent prayer of
a righteous man avails much" (James 5:16).*

Take time to fill in this prayer list for today. Then, pray for one another.

"Heavenly Father, please be with your church, and bless our every effort as we strive to glorify and honor your name. Please be with my brothers and sisters in Christ today. Strengthen us and draw each of us closer to you. Give us greater faith, love, courage and peace. Today, please be especially with:

_____

_____

_____

_____

_____

_____

_____

_____

First Special Category of Intercession for Day #24:
Make a special plea to God today for
Those Who Are Discouraged By the Trials & Distresses of Life.

Second Special Category of Intercession for Day #24:
Make a special plea to God today (by name) for
Specific brethren in your Church Directory.

Let some folks know that you are praying for them today.

Day #25 to Pray for One Another

"Pray for one another...The effective, fervent prayer of
a righteous man avails much" (James 5:16).

Take time to fill in this prayer list for today. Then, pray for one another.

"Heavenly Father, please be with your church, and bless our every effort as we strive to glorify and honor your name. Please be with my brothers and sisters in Christ today. Strengthen us and draw each of us closer to you. Give us greater faith, love, courage and peace. Today, please be especially with:

_____

_____

_____

_____

_____

_____

_____

_____

_____

_____

First Special Category of Intercession for Day #25:
Make a special plea to God today for
Those Who Are Struggling with Faith & Devotion to the Lord.

Second Special Category of Intercession for Day #25:
Make a special plea to God today (by name) for
Specific brethren in your Church Directory.

Let some folks know that you are praying for them today.

Day #26 to Pray for One Another

*"Pray for one another...The effective, fervent prayer of
a righteous man avails much" (James 5:16).*

Take time to fill in this prayer list for today. Then, pray for one another.

"Heavenly Father, please be with your church, and bless our every effort as we strive to glorify and honor your name. Please be with my brothers and sisters in Christ today. Strengthen us and draw each of us closer to you. Give us greater faith, love, courage and peace. Today, please be especially with:

First Special Category of Intercession for Day #26:
Make a special plea to God today for
Those Who Are Struggling with Sin and the Wiles of the Devil.

Second Special Category of Intercession for Day #26:
Make a special plea to God today (by name) for
Specific brethren in your Church Directory.

Let some folks know that you are praying for them today.

Day #27 to Pray for One Another

"Pray for one another...The effective, fervent prayer of
a righteous man avails much" (James 5:16).

Take time to fill in this prayer list for today. Then, pray for one another.

"Heavenly Father, please be with your church, and bless our every effort as we strive to glorify and honor your name. Please be with my brothers and sisters in Christ today. Strengthen us and draw each of us closer to you. Give us greater faith, love, courage and peace. Today, please be especially with:

_____

_____

_____

_____

_____

_____

_____

_____

_____

_____

First Special Category of Intercession for Day #27:
Make a special plea to God today for
Every Christian to Grow Stronger in Personal Faith.

Second Special Category of Intercession for Day #27:
Make a special plea to God today (by name) for
Specific brethren in your Church Directory.

Let some folks know that you are praying for them today.

Day #28 to Pray for One Another

*"Pray for one another...The effective, fervent prayer of
a righteous man avails much" (James 5:16).*

Take time to fill in this prayer list for today. Then, pray for one another.

"Heavenly Father, please be with your church, and bless our every
effort as we strive to glorify and honor your name. Please be with my
brothers and sisters in Christ today. Strengthen us and draw each of
us closer to you. Give us greater faith, love, courage and peace.
Today, please be especially with:

First Special Category of Intercession for Day #28:
Make a special plea to God today for
Every Christian to Seek Doors of Opportunity to Teach & Serve.

Second Special Category of Intercession for Day #28:
Make a special plea to God today (by name) for
Specific brethren in your Church Directory.

Let some folks know that you are praying for them today.

Walking Daily with My Lord

AUGUST:

28DAYS

To Triumph Over Sin

"Lead us not into temptation

but deliver us from evil"

(Matthew 6:13).

28DAYS To Triumph Over Sin

The GOAL for these 28 Days: *Intentionally, consistently and successfully target a specific sin or spiritual weakness in your life and work (with God's help) on eradicating it from your life.*

The Bible teaches that sin is:
- Disease (Psa. 41:4; Isa. 1:6).
- Deceptive (Heb. 3:13; Gal. 6:7).
- Debilitating (Heb. 12:1).
- Destructive (1 Cor. 6:18; Rev. 3:14-22; Prov. 14:34).
- Divisive (Isa. 59:1-2; Jas. 4:4; 2 Thess. 1:7-9).
- Deadly (Ezek. 18:20; Jas. 1:13-15; Rom. 6:23; Rev. 21:8).

Fortunately, the Bible also teaches that sin is DEFEATABLE:
- With God's Word (Psa. 119:11; 1 John 2:1; Matt. 4:1-11).
- With God's help (Matt. 6:13; Eph. 6:13, 18; Col. 4:2).
- With the strength (Phil. 4:13), way of escape (1 Cor. 10:13) and forgiveness (1 John 1:8-10) that God gives us.
- When we separate ourselves from it (2 Cor. 6:17) and put it off (Col. 3:8).

Let's Follow These Three Steps to Triumph Over Sin:
1. **Examine yourself. Identify THE sin besetting you.**
2. **Intensely pray about it every day, throughout the day.**
3. **Meditate upon and memorize helpful Scriptures.**

Let's focus on triumphing over sin for 28 days...

☐ Day 1	☐ Day 8	☐ Day 15	☐ Day 22
☐ Day 2	☐ Day 9	☐ Day 16	☐ Day 23
☐ Day 3	☐ Day 10	☐ Day 17	☐ Day 24
☐ Day 4	☐ Day 11	☐ Day 18	☐ Day 25
☐ Day 5	☐ Day 12	☐ Day 19	☐ Day 26
☐ Day 6	☐ Day 13	☐ Day 20	☐ Day 27
☐ Day 7	☐ Day 14	☐ Day 21	☐ Day 28

Day #1 to Triumph Over Sin

"Lead us not into temptation but deliver us from evil" (Matthew 6:13).

Take time to work on triumphing over sin TODAY and EVERY day.

1. **Examine yourself. Do a personal introspection.**
   a. Ask yourself, *"What am I struggling with the most? What is my besetting sin(s), that is constantly plaguing me?"*
   b. Identify the #1 sin with which you struggle, or your TOP TWO. (No more than three.)
2. **Intensely pray about it today at least 2-3 (if not 5-6) times.**
   a. *"Lord, please help me with this! I'm begging you, please help! I need you!"*
   b. *"Lord, please help me to put this from my mind and put this behind me! I cannot do this without Your help!"*
   c. Thank God for (and earnestly contemplate) the Divine attribute of encouragement highlighted below for today.
3. **Meditate upon and memorize a specific Bible verse(s) that addresses this issue. (See pages 255-264 for possibilities.)**
   a. Recite this verse multiple times today.
   b. Handwrite this verse today (maybe even below).
   c. Quote this verse out loud every time you're tempted in this area (just as Jesus did in Matthew 4:1-11).

In triumphing over sin, remember that...
God "is for us"
(Rom. 8:31).

(Pray intensely, meditate deeply, recite repeatedly today.)

Day #2 to Triumph Over Sin

"Lead us not into temptation but deliver us from evil" (Matthew 6:13).

Take time to work on triumphing over sin TODAY and EVERY day.

1. **Examine yourself. Do a personal introspection.**
   a. Ask yourself, *"What am I struggling with the most? What is my besetting sin(s), that is constantly plaguing me?"*
   b. Identify the #1 sin with which you struggle, or your TOP TWO. (No more than three.)
2. **Intensely pray about it today at least 2-3 (if not 5-6) times.**
   a. *"Lord, please help me with this!*
      I'm begging you, please help! I need you!"
   b. *"Lord, please help me to put this from my mind and put this behind me! I cannot do this without Your help!"*
   c. Thank God for (and earnestly contemplate) the Divine attribute of encouragement highlighted below for today.
3. **Meditate upon and memorize a specific Bible verse(s) that addresses this issue. (See pages 255-264 for possibilities.)**
   a. Recite this verse multiple times today.
   b. Handwrite this verse today (maybe even below).
   c. Quote this verse out loud every time you're tempted in this area (just as Jesus did in Matthew 4:1-11).

In triumphing over sin, remember that...
God "is able"
(Eph. 3:20).

(Pray intensely, meditate deeply, recite repeatedly today.)

Day #3 to Triumph Over Sin

"Lead us not into temptation but deliver us from evil" (Matthew 6:13).

Take time to work on triumphing over sin TODAY and EVERY day.

1. **Examine yourself. Do a personal introspection.**
   a. Ask yourself, *"What am I struggling with the most? What is my besetting sin(s), that is constantly plaguing me?"*
   b. Identify the #1 sin with which you struggle, or your TOP TWO. (No more than three.)
2. **Intensely pray about it today at least 2-3 (if not 5-6) times.**
   a. *"Lord, please help me with this! I'm begging you, please help! I need you!"*
   b. *"Lord, please help me to put this from my mind and put this behind me! I cannot do this without Your help!"*
   c. Thank God for (and earnestly contemplate) the Divine attribute of encouragement highlighted below for today.
3. **Meditate upon and memorize a specific Bible verse(s) that addresses this issue. (See pages 255-264 for possibilities.)**
   a. Recite this verse multiple times today.
   b. Handwrite this verse today (maybe even below).
   c. Quote this verse out loud every time you're tempted in this area (just as Jesus did in Matthew 4:1-11).

In triumphing over sin, remember that...
God "is faithful"
(1 Cor. 10:13).

(Pray intensely, meditate deeply, recite repeatedly today.)

Day #4 to Triumph Over Sin

"Lead us not into temptation but deliver us from evil" (Matthew 6:13).

Take time to work on triumphing over sin TODAY and EVERY day.

1. **Examine yourself. Do a personal introspection.**
   a. Ask yourself, *"What am I struggling with the most? What is my besetting sin(s), that is constantly plaguing me?"*
   b. Identify the #1 sin with which you struggle, or your TOP TWO. (No more than three.)
2. **Intensely pray about it today at least 2-3 (if not 5-6) times.**
   a. *"Lord, please help me with this!*
      I'm begging you, please help! I need you!"
   b. *"Lord, please help me to put this from my mind and put this behind me! I cannot do this without Your help!"*
   c. Thank God for (and earnestly contemplate) the Divine attribute of encouragement highlighted below for today.
3. **Meditate upon and memorize a specific Bible verse(s) that addresses this issue. (See pages 255-264 for possibilities.)**
   a. Recite this verse multiple times today.
   b. Handwrite this verse today (maybe even below).
   c. Quote this verse out loud every time you're tempted in this area (just as Jesus did in Matthew 4:1-11).

In triumphing over sin, remember that...
God "is with you"
(Josh. 1:9).

(Pray intensely, meditate deeply, recite repeatedly today.)

Day #5 to Triumph Over Sin

"Lead us not into temptation but deliver us from evil" (Matthew 6:13).

Take time to work on triumphing over sin TODAY and EVERY day.

1. **Examine yourself. Do a personal introspection.**
   a. Ask yourself, *"What am I struggling with the most? What is my besetting sin(s), that is constantly plaguing me?"*
   b. Identify the #1 sin with which you struggle, or your TOP TWO. (No more than three.)
2. **Intensely pray about it today at least 2-3 (if not 5-6) times.**
   a. *"Lord, please help me with this!*
      I'm begging you, please help! I need you!"
   b. *"Lord, please help me to put this from my mind and put this behind me! I cannot do this without Your help!"*
   c. Thank God for (and earnestly contemplate) the Divine attribute of encouragement highlighted below for today.
3. **Meditate upon and memorize a specific Bible verse(s) that addresses this issue. (See pages 255-264 for possibilities.)**
   a. Recite this verse multiple times today.
   b. Handwrite this verse today (maybe even below).
   c. Quote this verse out loud every time you're tempted in this area (just as Jesus did in Matthew 4:1-11).

In triumphing over sin, remember that...
God "is greater"
(1 John 4:4).

(Pray intensely, meditate deeply, recite repeatedly today.)

Day #6 to Triumph Over Sin

"Lead us not into temptation but deliver us from evil" (Matthew 6:13).

Take time to work on triumphing over sin TODAY and EVERY day.

1. **Examine yourself. Do a personal introspection.**
   a. Ask yourself, *"What am I struggling with the most? What is my besetting sin(s), that is constantly plaguing me?"*
   b. Identify the #1 sin with which you struggle, or your TOP TWO. (No more than three.)
2. **Intensely pray about it today at least 2-3 (if not 5-6) times.**
   a. *"Lord, please help me with this! I'm begging you, please help! I need you!"*
   b. *"Lord, please help me to put this from my mind and put this behind me! I cannot do this without Your help!"*
   c. Thank God for (and earnestly contemplate) the Divine attribute of encouragement highlighted below for today.
3. **Meditate upon and memorize a specific Bible verse(s) that addresses this issue. (See pages 255-264 for possibilities.)**
   a. Recite this verse multiple times today.
   b. Handwrite this verse today (maybe even below).
   c. Quote this verse out loud every time you're tempted in this area (just as Jesus did in Matthew 4:1-11).

In triumphing over sin, remember that...
God "is our refuge and strength" (Psa. 46:1).

(Pray intensely, meditate deeply, recite repeatedly today.)

Day #7 to Triumph Over Sin

"Lead us not into temptation but deliver us from evil" (Matthew 6:13).

Take time to work on triumphing over sin TODAY and EVERY day.

1. **Examine yourself. Do a personal introspection.**
   a. Ask yourself, *"What am I struggling with the most? What is my besetting sin(s), that is constantly plaguing me?"*
   b. Identify the #1 sin with which you struggle, or your TOP TWO. (No more than three.)
2. **Intensely pray about it today at least 2-3 (if not 5-6) times.**
   a. *"Lord, please help me with this! I'm begging you, please help! I need you!"*
   b. *"Lord, please help me to put this from my mind and put this behind me! I cannot do this without Your help!"*
   c. Thank God for (and earnestly contemplate) the Divine attribute of encouragement highlighted below for today.
3. **Meditate upon and memorize a specific Bible verse(s) that addresses this issue. (See pages 255-264 for possibilities.)**
   a. Recite this verse multiple times today.
   b. Handwrite this verse today (maybe even below).
   c. Quote this verse out loud every time you're tempted in this area (just as Jesus did in Matthew 4:1-11).

In triumphing over sin, remember that...
God "is the Rock of our salvation" (Psa. 95:1).

(Pray intensely, meditate deeply, recite repeatedly today.)

Day #8 to Triumph Over Sin

"Lead us not into temptation but deliver us from evil" (Matthew 6:13).

Take time to work on triumphing over sin TODAY and EVERY day.

1. **Examine yourself. Do a personal introspection.**
    a. Ask yourself, *"What am I struggling with the most? What is my besetting sin(s), that is constantly plaguing me?"*
    b. Identify the #1 sin with which you struggle, or your TOP TWO. (No more than three.)
2. **Intensely pray about it today at least 2-3 (if not 5-6) times.**
    a. *"Lord, please help me with this!*
       I'm begging you, please help! I need you!"
    b. *"Lord, please help me to put this from my mind and put this behind me! I cannot do this without Your help!"*
    c. Thank God for (and earnestly contemplate) the Divine attribute of encouragement highlighted below for today.
3. **Meditate upon and memorize a specific Bible verse(s) that addresses this issue. (See pages 255-264 for possibilities.)**
    a. Recite this verse multiple times today.
    b. Handwrite this verse today (maybe even below).
    c. Quote this verse out loud every time you're tempted in this area (just as Jesus did in Matthew 4:1-11).

In triumphing over sin, remember that...
God "forgives"
(Psa. 103:3).

(Pray intensely, meditate deeply, recite repeatedly today.)

Day #9 to Triumph Over Sin

"Lead us not into temptation but deliver us from evil" (Matthew 6:13).

Take time to work on triumphing over sin TODAY and EVERY day.

1. **Examine yourself. Do a personal introspection.**
   a. Ask yourself, *"What am I struggling with the most? What is my besetting sin(s), that is constantly plaguing me?"*
   b. Identify the #1 sin with which you struggle, or your TOP TWO. (No more than three.)
2. **Intensely pray about it today at least 2-3 (if not 5-6) times.**
   a. *"Lord, please help me with this! I'm begging you, please help! I need you!"*
   b. *"Lord, please help me to put this from my mind and put this behind me! I cannot do this without Your help!"*
   c. Thank God for (and earnestly contemplate) the Divine attribute of encouragement highlighted below for today.
3. **Meditate upon and memorize a specific Bible verse(s) that addresses this issue. (See pages 255-264 for possibilities.)**
   a. Recite this verse multiple times today.
   b. Handwrite this verse today (maybe even below).
   c. Quote this verse out loud every time you're tempted in this area (just as Jesus did in Matthew 4:1-11).

In triumphing over sin, remember that...
God "knows"
(Psa. 1:6).

(Pray intensely, meditate deeply, recite repeatedly today.)

Day #10 to Triumph Over Sin

"Lead us not into temptation but deliver us from evil" (Matthew 6:13).

Take time to work on triumphing over sin TODAY and EVERY day.

1. **Examine yourself. Do a personal introspection.**
   a. Ask yourself, *"What am I struggling with the most? What is my besetting sin(s), that is constantly plaguing me?"*
   b. Identify the #1 sin with which you struggle, or your TOP TWO. (No more than three.)
2. **Intensely pray about it today at least 2-3 (if not 5-6) times.**
   a. *"Lord, please help me with this! I'm begging you, please help! I need you!"*
   b. *"Lord, please help me to put this from my mind and put this behind me! I cannot do this without Your help!"*
   c. Thank God for (and earnestly contemplate) the Divine attribute of encouragement highlighted below for today.
3. **Meditate upon and memorize a specific Bible verse(s) that addresses this issue. (See pages 255-264 for possibilities.)**
   a. Recite this verse multiple times today.
   b. Handwrite this verse today (maybe even below).
   c. Quote this verse out loud every time you're tempted in this area (just as Jesus did in Matthew 4:1-11).

In triumphing over sin, remember that...
God "cannot lie"
(Tit. 1:2).

(Pray intensely, meditate deeply, recite repeatedly today.)

Day #11 to Triumph Over Sin

"Lead us not into temptation but deliver us from evil" (Matthew 6:13).

Take time to work on triumphing over sin TODAY and EVERY day.

1. **Examine yourself. Do a personal introspection.**
   a. Ask yourself, *"What am I struggling with the most? What is my besetting sin(s), that is constantly plaguing me?"*
   b. Identify the #1 sin with which you struggle, or your TOP TWO. (No more than three.)
2. **Intensely pray about it today at least 2-3 (if not 5-6) times.**
   a. *"Lord, please help me with this! I'm begging you, please help! I need you!"*
   b. *"Lord, please help me to put this from my mind and put this behind me! I cannot do this without Your help!"*
   c. Thank God for (and earnestly contemplate) the Divine attribute of encouragement highlighted below for today.
3. **Meditate upon and memorize a specific Bible verse(s) that addresses this issue. (See pages 255-264 for possibilities.)**
   a. Recite this verse multiple times today.
   b. Handwrite this verse today (maybe even below).
   c. Quote this verse out loud every time you're tempted in this area (just as Jesus did in Matthew 4:1-11).

In triumphing over sin, remember that...
God is "a very present help"
(Psa. 46:1).

(Pray intensely, meditate deeply, recite repeatedly today.)

Day #12 to Triumph Over Sin

"Lead us not into temptation but deliver us from evil" (Matthew 6:13).

Take time to work on triumphing over sin TODAY and EVERY day.

1. **Examine yourself. Do a personal introspection.**
   a. Ask yourself, *"What am I struggling with the most? What is my besetting sin(s), that is constantly plaguing me?"*
   b. Identify the #1 sin with which you struggle, or your TOP TWO. (No more than three.)
2. **Intensely pray about it today at least 2-3 (if not 5-6) times.**
   a. *"Lord, please help me with this! I'm begging you, please help! I need you!"*
   b. *"Lord, please help me to put this from my mind and put this behind me! I cannot do this without Your help!"*
   c. Thank God for (and earnestly contemplate) the Divine attribute of encouragement highlighted below for today.
3. **Meditate upon and memorize a specific Bible verse(s) that addresses this issue. (See pages 255-264 for possibilities.)**
   a. Recite this verse multiple times today.
   b. Handwrite this verse today (maybe even below).
   c. Quote this verse out loud every time you're tempted in this area (just as Jesus did in Matthew 4:1-11).

In triumphing over sin, remember that...
God is "not willing that any should perish" (2 Pet. 3:9).

(Pray intensely, meditate deeply, recite repeatedly today.)

Day #13 to Triumph Over Sin

"Lead us not into temptation but deliver us from evil" (Matthew 6:13).

Take time to work on triumphing over sin TODAY and EVERY day.

1. **Examine yourself. Do a personal introspection.**
    a. Ask yourself, *"What am I struggling with the most? What is my besetting sin(s), that is constantly plaguing me?"*
    b. Identify the #1 sin with which you struggle, or your TOP TWO. (No more than three.)
2. **Intensely pray about it today at least 2-3 (if not 5-6) times.**
    a. *"Lord, please help me with this!*
        I'm begging you, please help! I need you!"
    b. *"Lord, please help me to put this from my mind and put this behind me! I cannot do this without Your help!"*
    c. Thank God for (and earnestly contemplate) the Divine attribute of encouragement highlighted below for today.
3. **Meditate upon and memorize a specific Bible verse(s) that addresses this issue. (See pages 255-264 for possibilities.)**
    a. Recite this verse multiple times today.
    b. Handwrite this verse today (maybe even below).
    c. Quote this verse out loud every time you're tempted in this area (just as Jesus did in Matthew 4:1-11).

In triumphing over sin, remember that...
God "loves you"
(John 16:27).

(Pray intensely, meditate deeply, recite repeatedly today.)

Day #14 to Triumph Over Sin

"Lead us not into temptation but deliver us from evil" (Matthew 6:13).

Take time to work on triumphing over sin TODAY and EVERY day.

1. **Examine yourself. Do a personal introspection.**
   a. Ask yourself, *"What am I struggling with the most? What is my besetting sin(s), that is constantly plaguing me?"*
   b. Identify the #1 sin with which you struggle, or your TOP TWO. (No more than three.)
2. **Intensely pray about it today at least 2-3 (if not 5-6) times.**
   a. *"Lord, please help me with this! I'm begging you, please help! I need you!"*
   b. *"Lord, please help me to put this from my mind and put this behind me! I cannot do this without Your help!"*
   c. Thank God for (and earnestly contemplate) the Divine attribute of encouragement highlighted below for today.
3. **Meditate upon and memorize a specific Bible verse(s) that addresses this issue. (See pages 255-264 for possibilities.)**
   a. Recite this verse multiple times today.
   b. Handwrite this verse today (maybe even below).
   c. Quote this verse out loud every time you're tempted in this area (just as Jesus did in Matthew 4:1-11).

In triumphing over sin, remember that...
God "is longsuffering toward us"
(2 Pet. 3:9).

(Pray intensely, meditate deeply, recite repeatedly today.)

Day #15 to Triumph Over Sin

"Lead us not into temptation but deliver us from evil" (Matthew 6:13).

Take time to work on triumphing over sin TODAY and EVERY day.

1. **Examine yourself. Do a personal introspection.**
   a. Ask yourself, *"What am I struggling with the most? What is my besetting sin(s), that is constantly plaguing me?"*
   b. Identify the #1 sin with which you struggle, or your TOP TWO. (No more than three.)
2. **Intensely pray about it today at least 2-3 (if not 5-6) times.**
   a. *"Lord, please help me with this! I'm begging you, please help! I need you!"*
   b. *"Lord, please help me to put this from my mind and put this behind me! I cannot do this without Your help!"*
   c. Thank God for (and earnestly contemplate) the Divine attribute of encouragement highlighted below for today.
3. **Meditate upon and memorize a specific Bible verse(s) that addresses this issue. (See pages 255-264 for possibilities.)**
   a. Recite this verse multiple times today.
   b. Handwrite this verse today (maybe even below).
   c. Quote this verse out loud every time you're tempted in this area (just as Jesus did in Matthew 4:1-11).

In triumphing over sin, remember that...
God "is rich in mercy"
(Eph. 2:4).

(Pray intensely, meditate deeply, recite repeatedly today.)

Day #16 to Triumph Over Sin

"Lead us not into temptation but deliver us from evil" (Matthew 6:13).

Take time to work on triumphing over sin TODAY and EVERY day.

1. **Examine yourself. Do a personal introspection.**
   a. Ask yourself, *"What am I struggling with the most? What is my besetting sin(s), that is constantly plaguing me?"*
   b. Identify the #1 sin with which you struggle, or your TOP TWO. (No more than three.)
2. **Intensely pray about it today at least 2-3 (if not 5-6) times.**
   a. *"Lord, please help me with this! I'm begging you, please help! I need you!"*
   b. *"Lord, please help me to put this from my mind and put this behind me! I cannot do this without Your help!"*
   c. Thank God for (and earnestly contemplate) the Divine attribute of encouragement highlighted below for today.
3. **Meditate upon and memorize a specific Bible verse(s) that addresses this issue. (See pages 255-264 for possibilities.)**
   a. Recite this verse multiple times today.
   b. Handwrite this verse today (maybe even below).
   c. Quote this verse out loud every time you're tempted in this area (just as Jesus did in Matthew 4:1-11).

In triumphing over sin, remember that...
God "is slow to anger"
(Nah. 1:3).

(Pray intensely, meditate deeply, recite repeatedly today.)

Day #17 to Triumph Over Sin

"Lead us not into temptation but deliver us from evil" (Matthew 6:13).

Take time to work on triumphing over sin TODAY and EVERY day.

1. **Examine yourself. Do a personal introspection.**
   a. Ask yourself, *"What am I struggling with the most? What is my besetting sin(s), that is constantly plaguing me?"*
   b. Identify the #1 sin with which you struggle, or your TOP TWO. (No more than three.)
2. **Intensely pray about it today at least 2-3 (if not 5-6) times.**
   a. *"Lord, please help me with this!*
      I'm begging you, please help! I need you!"
   b. *"Lord, please help me to put this from my mind and put this behind me! I cannot do this without Your help!"*
   c. Thank God for (and earnestly contemplate) the Divine attribute of encouragement highlighted below for today.
3. **Meditate upon and memorize a specific Bible verse(s) that addresses this issue. (See pages 255-264 for possibilities.)**
   a. Recite this verse multiple times today.
   b. Handwrite this verse today (maybe even below).
   c. Quote this verse out loud every time you're tempted in this area (just as Jesus did in Matthew 4:1-11).

In triumphing over sin, remember that...
God is "full of compassion"
(Psa. 145:8).

(Pray intensely, meditate deeply, recite repeatedly today.)

Day #18 to Triumph Over Sin

"Lead us not into temptation but deliver us from evil" (Matthew 6:13).

Take time to work on triumphing over sin TODAY and EVERY day.

1. **Examine yourself. Do a personal introspection.**
    a. Ask yourself, *"What am I struggling with the most? What is my besetting sin(s), that is constantly plaguing me?"*
    b. Identify the #1 sin with which you struggle, or your TOP TWO. (No more than three.)
2. **Intensely pray about it today at least 2-3 (if not 5-6) times.**
    a. *"Lord, please help me with this!*
       I'm begging you, please help! I need you!"
    b. *"Lord, please help me to put this from my mind and put this behind me! I cannot do this without Your help!"*
    c. Thank God for (and earnestly contemplate) the Divine attribute of encouragement highlighted below for today.
3. **Meditate upon and memorize a specific Bible verse(s) that addresses this issue. (See pages 255-264 for possibilities.)**
    a. Recite this verse multiple times today.
    b. Handwrite this verse today (maybe even below).
    c. Quote this verse out loud every time you're tempted in this area (just as Jesus did in Matthew 4:1-11).

In triumphing over sin, remember that...
God "hears us"
(1 John 5:14).

(Pray intensely, meditate deeply, recite repeatedly today.)

Day #19 to Triumph Over Sin

"Lead us not into temptation but deliver us from evil" (Matthew 6:13).

Take time to work on triumphing over sin TODAY and EVERY day.

1. **Examine yourself. Do a personal introspection.**
   a. Ask yourself, *"What am I struggling with the most? What is my besetting sin(s), that is constantly plaguing me?"*
   b. Identify the #1 sin with which you struggle, or your TOP TWO. (No more than three.)
2. **Intensely pray about it today at least 2-3 (if not 5-6) times.**
   a. *"Lord, please help me with this!*
       I'm begging you, please help! I need you!"
   b. *"Lord, please help me to put this from my mind and put this behind me! I cannot do this without Your help!"*
   c. Thank God for (and earnestly contemplate) the Divine attribute of encouragement highlighted below for today.
3. **Meditate upon and memorize a specific Bible verse(s) that addresses this issue. (See pages 255-264 for possibilities.)**
   a. Recite this verse multiple times today.
   b. Handwrite this verse today (maybe even below).
   c. Quote this verse out loud every time you're tempted in this area (just as Jesus did in Matthew 4:1-11).

In triumphing over sin, remember that...
God "is able to keep you from stumbling" (Jude 24).

(Pray intensely, meditate deeply, recite repeatedly today.)

Day #20 to Triumph Over Sin

"Lead us not into temptation but deliver us from evil" (Matthew 6:13).

Take time to work on triumphing over sin TODAY and EVERY day.

1. **Examine yourself. Do a personal introspection.**
   a. Ask yourself, *"What am I struggling with the most? What is my besetting sin(s), that is constantly plaguing me?"*
   b. Identify the #1 sin with which you struggle, or your TOP TWO. (No more than three.)
2. **Intensely pray about it today at least 2-3 (if not 5-6) times.**
   a. *"Lord, please help me with this!*
      I'm begging you, please help! I need you!"
   b. *"Lord, please help me to put this from my mind and put this behind me! I cannot do this without Your help!"*
   c. Thank God for (and earnestly contemplate) the Divine attribute of encouragement highlighted below for today.
3. **Meditate upon and memorize a specific Bible verse(s) that addresses this issue. (See pages 255-264 for possibilities.)**
   a. Recite this verse multiple times today.
   b. Handwrite this verse today (maybe even below).
   c. Quote this verse out loud every time you're tempted in this area (just as Jesus did in Matthew 4:1-11).

In triumphing over sin, remember that...
God "is able to aid [when] tempted" (Heb. 2:18).

(Pray intensely, meditate deeply, recite repeatedly today.)

Day #21 to Triumph Over Sin

"Lead us not into temptation but deliver us from evil" (Matthew 6:13).

Take time to work on triumphing over sin TODAY and EVERY day.

1. **Examine yourself. Do a personal introspection.**
    a. Ask yourself, *"What am I struggling with the most? What is my besetting sin(s), that is constantly plaguing me?"*
    b. Identify the #1 sin with which you struggle, or your TOP TWO. (No more than three.)
2. **Intensely pray about it today at least 2-3 (if not 5-6) times.**
    a. *"Lord, please help me with this!*
       I'm begging you, please help! I need you!"
    b. *"Lord, please help me to put this from my mind and put this behind me! I cannot do this without Your help!"*
    c. Thank God for (and earnestly contemplate) the Divine attribute of encouragement highlighted below for today.
3. **Meditate upon and memorize a specific Bible verse(s) that addresses this issue. (See pages 255-264 for possibilities.)**
    a. Recite this verse multiple times today.
    b. Handwrite this verse today (maybe even below).
    c. Quote this verse out loud every time you're tempted in this area (just as Jesus did in Matthew 4:1-11).

In triumphing over sin, remember that...
God "knows how to deliver" (2 Pet. 2:9).

(Pray intensely, meditate deeply, recite repeatedly today.)

Day #22 to Triumph Over Sin

"Lead us not into temptation but deliver us from evil" (Matthew 6:13).

Take time to work on triumphing over sin TODAY and EVERY day.

1. **Examine yourself. Do a personal introspection.**
   a. Ask yourself, *"What am I struggling with the most? What is my besetting sin(s), that is constantly plaguing me?"*
   b. Identify the #1 sin with which you struggle, or your TOP TWO. (No more than three.)
2. **Intensely pray about it today at least 2-3 (if not 5-6) times.**
   a. *"Lord, please help me with this!*
      I'm begging you, please help! I need you!"
   b. *"Lord, please help me to put this from my mind and put this behind me! I cannot do this without Your help!"*
   c. Thank God for (and earnestly contemplate) the Divine attribute of encouragement highlighted below for today.
3. **Meditate upon and memorize a specific Bible verse(s) that addresses this issue. (See pages 255-264 for possibilities.)**
   a. Recite this verse multiple times today.
   b. Handwrite this verse today (maybe even below).
   c. Quote this verse out loud every time you're tempted in this area (just as Jesus did in Matthew 4:1-11).

In triumphing over sin, remember that...
God "will deliver"
(2 Tim. 4:18).

(Pray intensely, meditate deeply, recite repeatedly today.)

Day #23 to Triumph Over Sin

"Lead us not into temptation but deliver us from evil" (Matthew 6:13).

Take time to work on triumphing over sin TODAY and EVERY day.

1. **Examine yourself. Do a personal introspection.**
   a. Ask yourself, *"What am I struggling with the most? What is my besetting sin(s), that is constantly plaguing me?"*
   b. Identify the #1 sin with which you struggle, or your TOP TWO. (No more than three.)
2. **Intensely pray about it today at least 2-3 (if not 5-6) times.**
   a. *"Lord, please help me with this!*
      I'm begging you, please help! I need you!"
   b. *"Lord, please help me to put this from my mind and put this behind me! I cannot do this without Your help!"*
   c. Thank God for (and earnestly contemplate) the Divine attribute of encouragement highlighted below for today.
3. **Meditate upon and memorize a specific Bible verse(s) that addresses this issue. (See pages 255-264 for possibilities.)**
   a. Recite this verse multiple times today.
   b. Handwrite this verse today (maybe even below).
   c. Quote this verse out loud every time you're tempted in this area (just as Jesus did in Matthew 4:1-11).

In triumphing over sin, remember that...
God "knows those who are His"
(2 Tim. 2:19).

(Pray intensely, meditate deeply, recite repeatedly today.)

Day #24 to Triumph Over Sin

"Lead us not into temptation but deliver us from evil" (Matthew 6:13).

Take time to work on triumphing over sin TODAY and EVERY day.

1. **Examine yourself. Do a personal introspection.**
   a. Ask yourself, *"What am I struggling with the most? What is my besetting sin(s), that is constantly plaguing me?"*
   b. Identify the #1 sin with which you struggle, or your TOP TWO. (No more than three.)
2. **Intensely pray about it today at least 2-3 (if not 5-6) times.**
   a. *"Lord, please help me with this!*
      I'm begging you, please help! I need you!"
   b. *"Lord, please help me to put this from my mind and put this behind me! I cannot do this without Your help!"*
   c. Thank God for (and earnestly contemplate) the Divine attribute of encouragement highlighted below for today.
3. **Meditate upon and memorize a specific Bible verse(s) that addresses this issue. (See pages 255-264 for possibilities.)**
   a. Recite this verse multiple times today.
   b. Handwrite this verse today (maybe even below).
   c. Quote this verse out loud every time you're tempted in this area (just as Jesus did in Matthew 4:1-11).

In triumphing over sin, remember that...
God "knows what you need"
(Matt. 6:8).

(Pray intensely, meditate deeply, recite repeatedly today.)

Day #25 to Triumph Over Sin

"Lead us not into temptation but deliver us from evil" (Matthew 6:13).

Take time to work on triumphing over sin TODAY and EVERY day.

1. **Examine yourself. Do a personal introspection.**
   a. Ask yourself, *"What am I struggling with the most? What is my besetting sin(s), that is constantly plaguing me?"*
   b. Identify the #1 sin with which you struggle, or your TOP TWO. (No more than three.)
2. **Intensely pray about it today at least 2-3 (if not 5-6) times.**
   a. *"Lord, please help me with this!*
      I'm begging you, please help! I need you!"
   b. *"Lord, please help me to put this from my mind and put this behind me! I cannot do this without Your help!"*
   c. Thank God for (and earnestly contemplate) the Divine attribute of encouragement highlighted below for today.
3. **Meditate upon and memorize a specific Bible verse(s) that addresses this issue. (See pages 255-264 for possibilities.)**
   a. Recite this verse multiple times today.
   b. Handwrite this verse today (maybe even below).
   c. Quote this verse out loud every time you're tempted in this area (just as Jesus did in Matthew 4:1-11).

In triumphing over sin, remember that...
God "will establish you and guard you" (2 Thess. 3:3).

(Pray intensely, meditate deeply, recite repeatedly today.)

Day #26 to Triumph Over Sin

"Lead us not into temptation but deliver us from evil" (Matthew 6:13).

Take time to work on triumphing over sin TODAY and EVERY day.

1. **Examine yourself. Do a personal introspection.**
   a. Ask yourself, *"What am I struggling with the most? What is my besetting sin(s), that is constantly plaguing me?"*
   b. Identify the #1 sin with which you struggle, or your TOP TWO. (No more than three.)
2. **Intensely pray about it today at least 2-3 (if not 5-6) times.**
   a. *"Lord, please help me with this!*
      I'm begging you, please help! I need you!"
   b. *"Lord, please help me to put this from my mind and put this behind me! I cannot do this without Your help!"*
   c. Thank God for (and earnestly contemplate) the Divine attribute of encouragement highlighted below for today.
3. **Meditate upon and memorize a specific Bible verse(s) that addresses this issue. (See pages 255-264 for possibilities.)**
   a. Recite this verse multiple times today.
   b. Handwrite this verse today (maybe even below).
   c. Quote this verse out loud every time you're tempted in this area (just as Jesus did in Matthew 4:1-11).

In triumphing over sin, remember that...
God will "make the way of escape"
(1 Cor. 10:13).

(Pray intensely, meditate deeply, recite repeatedly today.)

Day #27 to Triumph Over Sin

"Lead us not into temptation but deliver us from evil" (Matthew 6:13).

Take time to work on triumphing over sin TODAY and EVERY day.

1. **Examine yourself. Do a personal introspection.**
   a. Ask yourself, *"What am I struggling with the most? What is my besetting sin(s), that is constantly plaguing me?"*
   b. Identify the #1 sin with which you struggle, or your TOP TWO. (No more than three.)
2. **Intensely pray about it today at least 2-3 (if not 5-6) times.**
   a. *"Lord, please help me with this!*
      I'm begging you, please help! I need you!"
   b. *"Lord, please help me to put this from my mind and put this behind me! I cannot do this without Your help!"*
   c. Thank God for (and earnestly contemplate) the Divine attribute of encouragement highlighted below for today.
3. **Meditate upon and memorize a specific Bible verse(s) that addresses this issue. (See pages 255-264 for possibilities.)**
   a. Recite this verse multiple times today.
   b. Handwrite this verse today (maybe even below).
   c. Quote this verse out loud every time you're tempted in this area (just as Jesus did in Matthew 4:1-11).

In triumphing over sin, remember that...
God will "will never leave you"
(Heb. 13:5).

(Pray intensely, meditate deeply, recite repeatedly today.)

Day #28 to Triumph Over Sin

"Lead us not into temptation but deliver us from evil" (Matthew 6:13).

Take time to work on triumphing over sin TODAY and EVERY day.

1. **Examine yourself. Do a personal introspection.**
    a. Ask yourself, *"What am I struggling with the most? What is my besetting sin(s), that is constantly plaguing me?"*
    b. Identify the #1 sin with which you struggle, or your TOP TWO. (No more than three.)
2. **Intensely pray about it today at least 2-3 (if not 5-6) times.**
    a. *"Lord, please help me with this! I'm begging you, please help! I need you!"*
    b. *"Lord, please help me to put this from my mind and put this behind me! I cannot do this without Your help!"*
    c. Thank God for (and earnestly contemplate) the Divine attribute of encouragement highlighted below for today.
3. **Meditate upon and memorize a specific Bible verse(s) that addresses this issue. (See pages 255-264 for possibilities.)**
    a. Recite this verse multiple times today.
    b. Handwrite this verse today (maybe even below).
    c. Quote this verse out loud every time you're tempted in this area (just as Jesus did in Matthew 4:1-11).

In triumphing over sin, remember that...
**God "is faithful and just to forgive"
(1 John 1:9).**

(Pray intensely, meditate deeply, recite repeatedly today.)

Bible Verses from God
to Read, Study, Write, Memorize and Quote
in an Effort to Triumph Over Sin

Adultery (Gen. 2:24; Ex. 20:14; Psa. 24:3-4; 51:10; Prov. 6:32; Matt. 5:8; 14:4; 19:3-9; Mark 7:21-23; 10:11-12; Rom. 1:28-32; 12:1-2; 13:14; 1 Cor. 6:9-11, 18 -20; 7:10-11; 2 Cor. 6:17; Gal. 5:19-21; Eph. 5:3-5; Col. 3:5; 1 Thess. 4:3-7; 1 Tim. 5:22b; Heb. 13:4; Jas. 3:17; Rev. 21:8)

Anger (Psa. 37:8; Prov. 14:17, 29; 15:1; 16:32; 17:14; 19:11; 25:28; 29:22; Ecc. 7:9; Matt. 5:22; Rom. 12:18; Gal. 5:19-21, 22-23; Eph. 4:31-32; Phil. 4:6-7; Col. 3:8, 12-15; Tit. 3:2; Jas. 1:19-20; 3:17-18)

Anxiety (Josh. 1:9; Psa. 23:1-6; 37:7-8, 25; 46:1-11; 55:22; 119:165; Prov. 3:5-7; 12:25; Isa. 41:10; Matt. 6:24-34; 11:28-30; Luke 1:37; 8:14; John 14:1, 27; 16:33; Rom. 8:28, 31; Phil. 4:6-7, 13; Col. 3:15; 2 Tim. 2:19; Heb. 13:5-6; 1 Pet. 5:7)

Apathy (Matt. 6:33; 25:3, 18, 24-26; 25:26; Luke 9:23; 14:16-20; John 9:4; Acts 24:25; Rom. 12:11; 1 Cor. 6:19-20; 15:58; Gal. 6:9; Eph. 2:10; 5:16; 6:10-18; Col. 3:23-24; 2 Tim. 2:3-6; Tit. 2:7, 14; 3:8, 14; Heb. 5:11; 6:10-12; Jas. 4:7-10, 17; Rev. 2:5; 3:15-16; 21:8)

Argumentative spirit (Psa. 140:1-2; Prov. 10:12; 15:1, 18; 17:14; 18:6; 20:3; 26:17, 21; Matt. 7:12; Rom. 12:17-21; 14:19; 2 Cor. 12:20-21; Gal. 5:19-21; Eph. 4:31-32; Phil. 2:3-5; Col. 3:15; 2 Tim. 2:24; Tit. 3:2; Heb. 12:14; Jas. 1:19-20; 3:17-18)

Arrogance (1 Sam. 2:3; Psa. 10:4; 31:23; Prov. 3:5-7; 6:16-17; 8:13; 11:2; 13:10; 16:5, 18; 18:12; 21:4, 24; 26:12; 29:23; Isa. 5:21; Matt. 18:4; 23:12; Mark 7:21-23; Luke 18:9-14; Rom. 1:28-32; 12:3, 16; 1 Cor. 10:12; 2 Cor. 12:20 -21; Gal. 5:26; 6:3; Phil. 2:3-5; Col. 3:12; 2 Tim. 3:2-4; Tit. 3:2; Jas. 4:6, 10, 16; 1 Pet. 5:5; 1 John 2:16)

Backbiting (Ex. 23:1; Lev. 19:16; Psa. 15:1-3; 19:14; 34:13; 101:5; 141:3; Prov. 10:18; 11:13; 16:28; 17:9; 20:19; 21:23; 26:20; Matt. 7:12; 12:36; John 13:34-35; Rom. 1:29-32; 12:14; 2 Cor. 12:20-21; Gal. 5:15, 26; Eph. 4:29; Phil. 4:8; 2 Thess. 3:11; 1 Tim. 5:13; Tit. 2:3; 3:2; Jas. 1:26; 4:11; 1 Pet. 2:1; 3:10; 4:15)

Bitterness (Prov. 10:12; 14:29; 15:1, 18; 19:11; 17:14; 20:22; Ecc. 7:9; Jer. 4:18; Matt. 6:14-15; 7:12; Rom. 12:17-21; Gal. 5:19-21; Eph. 4:26-27, 31-32; Col. 3:15, 19; Heb. 12:14-15; Jas. 1:19-20; 3:11, 14-16; 1 Pet. 2:1; 4:8)

Blasphemy (Psa. 15:1-3; 19:14; 34:13; 141:3; Prov. 10:18; 12:18; 13:3; 15:1; 21:23; Matt. 7:12; 12:34-37; Mark 7:21-23; Luke 6:28; Rom. 1:28-32; 12:10, 14, 17-21; 14:19; 1 Cor. 13:4-7; Gal. 5:15, 26; Eph. 4:29, 31-32; 5:4; Phil. 2:3-5; 4:8; Col. 3:8, 12-13; 4:6; 1 Tim. 1:20; 2 Tim. 3:2-3; Tit. 3:2; Heb. 12:14; Jas. 1:26; 3:1-12; 4:11; 1 Pet. 2:1; 3:8-10)

Boasting (Psa. 10:4; 31:23; Prov. 3:5-7; 6:16-17; 8:13; 13:10; 16:5, 18; 18:12; 21:4, 23, 24; 26:12; 29:23; Isa. 5:21; Matt. 18:4; 23:12; Mark 7:21-23; Luke 18:9-14; Rom. 1:28-32; 12:3, 16; 1 Cor. 10:12; 2 Cor. 12:20-21; Gal. 5:26; 6:3; Phil. 2:3-5; Col. 3:12; 2 Tim. 3:2; Jas. 3:1-12; 4:6, 10, 16; 1 Pet. 5:5)

Cheating (Lev. 19:35-36; Deut. 25:13-16; Psa. 101:7; Prov. 6:16-19; 11:1; 13:5; 16:11; 20:10, 17, 23; 21:6; Jer. 17:11; 2 Cor. 8:21; Jas. 4:17; Rev. 21:8)

Complaining (Prov. 21:23; Matt. 7:12; 1 Cor. 10:10; Eph. 4:29, 31-32; 5:20; Phil. 2:3-5, 14; 4:6, 8, 11; Col. 3:13; 1 Thess. 5:16-18; Jas. 1:17; 5:9; 1 Pet. 4:9; 5:7)

Conceit (Psa. 10:4; 31:23; Prov. 3:5-7; 6:16-17; 8:13; 13:10; 16:5, 18; 18:12; 21:4, 24; 26:12; 29:23; Isa. 5:21; Matt. 18:4; 23:12; Mark 7:21-23; Luke 18:9-14; Rom. 12:3, 16; 1 Cor. 10:12; 2 Cor. 12:20-21; Gal. 5:26; 6:3; Phil. 2:3-5; Col. 3:12; Jas. 4:6, 10, 16; 1 Pet. 5:5)

Contentiousness (Psa. 140:1-2; Prov. 10:12; 15:1, 18; 17:14; 18:6; 20:3; 26:17, 21; Matt. 7:12; Rom. 12:17-21; 14:19; 2 Cor. 12:20-21; Gal. 5:19-21; Eph. 4:31-32; Phil. 2:3-5; Col. 3:15; 2 Tim. 2:24; Tit. 3:2; Heb. 12:14; Jas. 1:19-20; 3:17-18)

Corrupt language (Ex. 20:7; Psa. 19:14; 141:3; Prov. 12:18; 13:3; 20:17; 21:23; Matt. 7:12; 12:34-37; Luke 6:28; Rom. 12:14; Col. 3:8; 4:6; Eph. 4:29, 31-32; 5:4; Col. 3:8; 1 Tim. 1:9; 4:12; Jas. 1:26; 3:1-12; 1 Pet. 3:10)

Covetousness (Ex. 20:17; Psa. 37:3-5, 16; 119:36; Prov. 16:8; 28:16; 30:8-9; Hab. 2:9; Matt. 5:6; 6:19-21, 24-25, 33; 16:26; Mark 7:21-23; Luke 12:15-21; Acts 20:35; Rom. 1:28-32; 1 Cor. 6:9-11; Eph. 5:3-5; Phil. 4:11-13, 19; Col. 3:1-5; 1 Tim. 6:6-11; 2 Tim. 3:2; Heb. 13:5; Jas. 1:27; 2 Pet. 3:9-10; 1 John 2:15-17)

Crude joking (Psa. 15:1-3; 19:14; 34:13; 141:3; Prov. 12:18; 13:3; 21:23; 26:18 -19; Matt. 7:12; 12:34-37; Mark 7:21-23; Rom. 12:10, 14, 18; 14:19; 1 Cor. 13:4-7; 15:33; Gal. 5:15, 26; Eph. 4:29, 31-32; 5:4; Col. 3:12-13; 4:6; Tit. 3:2; Heb. 12:14; Jas. 1:26; 3:1-12; 4:11; 1 Pet. 2:1; 3:8-10)

Cursing (Ex. 20:7; Psa. 19:14; 141:3; Prov. 12:18; 13:3; 20:17; 21:23; Matt. 7:12; 12:34-37; Luke 6:28; Rom. 12:14; Eph. 4:29, 31-32; 5:4; Col. 3:8; 4:6; 1 Tim. 1:9; 4:12; Jas. 1:26; 3:1-12; 1 Pet. 3:10)

Deceit (Deut. 25:13-16; Psa. 101:7; 120:2; Psa. 15:1-2; 101:7; 120:2; Prov. 6:16-19; 19:9; Matt. 7:12; Mark 7:21-23; Rom. 1:28-32; 2 Cor. 8:21; Phil. 4:8; Jas. 4:17; 1 Pet. 2:1; 3:10; Rev. 21:8)

Dishonesty (Ex. 20:16; Deut. 25:13-16; Psa. 15:1-2; 101:7; 119:163; 120:2; Prov. 6:16-19; 12:22; 13:5; 19:9; Matt. 7:12; 2 Cor. 8:21; Eph. 4:25; Phil. 4:8; Col. 3:9; 1 Tim. 1:9-10; 1 Pet. 3:10; Rev. 21:8)

Disobeying parents (Ex. 20:12; Deut. 27:16; Prov. 1:8; 6:20; 10:1; 15:20; 20:11; 23:22; Matt. 15:4; Rom. 1:28-32; Eph. 6:1-3; Col. 3:20; 2 Tim. 3:2)

Divisiveness (Psa. 133:1-3; Prov. 6:16-19; Matt. 7:12; John 17:20-21; Acts 4:32; Rom. 12:16; 15:5; 16:17; 1 Cor. 1:10-11; 3:3; 2 Cor. 12:20-21; 13:11; Gal. 5:15, 19-21, 26; Phil. 1:27; 2:2-5; Jas. 3:16; 4:1-2; 1 Pet. 3:8)

Doubt (Psa. 3:4-8; 27:13-14; 31:24; 37:3-8; 55:22; Prov. 3:5-7; Isa. 41:10; Matt. 6:25-34; 8:25-26; 14:27, 31; 21:21-22; Mark 11:23-24; John 14:1; 16:33; 20:27; Rom. 8:28, 31; 1 Cor. 1:9; Phil. 4:6-7, 13; Col. 3:15; 1 Thess. 5:24; 2 Thess. 3:3; 2 Tim. 1:12; Heb. 6:18; 11:6; 13:5-6; Jas. 1:5-8; 1 Pet. 5:7; 1 John 5:13)

Drinking (Lev. 10:8-11; Prov. 20:1; 23:29-35; Isa. 5:11; Hab. 2:15; Rom. 13:14; 14:21; 1 Cor. 6:19-20; Gal. 5:19-21; Eph. 5:18; Phil. 1:20; 1 Thess. 5:5-8; 1 Tim. 5:22b; 2 Tim. 2:22; 1 Pet. 2:11-12; 4:3; 5:8)

Drinking parties (Hab. 2:15; Matt. 5:16; Rom. 13:13-14; 14:21; 1 Cor. 6:19-20; 15:33; Gal. 5:19-21; 1 Tim. 4:12; 5:22b; 2 Tim. 2:22; 1 Pet. 2:11-12; 4:3; 5:8)

Drug abuse (Prov. 20:1; 23:29-35; Matt. 5:16; Rom. 12:1-2; 13:14; 1 Cor. 6:19-20; Gal. 5:19-21; Eph. 5:18; 1 Tim. 5:22b; 2 Tim. 2:22; 1 Pet. 2:11-12; 5:8)

Drunkenness (Lev. 10:8-11; Prov. 20:1; 23:29-35; Isa. 5:11; Luke 21:34; Rom. 13:13-14; 14:21; 1 Cor. 6:9-11; Gal. 5:19-21; Eph. 5:5, 18; 1 Thess. 5:5-8; 1 Tim. 5:22b; 2 Tim. 2:22; 1 Pet. 2:11-12; 4:3; 5:8)

Envy (Psa. 37:1; Prov. 3:31; 14:30; 23:17; 24:1, 19; 27:4; Matt. 7:12; Acts 7:9; Rom. 1:28-32; 12:14-16, 17-21; 13:13-14; 1 Cor. 3:3; 13:4; 2 Cor. 12:20-21; Gal. 5:19-21, 26; Phil. 2:3-5; 4:11-13; Col. 3:15; Tit. 3:3; Jas. 3:14-16; 1 Pet. 2:1)

Euphemisms (Ex. 20:7; Psa. 19:14; 141:3; Prov. 12:18; 13:3; 20:17; 21:23; Matt. 7:12; 12:34-37; Rom. 12:14; Eph. 4:29, 31-32; 5:4; Col. 3:8; 4:6; 1 Thess. 5:21-22; 1 Tim. 1:9; 4:12; Jas. 1:26; 3:1-12; 1 Pet. 3:10)

Evil desires (Job 31:1; Psa. 10:3; 19:14; 24:3-4; 101:3; Prov. 6:16-19; 21:20; 24:1; Mark 7:21-23; Rom. 1:28-32; 7:8; 12:21; 1 Cor. 10:6; Phil. 4:8; Col. 3:5, 8; 1 Thess. 5:22; Jas. 1:13-15; 3:17; 1 Pet. 4:15; 1 John 2:15-17; 3 John 11)

Evil thoughts (Gen. 6:5; Job 31:1; Psa. 19:14; 24:3-4; 51:10; 94:11; Prov. 6:16-19; 15:26; 23:7; Mark 7:21-23; Rom. 1:28-32; 12:21; 1 Cor. 4:6; 2 Cor. 10:5; Phil. 4:8; Col. 3:5, 8; Jas. 2:4; 3:17; 1 Pet. 2:11-12)

Extortion (Lev. 19:35-36; Deut. 25:13-16; Psa. 62:10; Prov. 6:16-19; 11:1; 13:5; 16:11; 20:10, 17, 23; 21:6; Jer. 17:11; 22:13; Matt. 7:12; 1 Cor. 6:9-11; 2 Cor. 8:21; Jas. 4:17)

Faultfinding (1 Sam. 16:7; Matt. 6:14-15; 7:1-5, 12; Luke 6:37-46; John 3:17; 7:24; Rom. 12:3; 1 Cor. 13:4-7; 2 Cor. 10:12; Gal. 6:1-2; Phil. 2:3-5; Col. 3:12; Jas. 2:1-9, 13; 3:17-18; 4:11-12; 5:9; 1 Pet. 4:8; 2 Pet. 3:9)

Fear (Josh. 1:9; Psa. 3:4-8; 27:13-14; 31:24; 37:3-8; 55:22; 56:3, 11; Prov. 3:5-7; Isa. 41:10; 43:1-3; 44:6-8; Matt. 6:25-34; 8:25-26; 14:27, 31; Mark 4:40; John 14:1, 27; 16:33; Rom. 8:28, 31; Phil. 4:6-7, 13; Col. 3:15; 1 Thess. 5:24; 2 Thess. 3:3; 2 Tim. 1:7, 12; Heb. 6:18; 13:5-6; 1 Pet. 5:7)

Filthy language (Ex. 20:7; Psa. 19:14; 141:3; Prov. 12:18; 13:3; 20:17; 21:23; Matt. 7:12; 12:34-37; Luke 6:28; Rom. 12:14; Eph. 4:29, 31-32; 5:4; Col. 3:8; 4:6; 1 Tim. 1:9; 4:12; Jas. 1:26; 3:1-12; 1 Pet. 3:10)

Fornication (Psa. 24:3-4; 38:1-8; Matt. 5:8; Mark 7:21-23; Rom. 1:28-32; 12:1-2; 13:14; 1 Cor. 6:9-11, 18-20; 7:2; 10:8; 2 Cor. 12:20-21; Gal. 5:19-21; Eph. 5:3-5; Col. 3:5; 1 Thess. 4:3-7; 1 Tim. 1:9-10; 2 Tim. 2:22; Heb. 13:4; Rev. 21:8)

Forsaking the assembly (Matt. 6:33; 22:37; 26:29; Acts 2:42; 20:7; Col. 1:18; Heb. 2:12; 10:24-25)

Gambling (Ex. 20:17; Prov. 22:16; 28:20, 22; Ecc. 5:10; Jer. 17:11; 22:13; Matt. 6:19-21, 24; 7:12; Mark 7:21-23; Luke 12:15-21; Acts 20:35; 1 Cor. 4:2; 6:12; 2 Cor. 8:21; Gal. 5:19-21; Eph. 4:28; Phil. 2:3-5; 4:11-13; Col. 3:1-5; 1 Thess. 5:22; 2 Thess. 3:10; 1 Tim. 6:6-11; Heb. 13:5; Jas. 1:27)

Gluttony (Num. 11:32-33; Prov. 23:20-21; Matt. 4:4; 5:6, 16; Rom. 12:1-2; 14:21; Gal. 5:24; 1 Cor. 6:19-20; 10:31)

Lack of self-control (Psa. 15:1-3; 19:14; 34:13; 37:8; 119:133; 141:3; Prov. 14:17, 29; 15:18; 16:32; 17:14; 19:11; 20:22; 21:23; 25:28; 29:22; Ecc. 7:9; Matt. 6:14-15; 7:12; Mark 7:21-23; Luke 6:28; Acts 24:25; Rom. 6:12; 12:1-2, 14, 17-21; 13:14; 14:19; 1 Cor. 6:19-20; 9:27; 13:4-7; Gal. 5:19-21, 22-23; Eph. 4:27, 31-32; Phil. 2:3-5; 4:8; Col. 3:12-15; 2 Tim. 2:24; 3:3; Tit. 2:12; Heb. 12:14; Jas. 1:19-20; 3:17-18; 1 Pet. 4:7; 5:8; 2 Pet. 1:6)

Gossip (Ex. 23:1; Lev. 19:16; Psa. 15:1-3; 19:14; 34:13; 101:5; 141:3; Prov. 10:18; 11:13; 16:28; 17:9; 20:19; 21:23; 26:17, 20; Matt. 7:12; 12:36; John 13:34-35; Rom. 1:29-32; 12:14; 2 Cor. 12:20-21; Gal. 5:15, 26; Eph. 4:29; Phil. 4:8; 2 Thess. 3:11; 1 Tim. 5:13; Tit. 2:3; 3:2; Jas. 1:26; 4:11; 1 Pet. 2:1; 3:10; 4:15)

Greed (Ex. 20:17; Psa. 37:3-5, 16; 119:36; Prov. 16:8; 28:16; 30:8-9; Hab. 2:9; Matt. 5:6; 6:19-21, 24-25, 33; 16:26; Mark 7:21-23; Luke 12:15-21; Acts 20:35; Rom. 1:28-32; 1 Cor. 6:9-11; Eph. 5:3-5; Phil. 4:11-13, 19; Col. 3:1-5; Heb. 13:5; 1 Tim. 6:6-11; 2 Tim. 3:2; Jas. 1:27; 2 Pet. 3:9-10; 1 John 2:15-17)

Hatred (Lev. 19:17; Prov. 10:12, 18; 15:17; 26:24-26; Matt. 5:22, 43-44; 6:14-15; 7:12; Luke 6:28; John 13:34-35; Rom. 1:28-32; 12:17-21; 1 Cor. 13:4-7; Gal. 5:19-21; Eph. 4:31-32; Phil. 2:3-5; Tit. 3:3; Jas. 1:19-20; 1 John 2:9-11; 3:15; 4:20)

Homosexuality (Gen. 1:26-28; 2:24; 19:1-38; Lev. 18:22; 20:13; Matt. 19:4-6; Rom. 1:23-32; 1 Cor. 6:9-11; 7:2; Gal. 5:19-21; 1 Tim. 1:9-10; Heb. 13:4; Jude 7; Rev. 21:8)

Hypocrisy (Josh. 24:14; Prov. 23:7; 26:25-26; Ecc. 12:14; Matt. 6:1-18; 7:1-5; 15:7-9; 23:1-39; Luke 12:1-2; Rom. 12:9; Phil. 1:10; Tit. 1:16; 2:7; Heb. 4:13; Jas. 1:26; 2:15-17; 3:17; 1 Pet. 1:22; 2:1; 1 John 2:4, 9; 3:18; 4:20)

Idolatry (Ex. 20:4; 34:17; Deut. 11:16; 12:2-4; Isa. 42:8; Matt. 4:10; 6:33; Acts 17:24-29; Rom. 1:22-23; 1 Cor. 6:9-11; 10:14; Gal. 5:19-21; Eph. 5:5; Col. 1:18; 3:5; 1 Pet. 4:3; 1 John 5:21; Rev. 21:8)

Immodesty (Job 31:1; Prov. 7:10; 11:22; 31:25, 30; Matt. 5:8, 16, 28-29; 18:6; Rom. 12:1-2; 14:21; 1 Cor. 6:19-20; 10:31; 1 Thess. 4:3-4; 1 Tim. 2:9-10; 4:12; 5:22b; Tit. 2:3-5; 1 Pet. 3:3-4; 1 John 2:16)

Impurity (Psa. 24:3-4; 51:10; Matt. 5:8; Mark 7:21-23; Rom. 12:1-2; 13:13-14; 1 Cor. 6:18-20; 10:31; 2 Cor. 8:21; 12:20-21; Gal. 5:19-21; Eph. 5:3-5; Phil. 4:8; Col. 3:5; 1 Thess. 4:3-7; 5:22; 1 Tim. 5:22b; 2 Tim. 2:22; Jas. 1:27; 3:17-18; 4:8; 1 Pet. 2:11-12; 4:3; 1 John 2:15-17)

Ingratitude (Prov. 17:13; Neh. 9:4-38; Ezek. 16:1-34; Luke 6:35; 17:11-19; Rom. 1:21; Eph. 5:4, 20; Phil. 4:6; Col. 3:15, 17; 4:2; 1 Thess. 5:18; 2 Tim. 3:2; Heb. 13:15)

Insincerity (Josh. 24:14; Prov. 23:7; 26:25-26; Ecc. 12:14; Matt. 6:1-18; 7:1-5; 15:7-9; 23:1-39; Luke 12:1-2; Rom. 12:9; Phil. 1:10; Tit. 1:16; 2:7; Heb. 4:13; Jas. 1:26; 2:15-17; 3:17; 1 Pet. 1:22; 2:1; 1 John 2:4, 9; 3:18; 4:20)

Insulting (Psa. 15:1-3; 19:14; 34:13; 141:3; Prov. 12:18; 13:3; 21:23; 26:18-19; Matt. 7:12; 12:34-37; Mark 7:21-23; Luke 6:28; Rom. 12:10, 14, 18; 14:19; 1 Cor. 6:9-11; 13:4-7; Gal. 5:15, 26; Eph. 4:29, 31-32; 5:4; Phil. 2:3-5; Col. 3:8, 11 -12; 4:6; Tit. 3:2; Heb. 12:14; Jas. 1:26; 3:1-12; 4:11; 1 Pet. 2:1; 3:8-10)

Jealousy (Psa. 37:1; Prov. 3:31; 14:30; 23:17; 24:1; 27:4; Matt. 7:12; Acts 7:9; Rom. 1:28-32; 12:14-16, 17-21; 13:13-14; 1 Cor. 3:3; 13:4; 2 Cor. 12:20-21; Gal. 5:19-21, 26; Phil. 2:3-5; 4:11-13; Col. 3:15; Tit. 3:3; Jas. 3:14-16; 1 Pet. 2:1)

Judgmental (inappropriately) (1 Sam. 16:7; Matt. 6:14-15; 7:1-5, 12; Luke 6:37-46; John 3:17; 7:24; Rom. 12:3; 1 Cor. 13:4-7; 2 Cor. 10:12; Gal. 6:1-2; Phil. 2:3-5; Col. 3:12; Jas. 2:1-9, 13; 3:17-18; 4:11-12; 5:9; 1 Pet. 4:8; 2 Pet. 3:9)

Lack of self-control (Psa. 15:1-3; 19:14; 34:13; 37:8; 119:133; 141:3; Prov. 14:17, 29; 15:18; 16:32; 17:14; 19:11; 20:22; 21:23; 25:28; 29:22; Ecc. 7:9; Matt. 6:14-15; 7:12; Mark 7:21-23; Luke 6:28; Acts 24:25; Rom. 6:12; 12:1-2, 14, 17-21; 13:14; 14:19; 1 Cor. 6:19-20; 9:27; 13:4-7; Gal. 5:19-21, 22-23; Eph. 4:27, 31-32; Phil. 2:3-5; 4:8; Col. 3:12-15; 2 Tim. 2:24; 3:3; Tit. 2:12; Heb. 12:14; Jas. 1:19-20; 3:17-18; 1 Pet. 4:7; 5:8; 2 Pet. 1:6)

Laziness (Prov. 10:4; 12:24, 27; 13:4; 15:19; 18:9; 19:15, 24; 20:4; 21:25; 26:13 -16; Ecc. 9:10; Matt. 25:26; Luke 2:49; John 9:4; Rom. 12:11; 1 Cor. 15:58; Eph. 2:10; Col. 3:23-24; 2 Thess. 3:10-12; 1 Tim. 5:8; Tit. 2:7, 14; 3:8, 14; Heb. 6:10-12; Jas. 4:17)

Lewd desires (Job 31:1; Psa. 24:3-4; 51:10; 101:3; Matt. 5:8, 27-28; Mark 7:21-23; Rom. 12:1-2; 13:13-14; 1 Cor. 6:18-20; 10:31; 2 Cor. 12:20-21; Gal. 5:19-21; Eph. 4:19-20; 5:3-5; Phil. 4:8; Col. 3:5; 1 Thess. 4:3-7; 5:22; 1 Tim. 5:22b; 2 Tim. 2:22; Heb. 13:4; Jas. 1:27; 1 Pet. 4:3; 5:8; 1 John 2:15-17)

Losing temper (Psa. 15:1-3; 19:14; 34:13; 37:8; 119:133; 141:3; Prov. 14:17, 29; 15:18; 16:32; 17:14; 19:11; 20:22; 21:23; 25:28; 29:22; Ecc. 7:9; Matt. 6:14 -15; 7:12; Mark 7:21-23; Luke 6:28; Acts 24:25; Rom. 6:12; 12:1-2, 14, 17-21; 13:14; 14:19; 1 Cor. 6:19-20; 9:27; 13:4-7; Gal. 5:19-21, 22-23; Eph. 4:27, 31-32; Phil. 2:3-5; 4:8; Col. 3:12-15; 2 Tim. 2:24; 3:3; Tit. 2:12; Heb. 12:14; Jas. 1:19-20; 3:17-18; 1 Pet. 4:7; 5:8; 2 Pet. 1:6)

Lust (Job 31:1; Psa. 24:3-4; 51:10; 101:3; Matt. 5:8, 27-28; Mark 7:21-23; Rom. 12:1-2; 13:13-14; 1 Cor. 6:18-20; 10:31; 2 Cor. 12:20-21; Gal. 5:19-21; Eph. 5:3 -5; Phil. 4:8; 1 Thess. 4:3-7; 5:22; 1 Tim. 5:22b; 2 Tim. 2:22; Jas. 1:27; 1 Pet. 4:3; 1 John 2:15-17)

Lying (Ex. 20:16; Deut. 25:13-16; Psa. 15:1-2; 101:7; 119:163; 120:2; Prov. 6:16-19; 12:22; 13:5; 19:9; Matt. 7:12; 2 Cor. 8:21; Eph. 4:25; Phil. 4:8; Col. 3:9; 1 Tim. 1:9-10; 1 Pet. 3:10; Rev. 21:8)

Maliciousness (Psa. 37:8-9; Prov. 10:12; 15:1, 18; 19:11; 20:22; Matt. 5:43-44; 6:14-15; 7:12; 22:39; Mark 7:21-23; Luke 6:28; John 13:34-35; Rom. 1:28-32; 12:10, 14, 17-21; 14:19; 1 Cor. 10:31; 13:4-7; Gal. 5:19-21; 6:10; Eph. 4:31-32; Phil. 2:3-5; Col. 3:8, 12-15; Tit. 3:3; Heb. 12:14; Jas. 1:19-20; 3:14-18 1 Pet. 2:1; 4:8)

Materialism (Ex. 20:17; Psa. 37:3-5, 16; 119:36; Prov. 16:8; 28:16; 30:8-9; Hab. 2:9; Matt. 5:6; 6:19-21, 24-25, 33; 16:26; Mark 7:21-23; Luke 12:15-21; Acts 20:35; Rom. 1:28-32; 1 Cor. 6:9-11; Eph. 5:3-5; Phil. 4:11-13, 19; Col. 3:1-5; Heb. 13:5; 1 Tim. 6:6-11; 2 Tim. 3:2; Jas. 1:27; 2 Pet. 3:9-10; 1 John 2:15-17)

Mean spirit (Psa. 15:1-3; 19:14; 34:13; 141:3; Prov. 3:30; 12:18; 13:3; 15:1; 21:23; 26:18-19; Matt. 7:12; 12:34-37; Mark 7:21-23; Luke 6:28; Rom. 12:10, 14, 18; 14:19; 1 Cor. 13:4-7; Gal. 5:15, 26; Eph. 4:29, 31-32; 5:4; Phil. 2:3-5; Col. 3:8, 12-13; 4:6; Tit. 3:2; Heb. 12:14; Jas. 1:26; 3:1-12; 4:11; 1 Pet. 2:1; 3:8-10)

Misplaced priorities (Ex. 20:3; Deut. 11:16; Psa. 90:12; Mic. 6:8; Matt. 5:6; 6:19-21, 24, 33; 16:26; 22:37-38; John 14:15; Rom. 12:1-2; 2 Cor. 4:16-18; 5:9; Phil. 1:21; 3:13-14; Col. 1:18; 3:1-2; 1 Tim. 4:8; Jas. 4:14-16)

Murder (Ex. 20:13; Prov. 6:16-17; Matt. 5:21-26; 5:43-44; 7:12; 22:39; Mark 7:21-23; John 13:34-35; Rom. 1:28-32; 12:17-21; 13:9; 14:19; 1 Cor. 10:31; 13:4-7; Gal. 5:19-21; 6:10; Phil. 2:3-5; Col. 3:8, 12-15; 1 Tim. 1:9-10; Jas. 1:19-20; 1 Pet. 4:15; 1 John 3:15; Rev. 21:8; 22:15)

Murmuring (Prov. 21:23; Matt. 7:12; 1 Cor. 10:10; Eph. 4:29, 31-32; 5:20; Phil. 2:3-5, 14; 4:6, 8, 11; Col. 3:13; 1 Thess. 5:16-18; Jas. 1:17; 5:9; 1 Pet. 4:9; 5:7)

Outbursts of anger (Psa. 15:1-3; 19:14; 34:13; 37:8; 119:133; 141:3; Prov. 14:17, 29; 15:18; 16:32; 17:14; 19:11; 20:22; 21:23; 25:28; 29:22; Ecc. 7:9; Matt. 6:14-15; 7:12; Mark 7:21-23; Luke 6:28; Acts 24:25; Rom. 6:12; 12:1-2, 14, 17-21; 13:14; 14:19; 1 Cor. 6:19-20; 9:27; 13:4-7; 2 Cor. 12:20-21; Gal. 5:19-21, 22-23; Eph. 4:27, 31-32; Phil. 2:3-5; 4:8; Col. 3:12-15; 2 Tim. 2:24; 3:3; Tit. 2:12; Heb. 12:14; Jas. 1:19-20; 3:17-18; 1 Pet. 4:7; 5:8; 2 Pet. 1:6)

Partiality (1 Sam. 16:7; Lev. 19:15; Deut. 1:17; Prov. 18:5; 24:23; 28:21; Matt. 7:12; 22:39; Acts 10:34; Rom. 2:11; 12:3; 1 Cor. 13:4-7; Gal. 2:6; Phil. 2:3-5; Col. 3:12; 1 Tim. 5:21; Jas. 2:1-9; 3:17-18; 1 Pet. 1:17; 4:8; 2 Pet. 3:9)

Pornography (Job 31:1; Psa. 24:3-4; 51:10; 101:3; Matt. 5:8, 27-28; Mark 7:21-23; Rom. 12:1-2; 13:13-14; 1 Cor. 6:18-20; 10:31; 2 Cor. 12:20-21; Gal. 5:19-21; Eph. 5:3-5; Phil. 4:8; 1 Thess. 4:3-7; 5:22; 1 Tim. 5:22b; 2 Tim. 2:22; Jas. 1:27; 1 Pet. 4:3; 1 John 2:15-17)

Prejudice (1 Sam. 16:7; Lev. 19:15; Deut. 1:17; Prov. 18:5; 24:23; 28:21; Matt. 7:12; 22:39; Acts 10:34; Rom. 2:11; 12:3; 1 Cor. 13:4-7; Gal. 2:6; Phil. 2:3-5; Col. 3:12; 1 Tim. 5:21; Jas. 2:1-9; 3:17-18; 1 Pet. 1:17; 4:8; 2 Pet. 3:9)

Pride (1 Sam. 2:3; Psa. 10:4; 31:23; Prov. 3:5-7; 6:16-17; 8:13; 11:2; 13:10; 16:5, 18; 18:12; 21:4, 24; 26:12; 29:23; Isa. 5:21; Matt. 18:4; 23:12; Mark 7:21-23; Luke 18:9-14; Rom. 1:28-32; 12:3, 16; 1 Cor. 10:12; 2 Cor. 12:20-21; Gal. 5:26; 6:3; Phil. 2:3-5; Col. 3:12; 2 Tim. 3:2-4; Tit. 3:2; Jas. 4:6, 10, 16; 1 Pet. 5:5; 1 John 2:16)

Profanity (Ex. 20:7; Psa. 19:14; 141:3; Prov. 12:18; 13:3; 20:17; 21:23; Matt. 7:12; 12:34-37; Luke 6:28; Rom. 12:14; Eph. 4:29, 31-32; 5:4; Col. 3:8; 4:6; 1 Tim. 1:9; 4:12; Jas. 1:26; 3:1-12; 1 Pet. 3:10)

Quarreling/Yelling (Psa. 15:1-3; 19:14; 34:13; 141:3; Prov. 3:30; 12:18; 13:3; 15:1, 18; 17:14; 20:3; 21:23; 26:17; Matt. 7:12; Mark 7:21-23; Luke 6:28; Rom. 12:10, 14, 18; 14:19; 1 Cor. 13:4-7; Gal. 5:15, 26; Eph. 4:3, 31-32; Phil. 2:3-5; Col. 3:12-15; 1 Thess. 5:13; 2 Tim. 2:24; Tit. 3:2; Heb. 12:14; Jas. 1:19-20, 26; 3:1-12, 17-18; 4:11; 1 Pet. 2:1)

Rage (Psa. 15:1-3; 19:14; 34:13; 37:8; 119:133; 141:3; Prov. 14:17, 29; 15:18; 16:32; 17:14; 19:11; 20:22; 21:23; 25:28; 29:22; Ecc. 7:9; Matt. 6:14-15; 7:12; Mark 7:21-23; Luke 6:28; Acts 24:25; Rom. 6:12; 12:1-2, 14, 17-21; 13:14; 14:19; 1 Cor. 6:19-20; 9:27; 13:4-7; Gal. 5:19-21, 22-23; Eph. 4:27, 31-32; Phil. 2:3-5; 4:8; Col. 3:12-15; 2 Tim. 2:24; 3:3; Tit. 2:12; Heb. 12:14; Jas. 1:19-20; 3:17-18; 1 Pet. 4:7; 5:8; 2 Pet. 1:6)

Rudeness (Psa. 15:1-3; 19:14; 34:13; 141:3; Prov. 12:18; 13:3; 15:1; 21:23; 26:18-19; Matt. 7:12; 12:34-37; Mark 7:21-23; Luke 6:28; Rom. 12:10, 14, 18; 14:19; 1 Cor. 13:4-7; Gal. 5:15, 26; Eph. 4:29, 31-32; 5:4; Phil. 2:3-5; 4:8; Col. 3:8, 12-13; 4:6; Tit. 3:2; Heb. 12:14; Jas. 1:26; 3:1-12; 4:11; 1 Pet. 2:1; 3:8-10)

Self-centeredness (Prov. 3:5-7; 16:5; 21:13; 25:6-7, 27; 26:12; 29:23; Isa. 5:21; Matt. 16:25; 18:4; 23:12; 25:34-46; Luke 9:23; 18:9-14; Acts 20:35; Rom. 2:8; 12:3, 10, 16; 14:21; 15:1-3; 1 Cor. 10:24; 13:4-7; 2 Cor. 12:20-21; Gal. 5:24; 6:1-3, 10; Eph. 5:21; Phil. 2:3-5, 21; 2 Tim. 3:2-4; Jas. 3:14-18; 4:10; 1 Pet. 5:5; 1 John 3:17-18)

Selfishness (Prov. 3:5-7; 16:5; 21:13; 25:6-7, 27; 26:12; 29:23; Isa. 5:21; Matt. 16:25; 18:4; 23:12; 25:34-46; Luke 9:23; 18:9-14; Acts 20:35; Rom. 2:8; 12:3, 10, 16; 14:21; 15:1-3; 1 Cor. 10:24; 13:4-7; 2 Cor. 12:20-21; Gal. 5:24; 6:1-3, 10; Eph. 5:21; Phil. 2:3-5, 21; 2 Tim. 3:2-4; Jas. 3:14-18; 4:10; 1 Pet. 5:5; 1 John 3:17-18)

Sensual touching (Job 31:1; Psa. 24:3-4; 51:10; 101:3; Matt. 5:8, 27-28; Mark 7:21-23; Rom. 12:1-2; 13:13-14; 1 Cor. 6:18-20; 10:31; 2 Cor. 12:20-21; Gal. 5:19-21; Eph. 4:19-20; 5:3-5; Phil. 4:8; Col. 3:5; 1 Thess. 4:3-7; 5:22; 1 Tim. 5:22b; 2 Tim. 2:22; Heb. 13:4; Jas. 1:27; 1 Pet. 4:3; 5:8; 1 John 2:15-17)

Sensuality (Job 31:1; Psa. 24:3-4; 51:10; 101:3; Matt. 5:8, 27-28; Mark 7:21-23; Rom. 12:1-2; 13:13-14; 1 Cor. 6:18-20; 10:31; 2 Cor. 12:20-21; Gal. 5:19-21; Eph. 4:19-20; 5:3-5; Phil. 4:8; Col. 3:5; 1 Thess. 4:3-7; 5:22; 1 Tim. 5:22b; 2 Tim. 2:22; Heb. 13:4; Jas. 1:27; 1 Pet. 4:3; 5:8; 1 John 2:15-17)

Sexual immorality (Psa. 24:3-4; 38:1-8; Matt. 5:8; Mark 7:21-23; Rom. 1:28-32; 12:1-2; 13:14; 1 Cor. 6:9-11, 18-20; 7:2; 10:8; 2 Cor. 12:20-21; Gal. 5:19-21; Eph. 5:3-5; Col. 3:5; 1 Thess. 4:3-7; 1 Tim. 1:9-10; 2 Tim. 2:22; Heb. 13:4; Rev. 21:8)

Slander (Psa. 15:1-3; 19:14; 34:13; 101:5; 141:3; Prov. 10:18; 12:18; 13:3; 21:23; Matt. 7:12; 12:34-37; Mark 7:21-23; Luke 6:28; Rom. 1:28-32; 12:10, 14, 17-21; 14:19; 1 Cor. 13:4-7; Gal. 5:15, 26; Eph. 4:29, 31-32; 5:4; Phil. 2:3-5; 4:8; Col. 3:8, 12-13; 4:6; 1 Tim. 1:20; 2 Tim. 3:2-3; Tit. 3:2; Heb. 12:14; Jas. 1:26; 3:1-12; 4:11; 1 Pet. 2:1; 3:8-10)

Slothfulness (Prov. 10:4; 12:24, 27; 13:4; 15:19; 18:9; 19:15, 24; 20:4; 21:25; 26:13-16; Ecc. 9:10; Matt. 25:26; Luke 2:49; John 9:4; Rom. 12:11; 1 Cor. 15:58; Eph. 2:10; Col. 3:23-24; 2 Thess. 3:10-12; 1 Tim. 5:8; Tit. 2:7, 14; 3:8, 14; Heb. 6:10-12; Jas. 4:17)

Smoking (Matt. 5:16; Rom. 12:1-2; 13:14; 14:21; 1 Cor. 6:12, 19-20; 10:31; Gal. 5:19-21; Phil. 1:20; 1 Tim. 4:12; 2 Tim. 2:22; 5:8)

Sorcery (Deut. 18:10; 1 Sam. 15:23; 2 Kgs. 9:22; 2 Chron. 33:6; Mal. 3:5; Acts 13:6-8; Gal. 5:19-21; Rev. 21:8; 22:15)

Speaking evil of others (Psa. 15:1-3; 19:14; 34:13; 141:3; Prov. 10:18; 12:18; 13:3; 21:23; Matt. 7:12; 12:34-37; Mark 7:21-23; Luke 6:28; Rom. 1:28-32; 12:10, 14, 17-21; 14:19; 1 Cor. 13:4-7; Gal. 5:15, 26; Eph. 4:29, 31-32; 5:4; Phil. 2:3-5; 4:8; Col. 3:8, 12-13; 4:6; 1 Tim. 1:20; 2 Tim. 3:2-3; Tit. 3:2; Heb. 12:14; Jas. 1:26; 3:1-12; 4:11; 1 Pet. 2:1; 3:8-10)

Stealing (Ex. 20:15; Lev. 19:11; Prov. 10:2; Matt. 5:16; 7:12; Mark 7:21-23; Rom. 13:0, 14; 1 Cor. 6:9-11; 10:31; Eph. 4:25, 28; 1 Pet. 4:15)

Strife (Prov. 3:30; 6:16-19; 10:12; 12:18; 13:10; 15:1, 18; 16:28; 17:14; 20:3; 26:17, 21; 29:22; Matt. 6:14-15; 7:12; Mark 7:21-23; Luke 6:28; John 13:34-35; Rom. 1:28-32; 12:10, 14, 17-21; 13:13-14; 14:19; 1 Cor. 13:4-7; Gal. 5:15, 19-21, 26; Eph. 4:31-32; Phil. 2:3-5; Col. 3:12-15; 2 Tim. 2:24; Tit. 3:2; Heb. 12:14; Jas. 1:19-20; 3:14-18; 4:1-2, 11; 1 Pet. 2:1; 4:8)

Swearing (Ex. 20:7; Psa. 19:14; 141:3; Prov. 12:18; 13:3; 20:17; 21:23; Matt. 7:12; 12:34-37; Luke 6:28; Rom. 12:14; Eph. 4:29, 31-32; 5:4; Col. 3:8; 4:6; 1 Tim. 1:9; 4:12; Jas. 1:26; 3:1-12; 1 Pet. 3:10)

Unforgiving (Matt. 6:14-15; 7:12; Mark 11:25-26; 18:21-35; Luke 17:1-4; Rom. 1:28-32; Eph. 4:31-32; Phil. 2:3-5; Col. 3:12-14; 2 Tim. 3:3; Jas. 2:13; 1 Pet. 3:9)

Unloving (Lev. 19:17; Prov. 10:12; 21:13; Matt. 5:43-44; 6:14-15; 7:12; John 13:34-35; Rom. 1:28-32; 1 Cor. 13:4-7; Eph. 4:31-32; Phil. 2:3-5; Col. 3:12-14; 2 Tim. 3:3; 1 John 2:9-11; 3:10-15; 4:7-21)

Unmerciful (Prov. 21:13; Matt. 6:14-15; 7:12; 18:21-35; Mark 11:25-26; 18:35; Luke 17:1-4; Rom. 1:28-32; Eph. 4:31-32; Phil. 2:3-5; Col. 3:12-14; Jas. 2:13; 3:17-18)

Unwarranted criticism (Psa. 15:1-3; 19:14; 34:13; 141:3; Prov. 3:30; 12:18; 13:3; 15:1; 21:23; Matt. 7:12; 12:34-37; Mark 7:21-23; Luke 6:28; Rom. 12:10, 14, 18; 14:19; 1 Cor. 13:4-7; Gal. 5:15, 26; Eph. 4:29, 31-32; 5:4; Phil. 2:3-5; 4:8; Col. 3:8, 12-13; 4:6; Tit. 3:2; Heb. 12:14; Jas. 1:26; 3:1-12; 4:11; 1 Pet. 2:1; 3:8-10)

Unwholesome speech (Ex. 20:7; Psa. 15:1-3; 19:14; 34:13; 141:3; Prov. 12:18; 13:3; 20:17; 21:23; Matt. 7:12; 12:34-37; Mark 7:21-23; Luke 6:28; Rom. 12:10, 14, 17-21; Eph. 4:29, 31-32; 5:4; Col. 3:8; 4:6; 1 Tim. 1:9; 4:12; Tit. 3:2; Heb. 12:14; Jas. 1:26; 3:1-12; 1 Pet. 2:1; 3:8-10)

Vanity (1 Sam. 2:3; Psa. 10:4; 31:23; Prov. 3:5-7; 6:16-17; 8:13; 11:2; 13:10; 16:5, 18; 18:12; 21:4, 24; 26:12; 29:23; Isa. 5:21; Matt. 18:4; 23:12; Mark 7:21-23; Luke 9:23; 18:9-14; Rom. 1:28-32; 12:3, 16; 14:21; 1 Cor. 10:12; 2 Cor. 12:20-21; Gal. 5:24, 26; 6:3; Phil. 2:3-5; Col. 3:12; 2 Tim. 3:2-4; Tit. 3:2; Jas. 4:6, 10, 16; 1 Pet. 5:5; 1 John 2:16)

Verbal abuse (Psa. 15:1-3; 19:14; 34:13; 141:3; Prov. 3:30; 12:18; 13:3; 15:1; 21:23; Matt. 7:12; 12:34-37; Mark 7:21-23; Luke 6:28; Rom. 12:10, 14, 18; 14:19; 1 Cor. 6:9-11; 13:4-7; Gal. 5:15, 26; Eph. 4:29, 31-32; 5:4; Phil. 2:3-5; Col. 3:8, 11-12; 4:6; 1 Tim. 1:20; 2 Tim. 3:2-3; Tit. 3:2; Heb. 12:14; Jas. 1:26; 3:1-12, 17-18; 4:11; 1 Pet. 2:1; 3:8-10)

Violence (Psa. 37:8-9; Prov. 10:12; 15:1, 18; 19:11; 20:22; Matt. 5:43-44; 6:14-15; 7:12; Mark 7:21-23; Luke 6:28; John 13:34-35; Rom. 1:28-32; 12:10, 14, 17-21; 14:19; 1 Cor. 10:31; 13:4-7; Gal. 5:19-21; Eph. 4:31-32; Phil. 2:3-5; Col. 3:8, 12-15; Tit. 3:3; Heb. 12:14; Jas. 1:19-20; 3:14-18 1 Pet. 2:1; 4:8)

Witchcraft (Deut. 18:10; 1 Sam. 15:23; 2 Kgs. 9:22; 2 Chron. 33:6; Mal. 3:5; Acts 13:6-8; Gal. 5:19-21; Rev. 21:8; 22:15)

Worldliness (Matt. 5:14-16; 6:24; 16:26; Luke 8:14; John 15:19; 17:11-16; Rom. 12:1-2; 13:12; 2 Cor. 6:14-7:1; Gal. 6:8; Eph. 4:17-24; 5:11; Col. 3:1-2, 8-10; 1 Thess. 4:3-7; 2 Thess. 3:6; 2 Tim. 2:4, 22; Tit. 2:12; Jas. 1:27; 4:4; 1 Pet. 1:14-16; 2:11-12; 4:2; 1 John 2:15-17; 5:19)

Worldly influences/friends (Ex. 23:2; 34:12; Psa. 1:1; Prov. 1:15; 4:14; 12:26; 22:24-25; Matt. 5:16; 1 Cor. 5:6; 15:33; 2 Cor. 6:14-7:1; 1 Pet. 2:11-12; 3 John 11)

Worry (Josh. 1:9; Psa. 23:1-6; 37:7-8, 25; 46:1-11; 55:22; 119:165; Prov. 3:5-7; 12:25; Isa. 41:10; Matt. 6:24-34; 11:28-30; Luke 1:37; 8:14; John 14:1, 27; 16:33; Rom. 8:28, 31; Phil. 4:6-7, 13; Col. 3:15; 2 Tim. 2:19; Heb. 13:5-6; 1 Pet. 5:7)

Wrath (Psa. 37:8; Prov. 14:17, 29; 15:1; 16:32; 17:14; 19:11; 25:28; 29:22; Ecc. 7:9; Matt. 5:22; Rom. 12:18; Gal. 5:19-21, 22-23; Eph. 4:31-32; Phil. 4:6-7; Col. 3:8, 12-15; Tit. 3:2; Jas. 1:19-20; 3:17-18)

Walking Daily with My Lord

SEPTEMBER:

28 DAYS
To Grow with
the Early Christians

"And they continued steadfastly
in the apostles' doctrine and fellowship,
in the breaking of bread,
and in prayers"
(Acts 2:42).

28DAYS To Grow Closer with the Early Christians

Christians Have a God-Given Responsibility to Grow!

- Spiritual growth is an imperative:
  "...Desire...the word, that you may grow thereby" (1 Pet. 2:2).
  "Grow in the grace and knowledge of our Lord" (2 Pet. 3:18).

- Spiritual growth requires great effort:
  "Giving all diligence" (2 Pet. 1:5).
  "Be even more diligent" (2 Pet. 1:10).

- Spiritual growth knows no limits:
  "If these things are yours and abound..." (2 Pet. 1:8).
  "...That it may bear more fruit" (John 15:2).

- Spiritual growth necessitates continual maturing:
  "Let us press on to maturity" (Heb. 6:1).
  "That we should no longer be children..." (Eph. 4:14-15).

One very effective way to grow as a Christian is to walk with, learn from and grow with the first-century Christians.

Step 1: READ a Chapter in the Book of Acts.

Step 2: REFLECT on the Passage and a Few Questions.

Step 3: REFRESH Your Faith Through Their Example.

Let's grow with the early Christians for 28 days...

❑	Acts 1	❑	Acts 8	❑	Acts 15	❑ Acts 22
❑	Acts 2	❑	Acts 9	❑	Acts 16	❑ Acts 23
❑	Acts 3	❑	Acts 10	❑	Acts 17	❑ Acts 24
❑	Acts 4	❑	Acts 11	❑	Acts 18	❑ Acts 25
❑	Acts 5	❑	Acts 12	❑	Acts 19	❑ Acts 26
❑	Acts 6	❑	Acts 13	❑	Acts 20	❑ Acts 27
❑	Acts 7	❑	Acts 14	❑	Acts 21	❑ Acts 28

Day #1 to Grow with the Early Christians

*"And **they continued steadfastly**
in the apostles' doctrine and fellowship,
in the breaking of bread, and in prayers"*
(Acts 2:42).

Read Acts 1

Moving Forward and Preparing for Future Service

1. What do you think it did for the faith and growth of the early disciples to spend 40 days with Jesus after His resurrection?

2. Why is it significant, based upon their previous conduct, that Jesus' brothers were gathered with the disciples of Christ?

3. What were the divine qualifications for being an apostle (according to verses 21-22)?

4. **What can I draw from this chapter to help me grow as a Christian?**

Answering the questions from this chapter is GOOD.

Applying the message of this chapter is BETTER.

Today's purpose: Read. Reflect. Refresh Your Faith.

One more thing: Pray about this today!

---

*"And **they continued steadfastly**
in the apostles' doctrine and fellowship,
in the breaking of bread, and in prayers"*
(Acts 2:42).

Read Acts 2

*The First Christians
in the Lord's Church*

1. In fulfillment of God's eternal plan, what came into existence in Acts 2?

2. According to Peter's sermon, what event/reality is the foundation of the Christian faith, and how absolutely certain is it?

3. What kind of unity did early Christians enjoy? How did it come about and how did they maintain it?

4. **What can I draw from this chapter to help me grow as a Christian?**

Answering the questions from this chapter is GOOD.

Applying the message of this chapter is BETTER.

Today's purpose: Read. Reflect. Refresh Your Faith.

One more thing: Pray about this today!

*"And **they continued steadfastly**
in the apostles' doctrine and fellowship,
in the breaking of bread, and in prayers"*
(Acts 2:42).

Read Acts 3

The Power and Authority of Jesus Christ in All Things

1. Like they did in New Testament times, what effect should reading about actual miracles in the Bible have on us today?

2. What significance do you think it has that Peter begins and ends his sermon referring to Jesus as God's "Servant"?

3. In prophecy 1,500 years before Christ, what did Moses emphasize about hearing (i.e., obeying) the words of Jesus?

4. **What can I draw from this chapter to help me grow as a Christian?**

Answering the questions from this chapter is GOOD.

Applying the message of this chapter is BETTER.

Today's purpose: Read. Reflect. Refresh Your Faith.

One more thing: Pray about this today!

*"And **they continued steadfastly**
in the apostles' doctrine and fellowship,
in the breaking of bread, and in prayers"*
(Acts 2:42).

Read Acts 4

Faithfully Enduring
Early Persecution

1. What was it about the apostles (and should be about us) that stood out and led people to conclude that they had been with Jesus?

2. Even though their lives were threatened, how did Peter and John respond to the command to never speak of Jesus again?

3. How was Barnabas an encourager in the early church? How can we emulate his example today?

4. **What can I draw from this chapter to help me grow as a Christian?**

Answering the questions from this chapter is GOOD.

Applying the message of this chapter is BETTER.

Today's purpose: Read. Reflect. Refresh Your Faith.

One more thing: Pray about this today!

Day #5 to Grow with the Early Christians

*"And **they continued steadfastly**
in the apostles' doctrine and fellowship,
in the breaking of bread, and in prayers"*
(Acts 2:42).

Read Acts 5

Determined Preaching
in the Face of Persecution

1. What positive, long-term effect did the harsh disciplinary action against Ananias and Sapphira have for the church?

2. In what situations today should we be ready to express the same commitment that the apostles did in 5:29?

3. At the end of chapter 5, how did the apostles respond to the command to stop preaching?

4. **What can I draw from this chapter to help me grow as a Christian?**

Answering the questions from this chapter is GOOD.

Applying the message of this chapter is BETTER.

Today's purpose: Read. Reflect. Refresh Your Faith.

One more thing: Pray about this today!

*"And **they continued steadfastly**
in the apostles' doctrine and fellowship,
in the breaking of bread, and in prayers"*
(Acts 2:42).

Read Acts 6

Special Servants
Needed in the Church

1. In the face of such severe persecution, why do you think the number of disciples kept multiplying?

2. Why would it be important for the men who served widows to meet certain qualifications?

3. When confronted with the truth, what were those men who had disputed with Stephen unable to do?

4. **What can I draw from this chapter to help me grow as a Christian?**

Answering the questions from this chapter is GOOD.

Applying the message of this chapter is BETTER.

Today's purpose: Read. Reflect. Refresh Your Faith.

One more thing: Pray about this today!

*"And **they continued steadfastly**
in the apostles' doctrine and fellowship,
in the breaking of bread, and in prayers"*
(Acts 2:42).

Read Acts 7

The First Christian Martyred for His Faith in Christ

1. Why was it necessary for Stephen to preach such a hard-hitting sermon on the Old Testament Jews' rebellion?

2. What made the response of the hearts in 7:54 different from those in 2:37?

3. How could Stephen be so calm and forgiving in the face of his own death?

4. **What can I draw from this chapter to help me grow as a Christian?**

Answering the questions from this chapter is GOOD.

Applying the message of this chapter is BETTER.

Today's purpose: Read. Reflect. Refresh Your Faith.

One more thing: Pray about this today!

*"And **they continued steadfastly**
in the apostles' doctrine and fellowship,
in the breaking of bread, and in prayers"*
(Acts 2:42).

Read Acts 8

Scattered Christians
Continue to Preach

1. Even though the Christians in Jerusalem were scattered because of their faith, what did they continue to do everywhere they went?

2. Why would it have been a big deal for Philip to go and preach in Samaria? (see John 4:9)

3. What are the instructions given to a Christian who sins in order to be made right with God?

4. **What can I draw from this chapter to help me grow as a Christian?**

Answering the questions from this chapter is GOOD.

Applying the message of this chapter is BETTER.

Today's purpose: Read. Reflect. Refresh Your Faith.

One more thing: Pray about this today!

Day #9 to Grow with the Early Christians

*"And **they continued steadfastly**
in the apostles' doctrine and fellowship,
in the breaking of bread, and in prayers"*
(Acts 2:42).

Read Acts 9

Complete Conversion of a Great Church Worker

1. What does the conversion of Saul of Tarsus teach us about the power of the gospel and the urgency of the Great Commission?

2. What did Barnabas do that no one else was willing to do?

3. What does the account about Dorcas show us about the impact one person can have in the church?

4. **What can I draw from this chapter to help me grow as a Christian?**

Answering the questions from this chapter is GOOD.

Applying the message of this chapter is BETTER.

Today's purpose: Read. Reflect. Refresh Your Faith.

One more thing: Pray about this today!

Day #10 to Grow with the Early Christians

*"And **they continued steadfastly**
in the apostles' doctrine and fellowship,
in the breaking of bread, and in prayers"
(Acts 2:42).*

Read Acts 10

*The Gospel
Really Is for All*

1. While the Biblical description of Cornelius is of a very religious man, how do we know that he was not saved, although he was so pious?

2. What can we learn from Cornelius' eagerness to hear Peter's preaching of the gospel and his desire for others to hear it with him?

3. What centrally key lesson to New Testament Christianity did Peter learn by being sent to the home of a Gentile (verses 34-35)?

4. **What can I draw from this chapter to help me grow as a Christian?**

Answering the questions from this chapter is GOOD.

Applying the message of this chapter is BETTER.

Today's purpose: Read. Reflect. Refresh Your Faith.

One more thing: Pray about this today!

Day #11 to Grow with the Early Christians

*"And **they continued steadfastly**
in the apostles' doctrine and fellowship,
in the breaking of bread, and in prayers"
(Acts 2:42).*

Read Acts 11

Christians Growing and Thriving Through Preaching

1. What personal application can we make today of Peter's realization, "Who was I that I could withstand God?"

2. What do we find Barnabas doing in this chapter and what great things resulted from his efforts?

3. Why is it important to use and define the word "Christian" in the way that the New Testament does and not as the world or denominationalism does today?

4. **What can I draw from this chapter to help me grow as a Christian?**

Answering the questions from this chapter is GOOD.

Applying the message of this chapter is BETTER.

Today's purpose: Read. Reflect. Refresh Your Faith.

One more thing: Pray about this today!

Day #12 to Grow with the Early Christians

*"And **they continued steadfastly**
in the apostles' doctrine and fellowship,
in the breaking of bread, and in prayers"*
(Acts 2:42).

Read Acts 12

Death Due to Faith vs.
Death Due to Pride

1. When peril came upon one of God's children, what did the church do on his behalf?

2. What happened to Herod when he allowed himself to be unduly exalted, and what can we learn from that for ourselves today?

3. An apostle was murdered and another apostle was imprisoned, but what did "the word of God" continue to do?

4. **What can I draw from this chapter to help me grow as a Christian?**

Answering the questions from this chapter is GOOD.

Applying the message of this chapter is BETTER.

Today's purpose: Read. Reflect. Refresh Your Faith.

One more thing: Pray about this today!

*"And **they continued steadfastly**
in the apostles' doctrine and fellowship,
in the breaking of bread, and in prayers"
(Acts 2:42).*

Read Acts 13

*Spreading the Gospel
on a Mission Trip*

1. Since Paul was trying to convert people to Christ and His gospel, why do you think he would spend so much time going to Jewish synagogues?

2. The Bible says that Sergius Paulus was "an intelligent man" (13:7), who was intelligent enough to do what (in verse 12)?

3. When the Jews rejected the gospel in Antioch Pisidia, why do you think Paul thought that the gospel would be more readily accepted among the Gentiles?

4. **What can I draw from this chapter to help me grow as a Christian?**

Answering the questions from this chapter is GOOD.

Applying the message of this chapter is BETTER.

Today's purpose: Read. Reflect. Refresh Your Faith.

One more thing: Pray about this today!

Day #14 to Grow with the Early Christians

*"And **they continued steadfastly**
in the apostles' doctrine and fellowship,
in the breaking of bread, and in prayers"*
(Acts 2:42).

Read Acts 14

Continuing in the Faith
Despite Persecution

1. What can we learn from the response of Paul and Barnabas to the people of Lystra who wanted to worship these men of God?

2. Why do you think that Paul went back into the city of Lystra after he had been dragged out of the city and stoned (supposing to death)?

3. While strengthening and exhorting new converts to continue in the faith, what did Paul warn them they must endure to enter the eternal kingdom?

4. **What can I draw from this chapter to help me grow as a Christian?**

Answering the questions from this chapter is GOOD.

Applying the message of this chapter is BETTER.

Today's purpose: Read. Reflect. Refresh Your Faith.

One more thing: Pray about this today!

Day #15 to Grow with the Early Christians

*"And **they continued steadfastly**
in the apostles' doctrine and fellowship,
in the breaking of bread, and in prayers"
(Acts 2:42).*

Read Acts 15

Handling Conflict
While Staying Properly Focused

1. What does it mean that God made "no distinction" between the Jews (i.e., "we") and the Gentiles (i.e., "them")? (Read verses 8 through 11.)

2. When some brethren tried to bind circumcision on the Gentiles, how did the leaders in Jerusalem prevent that issue from dividing the church?

3. How did Paul and Barnabas resolve their conflict, so that it did not hinder the work of the Lord (which was their top priority)?

4. **What can I draw from this chapter to help me grow as a Christian?**

Answering the questions from this chapter is GOOD.

Applying the message of this chapter is BETTER.

Today's purpose: Read. Reflect. Refresh Your Faith.

One more thing: Pray about this today!

Day #16 to Grow with the Early Christians

*"And **they continued steadfastly**
in the apostles' doctrine and fellowship,
in the breaking of bread, and in prayers"*
(Acts 2:42).

Read Acts 16

The Macedonian Call of Souls
Needing the Gospel

1. What can we learn from Paul's choice to take such a young man as Timothy with him on his missionary journey?

2. We sing a song that says, "We have heard the Macedonian call today." What does that mean in specific application for us today?

3. Although they were arrested, beaten with rods and thrown into the inner prison, how did Paul and Silas respond to this maltreatment?

4. **What can I draw from this chapter to help me grow as a Christian?**

Answering the questions from this chapter is GOOD.

Applying the message of this chapter is BETTER.

Today's purpose: Read. Reflect. Refresh Your Faith.

One more thing: Pray about this today!

---

*"And **they continued steadfastly***
in the apostles' doctrine and fellowship,
in the breaking of bread, and in prayers"
(Acts 2:42).

Read Acts 17

Coming to Know
the One God and His Scripture

1. What key efforts are necessary on our part to be Bible students like the Bereans?

2. When Paul preached about the true God of heaven to the Athenians, for what purpose did he state that the Lord had made man?

3. While repentance is not a fun topic to discuss or contemplate, what reason did Paul give that all must make necessary changes and preparations in their lives?

4. **What can I draw from this chapter to help me grow as a Christian?**

Answering the questions from this chapter is GOOD.

Applying the message of this chapter is BETTER.

Today's purpose: Read. Reflect. Refresh Your Faith.

One more thing: Pray about this today!

Day #18 to Grow with the Early Christians

*"And **they continued steadfastly**
in the apostles' doctrine and fellowship,
in the breaking of bread, and in prayers"*
(Acts 2:42).

Read Acts 18

Accurately Reasoning and Teaching God's Word

1. Paul regularly "reasoned" with individuals "from the Scriptures." What does that indicate about the understandable and logical nature of God's Word?

2. The Lord spoke directly to Paul to reassure him while in Corinth. Has the Lord said anything similar to us in His Word?

3. Why was it crucial for Apollos to not be "mostly right" in his preaching but to be taught "more accurately" all the truth of God?

4. **What can I draw from this chapter to help me grow as a Christian?**

Answering the questions from this chapter is GOOD.

Applying the message of this chapter is BETTER.

Today's purpose: Read. Reflect. Refresh Your Faith.

One more thing: Pray about this today!

*"And **they continued steadfastly**
in the apostles' doctrine and fellowship,
in the breaking of bread, and in prayers"*
(Acts 2:42).

Read Acts 19

*The Distinctive Nature
of God and His Plan*

1. Why was it necessary for the twelve men in Ephesus to be "baptized in the name of the Lord Jesus" when they had already been baptized before?

2. Multiple times in this book (and in this chapter) the Lord's church and doctrine is referred to as "the Way." What significance does that have?

3. What effect was the gospel having on the practice of idolatry (and those who profited from it) in the city of Ephesus?

4. **What can I draw from this chapter to help me grow as a Christian?**

Answering the questions from this chapter is GOOD.

Applying the message of this chapter is BETTER.

Today's purpose: Read. Reflect. Refresh Your Faith.

One more thing: Pray about this today!

*"And **they continued steadfastly**
in the apostles' doctrine and fellowship,
in the breaking of bread, and in prayers"*
(Acts 2:42).

Read Acts 20

*The Blessing of Worship
and Godly Church Leaders*

1. What was the central purpose of the weekly assembly of the Lord's church in the first century?

2. What charge did Paul give to the Ephesian elders regarding themselves and their oversight of the Lord's church in Ephesus?

3. How have you found this statement to be true in your life—"It is more blessed to give than to receive"?

4. **What can I draw from this chapter to help me grow as a Christian?**

Answering the questions from this chapter is GOOD.

Applying the message of this chapter is BETTER.

Today's purpose: Read. Reflect. Refresh Your Faith.

One more thing: Pray about this today!

Day #21 to Grow with the Early Christians

*"And **they continued steadfastly**
in the apostles' doctrine and fellowship,
in the breaking of bread, and in prayers"
(Acts 2:42).*

Read Acts 21

*Being Loved and Hated
for Preaching Jesus Christ*

1. When the brethren pleaded with Paul not to go to Jerusalem, what did he tell them that he was ready to do?

2. Paul regularly reported to the Jews "in detail those things which God had done among the Gentiles." Why do you think he kept doing that?

3. With an eerie similarity to the mob crying out against Jesus, why were the Jews determined to "do away with" Paul?

4. **What can I draw from this chapter to help me grow as a Christian?**

Answering the questions from this chapter is GOOD.

Applying the message of this chapter is BETTER.

Today's purpose: Read. Reflect. Refresh Your Faith.

One more thing: Pray about this today!

*"And **they continued steadfastly**
in the apostles' doctrine and fellowship,
in the breaking of bread, and in prayers"*
(Acts 2:42).

Read Acts 22

Defending Conversion to and Devotion to Christ

1. How extreme was Paul's conversion from where he had been before Christ to where he grew to be in Christ? What can we learn from this?

2. Why were the Jews so incensed when Paul mentioned the word "Gentiles"? Is there any modern-day parallel to that?

3. How did Paul use his legal/national citizenship as a Roman to benefit his spiritual/heavenly citizenship as a Christian?

4. **What can I draw from this chapter to help me grow as a Christian?**

Answering the questions from this chapter is GOOD.

Applying the message of this chapter is BETTER.

Today's purpose: Read. Reflect. Refresh Your Faith.

One more thing: Pray about this today!

*"And **they continued steadfastly**
in the apostles' doctrine and fellowship,
in the breaking of bread, and in prayers"*
(Acts 2:42).

Read Acts 23

*God's Deliverance
from Man's Wicked Schemes*

1. How could Paul say that he had lived in all good conscience, even while persecuting and killing Christians? What does that teach us about following our conscience?

2. While Paul may have felt alone in the midst of his horrible circumstances, who does it say "stood by him"? What comfort should that bring to us?

3. What do we learn about the power of just one individual from the account of Paul's nephew?

4. **What can I draw from this chapter to help me grow as a Christian?**

Answering the questions from this chapter is GOOD.

Applying the message of this chapter is BETTER.

Today's purpose: Read. Reflect. Refresh Your Faith.

One more thing: Pray about this today!

---

*"And **they continued steadfastly**
in the apostles' doctrine and fellowship,
in the breaking of bread, and in prayers"*
(Acts 2:42).

Read Acts 24

*The Foolishness of
the Convenient Season*

1. While Paul's accusers foolishly referred to the religion of Christ as a "sect," how did Paul describe it and how much confidence did he have in it?

2. What three things did Paul reason about from the Scriptures before Felix, which caused Felix to become afraid?

3. While we consider Felix's postponement for a "convenient time" to be foolish, in what ways do Christians today sometimes wait for their own "convenient time"?

4. **What can I draw from this chapter to help me grow as a Christian?**

Answering the questions from this chapter is GOOD.

Applying the message of this chapter is BETTER.

Today's purpose: Read. Reflect. Refresh Your Faith.

One more thing: Pray about this today!

*"And **they continued steadfastly**
in the apostles' doctrine and fellowship,
in the breaking of bread, and in prayers"*
(Acts 2:42).

Read Acts 25

*Taking the Message of God
to All in Authority*

1. How should we as Christians respond when others conspire against us and lay complaints down against us?

2. Why would Paul appeal to stand before Caesar? What possible benefits could outweigh the risks involved in that?

3. One significant proof of the resurrection of Christ is the conversion, faith and preaching of Paul. Why are Paul's before and after pictures strong evidence for the resurrection?

4. **What can I draw from this chapter to help me grow as a Christian?**

Answering the questions from this chapter is GOOD.

Applying the message of this chapter is BETTER.

Today's purpose: Read. Reflect. Refresh Your Faith.

One more thing: Pray about this today!

*"And **they continued steadfastly**
in the apostles' doctrine and fellowship,
in the breaking of bread, and in prayers"*
(Acts 2:42).

Read Acts 26

The Foolishness of Almost Persuaded

1. Why do you think Paul explained where he had come from in his life as a Jew and what he had previously done to Christians?

2. When Jesus appeared to Paul on the road to Damascus, what plans did the Lord tell Paul that He had for him?

3. "Almost" is such a devastating word when it comes to Christianity. How can the word "almost" stunt and even prevent our growth and service as a Christian?

4. **What can I draw from this chapter to help me grow as a Christian?**

Answering the questions from this chapter is GOOD.

Applying the message of this chapter is BETTER.

Today's purpose: Read. Reflect. Refresh Your Faith.

One more thing: Pray about this today!

*"And **they continued steadfastly**
in the apostles' doctrine and fellowship,
in the breaking of bread, and in prayers"*
(Acts 2:42).

Read Acts 27

*Deep Faith in God
in the Midst of Dreadful Storms*

1. Why do you suppose that the centurion was "more persuaded" by the advice of "the majority" than of Paul? How should we measure whose advice we follow today?

2. In order to convey his utter trust and dependence on God to these sailors, what three verbs did Paul use after the personal pronoun "I" in verses 23-25?

3. Just as physical lives were "saved" because the men obeyed the words of Paul, how could those men have made a parallel application to their spiritual lives being "saved"?

4. **What can I draw from this chapter to help me grow as a Christian?**

Answering the questions from this chapter is GOOD.

Applying the message of this chapter is BETTER.

Today's purpose: Read. Reflect. Refresh Your Faith.

One more thing: Pray about this today!

---

*"And **they continued steadfastly**
in the apostles' doctrine and fellowship,
in the breaking of bread, and in prayers"*
(Acts 2:42).

Read Acts 28

Unrelentingly Preaching Jesus and His Kingdom

1. While the Christian Way, which the Jews called a "sect," was "spoken against everywhere," was Paul embarrassed or did he back down? What can we learn from that?

2. Although Paul had been arrested, beaten, imprisoned and now could have his life taken for preaching about Jesus and His kingdom, what did he continue to preach while in prison?

3. Why is it that some people can hear the truth plainly preached but yet not believe it and not respond to it?

4. **What can I draw from this chapter to help me grow as a Christian?**

Answering the questions from this chapter is GOOD.

Applying the message of this chapter is BETTER.

Today's purpose: Read. Reflect. Refresh Your Faith.

One more thing: Pray about this today!

Walking Daily with My Lord

OCTOBER:

28 DAYS
To Teach the Gospel

"Him we preach,
warning every man and
teaching every man in all wisdom,
that we may present every man
perfect in Christ Jesus"
(Colossians 1:28).

28DAYS To Teach the Gospel

Christians Have the God-Given Responsibility to Teach the Gospel to Lost Souls in the World!

To some Christians, the thought of trying to teach someone the gospel brings a sense of fear and uncertainty.

- What do I say?
- Where do I start?
- What points need to be made?
- How do I proceed in an orderly manner?

However, this responsibility need not create trepidation or uneasiness.

The following 28 pages are designed to take someone through the saving message of the gospel from beginning to end.

Read through them over the next 28 days, and if you find them helpful, share them with souls who need the gospel.

Links to each article can be found at pblcoc.org:
"Let's Go Back to the Bible"

The series can be found in booklet form on Amazon.
Search for: Let's Go Back to the Bible by David Sproule.
Or, search for the ISBN: 1727484053.

Let's teach the gospel for 28 days...

☐ Day 1	☐ Day 8	☐ Day 15	☐ Day 22
☐ Day 2	☐ Day 9	☐ Day 16	☐ Day 23
☐ Day 3	☐ Day 10	☐ Day 17	☐ Day 24
☐ Day 4	☐ Day 11	☐ Day 18	☐ Day 25
☐ Day 5	☐ Day 12	☐ Day 19	☐ Day 26
☐ Day 6	☐ Day 13	☐ Day 20	☐ Day 27
☐ Day 7	☐ Day 14	☐ Day 21	☐ Day 28

Let's Go Back to the Bible!

What does God expect of me? How can I know what He wants me to do? How can I know if I am right with God? How can I know if I'm going to heaven?

These short, easy-to-read lessons have been designed to give each reader a Biblical foundation for faith and Biblical answers to the most essential matters of life regarding salvation and the promise of heaven.

Rather than survey the common answers among religious groups regarding these matters or accepting what a particular person or group might teach, *let's go back to the Bible!* *Let's allow the Bible to teach us.* Take out your personal Bible and let's study God's Word together. Let us "search the Scriptures" (Acts 17:11) as we study the following Biblical topics:

1. Foundational Questions Must Be Answered
2. The God of the Bible Exists
3. The Bible Really Is from God
4. The Bible Can Be Understood
5. Jesus Really Is the Son of God
6. God's Love Is Wonderfully Revealed in the Bible
7. Jesus Christ Has All Authority
8. The Bible Is God's All-Authoritative Truth
9. The Bible Must Be Respected and Obeyed
10. The Lord Established Only One Church
11. The Church Is Composed of Those Who Are Saved
12. The Lord's Church Holds to the Scriptural Pattern
13. The Lord's Church Is Scripturally Organized
14. The Lord's Church Wears a Scriptural Name
15. The Lord's Church Worships As Authorized
16. The Lord's Church Worships in Scriptural Avenues
17. The Lord's Church Still Exists Today
18. Sin Separates Man from God
19. God Wants All People to Be Saved
20. One Must Be Saved As Authorized in Scripture
21. One Must Believe Jesus Is God's Son to Be Saved
22. One Must Repent of His Sins to Be Saved
23. One Must Confess His Faith in Jesus to Be Saved
24. One Must Be Immersed into Christ to Be Saved
25. One Must Be "In Christ" to Be Saved
26. A Christian Must Live a Faithful Life to God
27. One Day Jesus Will Return from Heaven
28. How Do YOU Answer the Foundational Questions?

#1 Foundational Questions Must Be Answered

Life. It is the one thing (no matter who we are) that we all have in common. But, have you ever stopped to think about it? At some point in our existence on this earth, the thought will likely cross each person's mind—*What is life all about?* That's an important question—don't you think? But, once you've asked the question, how do you determine the answer? How do you know what source or sources to trust in your search for a reasonable response to such a fundamental question? As you contemplate that, consider for just a moment that there are three foundational questions that we must ponder in our quest for understanding "life."

First, each person must ask (and answer), "Where am I from?" This is not asking in what city or state were you born. This is asking, *where did life come from?* Are you the result of a tiny particle exploding billions of years ago? Are you the result of something inorganic and nonliving becoming organic and living? Are you the result of a single-celled organism evolving into the complex human machine you are today? Are you the result of mere chance, happenstance and randomness? Or are you the result of a meticulous, precise design and creation of human life? You must be able to answer the question of your origin. Human life had a beginning! What was it?

Second, each person must ask (and answer), "Why am I here?" This is not asking why you are presently in your specific location. This is asking, *what is the purpose of life?* Are you here to fulfill your greatest pleasures? Are you here to do whatever you want to do? Are you here without any specified purpose of any kind? Or are you here for a specific reason, and is that specific reason something that is tied back to your origin and to the one who gave you life? Human life has a purpose! What is it?

Third, each person must ask (and answer), "Where am I going?" This is not asking about your plans for the rest of your day or week or year. This is asking, *what is going to happen when life on this earth is over?* Is there anything beyond death? Is the graveyard your final destination? Will you cease to exist completely when you take your last breath on this earth? Is the limited and short life that you have now all that you will ever have and all that you were meant to have? Or is there life after death waiting for you? Will you continue to exist in a non-material realm once you are done with life on this material realm? Human life has an ultimate destination. What will it be?

These three foundational questions either have a definite answer or they are not meant to be answered at all. Which do you think is the case? If they do have a definite answer, then we're back to where we started—how do you determine the answer, and how do you know what source to trust? In this series, you will be able to use a proven source to confidently answer each of these questions. But, don't take my word for it. Check it out yourself!

Is there a God? That is a question that must be answered! But it cannot be answered based upon personal opinions or feelings on the matter, for that is completely subjective (and thus, in the end, unreliable). Obviously, not everyone believes in God. But what does the evidence show? Would it surprise you to know that the evidence for the existence of God (the God of the Bible) is absolutely overwhelming? Consider it for yourself. What is the only reasonable conclusion to the following lines of testimony?

First, consider the "Law of Cause and Effect." Basically, this states that "every material effect must have an adequate cause that existed before the effect." If you found your house crumbled to the ground, you could not blame it on the mosquito that you found flying over the debris. That would not be an adequate cause. Something quite substantial would have to cause that to happen. Would that also be true of our universe? Do you know that there are over 100 billion galaxies in our universe and each galaxy (like our Milky Way) has over 100 billion stars in it? Would a tiny ball of matter smaller than a proton be able to "Bang" Big enough to adequately cause this massive, material universe that we cannot even completely see, yet alone explore? No, that would not be an adequate cause! There must have been an original *cause* substantial enough to bring about the *effect* that is here.

Second, consider the "Law of Biogenesis." Basically, this states that "life in the material universe comes from previous life of its own kind." This has been proven over and over, and science itself has shown that life never arises except from life. It is evident that life is now here. (You are evidence that life is now here.) Where did it come from? It could not have come from non-life. (That's what the Law of Biogenesis proves.) Therefore, the origin of life on earth points back to an original life-giver. Who (not what) could that be?

Third, consider the "Law of Rationality." Basically, this states that "one must only draw and accept conclusions that are warranted by clear evidence." Specifically, think about the matter of design. If there is design, that demands the conclusion that there is a designer. A watch demands a watchmaker. A painting demands a painter. The design that is evident in the earth, the universe and the human body is millions of times more complex than a watch or a painting. What conclusion does that evidence warrant? What is the rational explanation? Doesn't that design also demand a designer? It is not rational to state that the intricate design around us is not by design!

There is no other explanation for the substantial amount of evidence than this conclusion: **There is a God!** This is not merely an opinion. The laws of science substantiate that a random event involving an explosion of non-living material is not a rational explanation for this universe or life we possess! But, the God of the Bible—the Creator—is! He is the only true God!

#3 The Bible Really Is from God

Is there anything special about the Bible? If so, can it be proven? There are certainly many different beliefs today about the Bible, but this is another topic that cannot be settled by personal opinions or feelings. What does the evidence (if there is any) show (if anything)? It may surprise you to know that the evidence for the divine origin of the Bible is incontrovertible when examined thoroughly and collectively. Take a moment and consider just a few things for yourself. Then, decide what the only reasonable conclusion is.

First, the Bible maintains complete unity from beginning to end. About 40 men from very diverse backgrounds and over a period of 1,600 years penned a book that remains united in the central theme and purpose of the coming of Jesus Christ to save mankind. And the penmen accomplish this task without contradicting themselves a single time. It's hard to explain that from a human standpoint, but easy if it is God!

Second, the Bible is completely accurate in its every detail. The Bible is full of historical and geographical data that has been found, upon repeated examination by historians and archaeologists, to be factually accurate, even when put to harsh, biased tests. (Many so-called "experts" set out with the purposeful intent to disprove the Bible, but they could not.) No man could have got every single detail precisely right in a book this size, but God could!

Third, the Bible contains hundreds of predictive prophecies that were fulfilled with exact precision. The prophecies contained in the Bible were made hundreds of years in advance of their fulfillment and included details about specific people, places and events that were impossible for the writers (or any others) to have known about, let alone to have effected in any way the complete and precise fulfillment. There is no human explanation for this, but God can explain it.

Fourth, the Bible includes staggering scientific foreknowledge. The writing of the Bible was completed more than 1,900 years ago, and yet there are scientific details in the book (including knowledge in the fields of astronomy, biology, medicine, oceanography, physics, etc.) that were not actually discovered by men until the last few centuries. How could men record these scientific facts hundreds of years (and even thousands, in some cases) before other men ever discovered them? The only reasonable answer is that man did not originate the words in the Bible, but God did!

The Bible is an amazing book! It claims to be "inspired by God" (2 Tim. 3:16) and that no human could or did produce it on their own (1 Cor. 2:10-13; 2 Pet. 1:20-21). It not only claims it; it proves it! The overwhelming evidence contained therein leads to only one rational conclusion—the Bible did not come from man but it really did come from God!

#4 The Bible Can Be Understood

Sometimes when people look at the Bible, they get a bit overwhelmed. They see a book with over a thousand pages and with some unfamiliar names and terminology in it. They have likely heard people talk about trying to read and understand the Bible, and they allow what they hear to shape their own expectations. Truthfully, they are just not really sure where to start. Perhaps some words of introduction and encouragement would be beneficial.

First, if the above paragraph describes you in any part, realize that everyone has been where you are. No one comes to the Bible the first time with all the knowledge and understanding of a longtime Bible scholar. It takes time and effort for everyone. Start small. It's not a race or a competition.

Second, it helps to recognize that God *intends* for His Word to be understood. The Almighty God made us and He made the Bible. Thus, He has the power to (1) write a book that is understandable and (2) give us the ability to understand it. Early Christians were reassured that when they read the Bible they would be able to "understand" it (Eph. 3:3-4), and they were challenged to "understand what the will of the Lord is" (Eph. 5:17). God would not call upon us to do something that He did not first give us the ability to do.

Third, start at the beginning (in the Table of Contents) and see the two main divisions. The Bible is divided into the Old Testament and the New Testament. In general, these two divisions represent two separate covenants that God made at two separate times with two separate peoples. The first covenant was made with the Jews when they were at Mt. Sinai (Deut. 5:2). The purpose of that first covenant was to prepare people for the coming of Jesus (Gal. 3:19-25). When Jesus came, that old covenant was "taken out of the way" (Col. 2:14), and Jesus "established the second" covenant, or the New Testament (Heb. 10:9), when He died on the cross for us (Heb. 9:15-17). Today, we do not live under the Old Testament (Gal. 5:1-4), but we live under the New Testament and are subject to obeying it (Heb. 5:8-9).

Fourth, know that Jesus Christ is the theme of the whole Bible. God had a plan before Creation to redeem mankind to Himself (Eph. 1:4-7), and the Bible unfolds how God fulfilled that plan completely and perfectly. The Bible can be summarized in three sentences: (1) "Jesus is coming" (the books of the Old Testament). (2) "Jesus is here" (the first four books of the New Testament). (3) "Jesus is coming again" (the last 23 books of the New Testament).

The Bible is a marvelous book. The best way to understand it is to just start reading it. If there are parts that are hard to understand, don't worry about those parts at first. The great thing is that the parts we do need to understand to be saved are very clear and understandable. God is good! He gave us the Bible so that we could come to know Him, love Him, believe in Him and obey Him. Let's get into it and let's study it.

Jesus Really Is the Son of God

Who is Jesus? That is a question that everyone must face! But we cannot base our conclusions on the various opinions of our modern day, for people have all sorts of different ideas about Jesus today. What does the evidence show? It is historically verified that Jesus of Nazareth really lived on this earth and had a tremendous impact on mankind. (The influence of His life still resonates to this day.) But Jesus was more than just a mere man! When the evidence is impartially examined, you will find that it is hard to escape this undeniable truth— Jesus is the Son of God!

First, Jesus fulfilled 332 prophecies that were made in the Old Testament. This fact is just astonishing. The prophecies were specific, detailed predictions made hundreds of years before Jesus was ever born (some more than 1,000 years earlier). One scientist and mathematician calculated that the chance of one man fulfilling just 48 prophecies was 1 in 10^{157}. But Jesus fulfilled 332 prophecies exactly and completely! There is no human explanation for that! This truth proves that Jesus is precisely who He claimed to be— the promised Messiah of the Old Testament (i.e., "the Christ, the Son of the living God" [Matt. 16:16; cf. Acts 2:36]).

Second, Jesus performed many astonishing miracles. He had power on this earth that was truly supernatural! There is no human explanation for the wonders that Jesus did on this earth! He demonstrated power over nature (like calming a storm), power over disease (like healing the blind), power over demons (by casting them out of people) and power over death (by raising people from the dead). These mighty works were recognized to be the power of God (John 3:2; Acts 2:22), and they proved to every honest observer that "Jesus is the Christ, the Son of God" (John 20:30-31).

Third, Jesus was raised from dead. Jesus died on a Friday afternoon, and to make sure that He was dead, soldiers thrust a spear through His side. Blood and water poured forth. They buried Him in a friend's tomb, and early on Sunday morning that tomb was empty. While many explanations have been offered for the empty tomb (and even secular historians have had to admit the tomb was occupied on Friday and Saturday, and then empty on Sunday), all human conjecture has failed to explain all of the evidence. The only reasoned explanation for the empty tomb (when examined honestly and without any prejudice) is that God truly raised Him from the dead, which "declared [Him] to be the Son of God with power" (Rom. 1:4). This truth must be reckoned with by every living soul!

Jesus was (and is) no ordinary man! All of the evidence, when weighed in the balance, points overwhelmingly to the conclusion that He is the Son of God, which means that He deserves our respect and our obedience. The inspired Word of the God of heaven establishes the deity of Jesus Christ!

#6 | God's Love Is Wonderfully Revealed in the Bible

The legendary Frank Sinatra expressed it this way in 1958: "To love and be loved—That's what life's all about!" If that's true of a human relationship, what about when that love comes from the Almighty God of heaven? How deep and breathtaking can you imagine His love would be? There is no way to fully wrap our minds around the enormity of His love, but think about this.

First, God's love reveals to us the truth about sin. Because He loves us, God unfolded His will for us in the pages of the Bible (2 Tim. 3:16-17). When we transgress or disobey God's will (Heb. 2:2), or when we choose to disregard or not follow His will (Jas. 4:17), the Bible says that we sin against God (1 John 3:4). This is a big deal for all of us (Rom. 3:23)!

Second, God's love reveals the consequences of sin. Is sin really all that bad? The Bible says that sin makes "a separation between you and your God" and causes "His face" to be "hidden" from you (Isa. 59:2). That's because God is holy and cannot "behold evil" or "look on wickedness" (Hab. 1:13). My sin separates me from God in this life (Rom. 6:23), and if I don't do anything to remove it, sin will separate me from God for all eternity (2 Thess. 1:8-9). This is a very serious matter! So, where is love in all of this?

Third, God's love is revealed in His answer for sin. Since sin is the result of man transgressing the will of God, it's amazing that God wants anything to do with us after that. But He does! In His amazing grace, God wants all of mankind to be saved from their sins (1 Tim. 2:4). His deep and unfathomable love prompted Him to send "His only begotten Son" to die on the cross (Phil. 2:6-8), so that we can be saved (Rom. 5:9-10) and spend an eternity with Him in heaven (John 3:16). Think about that! "The wages of sin is death" (Rom. 6:23). While Jesus never committed a single sin Himself (Heb. 4:15), the Bible says that all of our sins were "laid upon" Him while He died on that cross (Isa. 53:6). He "bore our sins" (1 Pet. 2:24) and died, so that we could be saved! That is an amazing love!

Fourth, God's love is revealed in His cleansing for sin. In the Bible, blood was used by God as a means by which to atone, cleanse and forgive sins (Ex. 12:1-13; Lev. 16:1-22). In the Old Testament, the blood of animals was used to make atonement, but that blood could not "take away sins" (Heb. 10:4). Only the blood of Jesus Himself, when He offered Himself as the sacrifice in our place (Heb. 9:11-28), can "wash" us (Rev. 1:5) and "save" us (Heb. 9:22) from our sins. There is no greater love than that (John 15:13)!

It is hard to fathom the depth of His love, which led Him to unconditionally and unselfishly sacrifice Himself for us! We do not deserve it! But we should be ever grateful that He has given us an opportunity to be saved from the eternal consequences of our sins and to live with Him forever!

#7 Jesus Christ Has All Authority

In all facets of life, it is essential to learn and to know who has authority. In the schoolhouse, it is essential to know who has authority. In the home, it is essential to know who has authority. On the sports field, it is essential to know who has authority. In the workplace, it is essential to know who has authority. We can readily understand how and why that is so important.

So, what about in religion? Who has authority (specifically—ALL authority) in religious matters today? Is it the preacher, the pastor, the elders, the church council, our family, our friends, a church manual, a creed book, my personal opinions, my personal beliefs, some church tradition, what is popular, what I feel in my heart, OR something else? How would we determine the answer to this crucial question? Let us see what the Bible has to say!

First, Jesus Christ has all authority in religious matters today because He created all things. "By Him all things were created that are in heaven and that are on earth" (Col. 1:16). Nothing exists that Jesus Himself did not create (John 1:3). "He is before all things," therefore, "in all things" He is to have "preeminence" (Col. 1:17-18). Jesus truly has all authority!

Second, Jesus Christ has all authority in religious matters today because He came down from heaven. When Jesus came to the earth, those who heard Him preach "were astonished at His teaching, for He taught them as one having authority, and not as the scribes" (Matt. 7:28-29). The God of heaven announced, "This is My beloved Son, in whom I am well pleased. Hear Him!" (Matt 17:5). Everyone who will not hear Him "shall be utterly destroyed from among the people" (Acts 3:22-23). Jesus truly has all authority!

Third, Jesus Christ has all authority in religious matters today because He was raised from the dead. After His resurrection and before He ascended back into heaven, Jesus proclaimed, "All authority has been given to Me in heaven and on earth" (Matt. 28:18). Jesus was then seated at the right hand of God, "far above all rule and authority and power and dominion, and every name that is named" (Eph. 1:21). Jesus truly has all authority!

Fourth, Jesus Christ has all authority in religious matters today because He will judge all mankind. The day will come when we will "all stand before the judgment seat of Christ" (Rom. 14:10). Jesus has been "ordained" by God to "judge the world" (Acts 17:31) at the end of time, and it is His word that "will judge [man] in the last day" (John 12:48). Jesus truly has all authority!

Whose authority should we follow in religion today? Whose standard must we use to acceptably serve God? There is no human authority or human standard that has been given all authority or will judge us in the end. Only Christ has all authority! Therefore, we must turn to Him, respect Him, submit to Him, follow Him and obey Him!

#8 The Bible Is God's All-Authoritative Truth

Jesus Christ truly has all authority (Matt. 28:18), and it is His word that is going to judge all of mankind at the end of time (John 12:48)! When Jesus ascended into heaven, He sent the Holy Spirit to His apostles to remind them of His words and to guide them into all truth (John 14:26; 16:13), as they recorded the words that we now have in our Bible today (2 Pet. 1:20-21). Thus, we can have great assurance in the truth revealed in Scripture that it bears the full authority of Jesus Christ and is essential to navigating the course of this life. Consider the fullness of God's truth that we have today in the Bible.

First, the Bible is absolute truth. Since the Bible is from God (2 Tim. 3:16), it stands on its own. God's truth is "settled" or "firmly fixed" in heaven "forever" (Psa. 119:89). Without needing any human corroboration, God's Word is truth (John 17:17).

Second, the Bible is objective truth. Because of its divine origin, the truth of God's Word has not been and is not now influenced by personal feelings, opinions, prejudice or beliefs. The Bible is truth regardless of anyone's "private" thoughts, wishes or convictions (2 Pet. 1:20-21).

Third, the Bible is universal truth. It is not limited to a certain segment of society, but God's truth has been directed toward and has application for every person ever living on earth (Mark 16:15), for it will be the universal, objective standard that will judge all mankind at the end of time (John 12:48).

Fourth, the Bible is enduring truth. God's truth is not going anywhere. It is not only going to be in existence forever, but it is always going to be truth (1 Pet. 1:22-25; Matt. 24:35).

Fifth, the Bible is unchanging truth. God has "once for all delivered" His truth (Jude 3), meaning it cannot and will not be added to, taken from or modified by anyone (Rev. 22:18-19).

Sixth, the Bible is comprehensive truth. In His Word, God has "given to us all things that pertain to life and godliness" (2 Pet. 1:3). The Bible has all of the answers all in one place (2 Tim. 3:17).

Seventh, the Bible is understandable truth. It is not hidden or mysterious, but God has given man the ability to "know" and to "understand" His truth as revealed in His word (John 8:32; Eph. 3:4; 5:17).

Eighth, the Bible is powerful truth. God's truth changes lives! This is not some meaningless or inconsequential matter! God's Word has the power to transform the way one lives on this earth and prepare him for an eternal dwelling with God in heaven (2 Cor. 3:18; 4:16-18; Rom. 1:16).

The Bible is such an amazing book! The authority of Jesus abides within His Word! Let us hear it, read it, respect it and obey it!

#9 The Bible Must Be Respected and Obeyed

The Bible is no ordinary book! The Bible is the inspired Word of the Almighty God of heaven, in which He reveals to us His will for our lives today! No, that's not an ordinary book! That's an extraordinary book! Thus, our response cannot be merely ordinary or superficial. What expectations does God have of us when it comes to His Word?

First, God wants us to fully respect what He says. The Lord makes it clear that He does not want us "to think beyond what is written" (1 Cor. 4:6). What an interesting statement! Additionally, He does not want us to speak beyond what is written, but to "speak as the oracles of God" (1 Pet. 4:11). Note also that He does not want us to step beyond His Word and thus create divisions among believers (1 Cor. 1:10). His Word demands our respect!

Second, God wants us to never modify what He says. The Lord issues severe warnings to anyone who "adds" to His Word or "takes away from" His Word (Rev. 22:18-19). Such warnings make it clear that one places his soul in jeopardy when he tampers with God's truth. In fact, Scripture warns that if anyone preaches "a different gospel" or does not "abide in the teaching of Christ," he "does not have God" (2 John 9-11) and "he is to be accursed" (Gal. 1:6-9). We must never modify God's Word to fit what we want it to say!

Third, God wants us to obey what He says. The Lord shows that the one who truly respects Him is the one who "keeps His commandments" (Ecc. 12:13) and "works righteousness" (Acts 10:34-35). An obedient heart does not question the will of God but humbles himself before the Almighty and learns to obey His will, just as Jesus Himself did (Heb. 5:8-9; Phil. 2:8). While doing the will of the Father leads to heaven (Matt. 7:21), neglecting to obey Him leads to eternal separation (2 Thess. 1:8-9). We must respect AND obey!

Fourth, God shows us examples of those who did not respect and obey His Word. The Lord makes it abundantly clear in Scripture that He is very serious about men obeying His Word. One only need to read the accounts of Nadab and Abihu who were devoured by fire (Lev. 10:1-3) and Uzzah who was struck dead (2 Sam. 6:3-7) to learn that good intentions are no substitute for doing exactly what God said. Numerous examples are provided of disobedience and its consequences to teach us that we must respect and obey God!

Fifth, God shows us supreme examples of those who did respect and obey His Word. While there are many human examples of such in Scripture, interestingly, the Bible says that Jesus Himself had enough respect for God's Word to limit Himself to it, respect it and obey it (John 6:38; 12:49-50), as did the Holy Spirit (John 16:13). If Jesus and the Holy Spirit respected and obeyed God's Word, what does God expect of me (Matt. 7:21-27)?

Let us love the Lord and the Bible enough to do as He says!

#10 The Lord Established Only One Church

It may seem strange to some people that the church is even included in a study like this—some may think such is out of place. However, when we come to understand what the Scripture teaches about the church, we see how empty and incomplete such a study would be without investigating the church that we read about in the Bible.

First, we need to understand the origin of the church. The church that we read about in the Bible did not originate in the mind of man. Much to the contrary! Before God ever created the world, the Bible teaches that "the church" was part of "the eternal purpose" of God (Eph. 3:10-11). God had a plan to establish His (one) church before He ever made the first man.

Second, we need to understand the price of the church. When Jesus came down to live on this earth, He promised, "I will build My church" (Matt. 16:18). It was not a building that He needed to erect but a redeemed people that He wanted to unite into one body (Eph. 2:13-22). He did this when He "purchased" the (one) church "with His own blood" (Acts 20:28).

Third, we need to understand the establishment of the church. The church began on Pentecost in Acts 2, in the very way that the Lord had prophesied it would happen. The Holy Spirit came with "power" (Mark 9:1; Acts 1:8) upon the apostles so that they could preach the gospel and do miracles to confirm that their message was from heaven. Upon hearing the glorious message about Jesus Christ's death, burial and resurrection, about 3,000 people were baptized that day and the Lord's (one) church began (Acts 2:41-47).

Fourth, we need to understand the intention for just one church. When the Old Testament prophets foretold the coming church (also called the house and kingdom of God), it was always singular (Isa. 2:2-3; Dan. 2:44). When Jesus promised to build His church, it was singular (Matt. 16:18). Just hours before His death, Jesus prayed that all believers would "be one" (John 17:20-21). The Lord always intended for there to be only one church!

Fifth, we need to understand the reality of just one church. About 30 years after the establishment of the church, Paul wrote, "There is one body" (Eph. 4:4), and he identified that one body as "the church" (1:22-23). In an earlier letter, Paul pleaded with the early church, "by the name of our Lord Jesus Christ, that you all speak the same thing, and that there be no divisions among you..." (1 Cor. 1:10). In the first century, there was only one church!

When the Lord started His church, there were no denominations. He established His one church in Acts 2 and emphatically called for that one church to preach one message and never be divided. Do you know that His one church still exists today and you can be a part of it? If we go back to the Bible, we can find God's pattern for His church and identify it today.

#11 The Church Is Composed of Those Who Are Saved

What is the church? That's a very good question. It is helpful to understand that the church is not the building. The walls, roof, windows and doors do not comprise the church. And, it is helpful to understand that the church is not some ecclesiastical (or hierarchical) institution that makes and disseminates laws and rules for people to follow. That is not how the Bible describes the church. Rather, the Bible presents the church as *the people.*

First, let us understand what the word "church" means. The original word for "church" literally means, "the called out." Thus, the church is made up of ones who have responded to the gospel (2 Thess. 2:14) and have been "called out of darkness into His marvelous light" (1 Pet. 2:9). They have been "delivered...from the power of darkness" of sin and the world, and "conveyed...into the kingdom," which is His church (Col. 1:13).

Second, let us understand who is in the church. The church is not a country club that someone joins. The church is comprised of those persons whom God has put into it. But who has God placed in His church? The Bible teaches that the church is composed of those who have been saved. In Acts 2, individuals responded to the complete gospel message for the first time. When they did, their sins were forgiven (2:38) and they were "saved" (2:47). Immediately, "the Lord added to the church...those who were being saved" (2:47). Jesus is "the Savior of the body" (Eph. 5:23), thus those whom the Savior saves are those who are in His body, the church (Eph. 1:22-23).

Third, let us understand the depictions used for the church. There are various images used for the church in the New Testament, and each of them helps us to understand the nature of the church even more. The church is depicted as a "body" (1 Cor. 12:12-27), a "family" (1 Tim. 3:15), a "kingdom" (Col. 1:13), a "bride" (Eph. 5:23-33), a "temple" (1 Cor. 3:16-17), a "flock" (1 Pet. 5:2), and an "army" (2 Tim. 2:3-4). Think about each of these. Think about how these help us to have a clearer grasp of the church, as well as a better understanding of those who are in the church.

Fourth, let us understand the destiny of the church. The Bible looks forward to the coming of Christ and teaches, "Then comes the end, when He delivers the kingdom to God the Father..." (1 Cor. 15:24). At the end of time, Jesus is going to take those in His kingdom (i.e., His church, Matt. 16:18-19) and hand them over to His Father in heaven. So, in order to go to heaven, one must be saved and must be in the church that belongs to Jesus Christ.

What is the church? The church is the people of God, who have been called out of the world, saved from their sins and have become an active part of His kingdom, as they await the return of Jesus and their home in heaven! Are you in His church? The one that we read about in the Bible?

#12 The Lord's Church Holds to the Scriptural Pattern

What if you were going to try to find the church of the New Testament today—the one that we read about in the pages of our Bible? How could you go about identifying it? Is there any way to know for sure, in one's examination of "churches" today, if a "church" that he finds is actually the one that Jesus established? As one reads through the New Testament, there are certainly a number of identifying marks of the Lord's church. Perhaps first and foremost is identifying the authoritative pattern that the church uses.

First, it is important to understand the authoritative pattern that the church of the Bible does *not* use. Many religious groups today are following doctrines that come from creed books, such as various church manuals, church disciplines, catechisms, etc. Is there anything wrong with that? Well, consider that man is not to "add to" or "take away from" God's Word (Rev. 22:18-19), and he is to "speak" only "the utterances of God" (1 Pet. 4:11). To find our teaching or authoritative direction in a book other than the Bible is to "go beyond what is written" (1 Cor. 4:6).

Second, it is critical to understand the authoritative pattern that the church of the Bible *must* certainly use. When Moses built the tabernacle in the Old Testament, he made "all things according to the pattern shown" to him by God (Heb. 8:5). Even more so, God gave a clear "pattern" for His church to follow in all things, and that "pattern of sound words" (2 Tim. 1:13) is His inspired Word (2 Tim. 3:16-17). The command is distinct and comprehensive—"Whatever you do in word or deed, do all in the name of the Lord Jesus" (Col. 3:17). His authoritative Word is the pattern for the church!

Third, it is vital to understand the consequences of not following the authoritative pattern prescribed in Scripture. Going beyond what God's Word authorizes and practicing a "Christianity" that is not firmly founded upon and grounded in the pure, unadulterated doctrine of the New Testament is not an insignificant matter. Such will result in being "accursed" (Gal. 1:8-9) and taken from "the Book of Life" (Rev. 22:19), for such action forfeits one's relationship with God Himself (2 John 9). That verse affirms, "Anyone who goes too far and does not abide in the teaching of Christ, does not have God." This is a matter of eternal consequence!

So, what if you were going to try to find the church of the New Testament today? What if, in your search, you found a church that uses some other book as their guide instead of the Bible? What if you found a church that uses the Bible some but also follows an additional creed or manual or catechism? The reality is that if a "church" today uses or follows any law system, doctrine, creed or discipline other than the New Testament, it is not the church that Jesus established on this earth. Our desire should be to find His church today and restore it to the pattern that He gave in Scripture.

#13 The Lord's Church Is Scripturally Organized

If you went on a search today of the various kinds of "churches" that are around, you would certainly encounter many different groups teaching and practicing many different things. Would there be a way to differentiate among them and identify the church that began in the New Testament? The Lord, in His wisdom, provided numerous identifying marks for His church, which help anyone on a genuine search for His church to be able to find it. One of those identifying marks is how the Lord organized His church.

First, consider *who* started the Lord's church. Jesus promised during His earthly ministry, "I will build My church" (Matt. 16:18). And He most certainly did. He became the Founder and the very foundation upon which the church was established (Eph. 2:20; 1 Cor. 3:11). Additionally, Jesus "purchased [the church] with His own blood" (Acts 20:28). It belongs to Him. As far as the organization of the church is concerned, the Bible says that "Christ is head of the church" (Eph. 5:23). Think about this. If a person finds a "church" that was founded by a man (other than Jesus) or has a man as head of the church (other than Jesus), then has that person found the church of the Bible?

Second, consider *when* and *where* the Lord's church started. The Lord's church came into existence in Acts 2. It was the day of Pentecost following the resurrection of Christ (2:1), and there was a large gathering of people in the city of Jerusalem (2:5), who would hear the gospel proclaimed for the first time (2:22-36). When 3,000 souls responded to the gospel that day and were baptized (2:41), the Lord Himself added them to His church (2:41, 47). Put all of this together. If a person finds a "church" that was founded at a different time and in a different place, then has he found the church of the Bible?

Third, consider the organizational structure the Lord gave to His church. The Lord designed His church to be comprised of autonomous congregations (Acts 14:23; 20:28), who were to have a plurality of qualified men called elders (1 Tim. 3:1-7) to oversee the work of the church (1 Pet. 5:1-4). Each congregation was to have their own elders (Tit. 1:5), who were responsible for shepherding the church only "among" which they themselves were a part (Acts 20:28; 1 Pet. 5:2; Heb. 13:17). Additionally, there were to be qualified men called deacons (1 Tim. 3:8-13), who would serve the church in special capacities. Evangelists were needed to preach the gospel, to edify, to comfort and to exhort (2 Tim. 4:2-5). The New Testament is very clear in these details. If a person finds a "church" that is organized in a way that is different from the Biblical pattern, then has that person found the church of the Bible?

These guidelines were not merely "a way to do it," but they are "God's way to do it." Our desire should be to find His church today and to make sure that it is restored precisely as He designed it to be organized in the very beginning. With Scripture in hand, this can be done.

#14 The Lord's Church Wears a Scriptural Name

If someone had a desire to search for a church to attend today, it is likely that he would get on the internet and search for "churches near me." What would those search results look like? There would be dozens (maybe hundreds) of different "churches" that would be listed—all with very different names. But, does the name of the church matter all that much? Well, does it matter what name they put on your diploma, or on your paycheck, or on your tax return? Having the right name does matter, doesn't it? So, what can we learn about the name of the Lord's church and how does that matter today?

First, the name of the church should be tied to the builder of the church. Often times, a building or a home is named after the person who built it. Jesus said, "I will build My church" (Matt. 16:18). Jesus built His one church. Would it not make sense for the church that He built to wear His name?

Second, the name of the church should be tied to the owner of the church. Often times, a business is named after the person who owns it. Jesus purchased the church "with His own blood" (Acts 20:28). The church belongs to Him. Would it not make sense for the church that He bought to wear His name?

Third, the name of the church should be tied to the "husband" of the church. Usually, a bride will take her husband's name when they marry. Interestingly, the church is referred to as "the bride" of Christ (Rev. 22:17), who is "married" to Christ (Rom. 7:4). Jesus is the "bridegroom" (Matt. 25:1-13; cf. Eph. 5:23-25). Would it not make sense for the church to which He is married to wear His name?

Fourth, the name of the church should be found in the New Testament. In the New Testament, the church is referred to by various designations—such as "the church" (Eph. 3:10), "the churches of Christ" (Rom. 16:16), "the church of God" (1 Cor. 1:2), "the body of Christ" (Eph. 4:12), "the church of the living God" (1 Tim. 3:15), "the kingdom of His dear Son" (Col. 1:13), etc. Compare these Scriptural designations with many that you see around you today. It is important to note that these Scriptural expressions and designations for the church are not "proper names" or "titles" but marks of ownership. The Lord's church belongs to Christ and will only wear one of the names which He has designated in His Word.

The name of the church is important to the Lord! In a search for the church of the Bible, what if one found a church that wears the name of some man or some religious act, or a name that is not even found in the Bible? If the name is not in the Bible, one could not rightly conclude that the church is the one in the Bible. Our desire today should be to find His church, and His church should be identifiable by wearing a name He has given to it.

#15 The Lord's Church Worships As Authorized

God created man with an instinctive need to worship. When man worships God as the Lord has instructed, there is something intensely thrilling and satisfying about being in His presence. But here's the question: Does it really matter how a person worships? Can a person worship God in any way that he chooses and in any way that feels good, and that worship be acceptable and pleasing to God? Let's investigate that for a moment.

First, the Bible teaches that not all worship is acceptable to God. The first record of worship in the Bible shows there is such a thing as acceptable worship and such a thing as unacceptable worship. "The Lord respected Abel and his offering, but He did not respect Cain and his offering" (Gen. 4:4-5). Not all worship is alike. This is seen again with Nadab and Abihu, when they "offered unauthorized fire before the Lord, which He had not commanded them. And fire came out from before the Lord and consumed them" (Lev. 10:1-2). Jesus Himself taught that some worship man offers is "in vain" (Matt. 15:8-9). So, how can we know if our worship is acceptable to God?

Second, the Bible teaches that God is both the object and the governor of true worship. Jesus taught an essential lesson about worship in John 4. Study His words carefully: "...true worshipers will worship the Father in spirit and truth; for the Father is seeking such to worship Him. God is Spirit, and those who worship Him must worship in spirit and truth" (4:23-24). By identifying "true worshipers," Jesus implied there can be "false worshipers." Jesus identified the proper object of worship ("God"), the proper attitude of worship ("in spirit") and the proper standard of worship ("truth"). As the Creator and focus of the worship of the church, God alone has the right to govern and regulate what happens in worship. To worship in "truth," we must look to His "Word," which "is truth" (John 17:17) and the only standard for worship.

Third, the Bible teaches that Sunday is the authorized day of worship. The day of worship, as authorized by God in the New Testament, is not optional. Man is not authorized to choose the day of worship or to teach that Saturday is as equally authorized as Sunday. God specified and authorized "the first day of the week" as the day of worship for the New Testament church. Jesus was raised on Sunday (Mark 16:9); He gathered with His disciples on Sunday (John 20:19, 26); the church was established on Sunday (Acts 2:1-47); and the church assembled in New Testament times on every Sunday to partake of the Lord's Supper (Acts 20:7; 1 Cor. 16:1-2; 11:20). To worship as God authorizes requires worshiping on the day that He specified.

Worshiping God is a sacred privilege. The very thought of coming into His presence ought to drive every worshiper to ensure that his every effort in worship is that which is authorized by and pleasing to the Lord. After all, we are not the object of worship. God is! Worship must be done His way!

#16 The Lord's Church Worships in Scriptural Avenues

The Lord designed His church to be very distinct. He placed a number of identifying marks for His church in Scripture, in order for man to be able to identify it when he finds it and to restore it as He desired it to be. One very recognizable characteristic of the Lord's church is its worship. It is quite noticeable today that different religious groups worship in different ways, but is that in accordance with God's standard and satisfaction? Let's study this.

First, the Bible teaches that the New Testament is God's pattern for acceptable worship in the church today. Colossians 3:17 comprehensively states, "Whatever you do...do all in the name of the Lord Jesus." "Whatever" certainly includes worship. Our worship must be authorized by Christ.

Second, the Bible teaches that there are five avenues of acceptable worship in the church today. In the New Testament, you will find that the church was authorized in its worship to have preaching of God's Word (2 Tim. 4:2; 1 Cor. 14:24-31), giving of our means (1 Cor. 16:1-2; 2 Cor. 9:6-7), praying to God (Acts 2:42; 1 Cor. 14:14-16), observance of the Lord's Supper (1 Cor. 11:23-29; Acts 20:7) and congregational singing (Eph. 5:19; Col. 3:16). The Lord authorized these five avenues only.

Third, the Bible teaches that the Lord's Supper is to be observed every Sunday. In the New Testament, the Lord's church worshiped every first day of the week (1 Cor. 16:1-2; Acts 20:7), and their purpose when they "came together" every Sunday was "to break bread" (Acts 20:7), which meant "to eat" the Lord's Supper (1 Cor. 11:20, 33). The Lord authorized the day of the week and the weekly frequency of this memorial.

Fourth, the Bible teaches that the church is to sing together as a congregation. In the New Testament, the Lord specified that the church is to sing "to one another" (Eph. 5:19; Col. 3:16), which involves every member and excludes one group singing to or singing in place of another group. Also, the Lord specified the music in worship as "singing and making melody in your heart to the Lord" (Eph. 5:19). By specifying one type of music (i.e., singing), He automatically excluded any other type of music (like playing an instrument). The Lord authorized exactly what He wants in His worship.

Fifth, the Bible teaches that the men are to lead the church in worship. In the New Testament, the Lord calls upon "the men" (i.e., males) to take the lead, and He does not "permit a woman to teach or to exercise authority over a man" in the church (1 Tim. 2:8, 12). This is not chauvinistic or oppression, but just the Divine standard for order in His worship (1 Cor. 14:40).

If someone was searching for the Lord's church today, there are some very specific avenues of worship that would help him to identify if what he finds is the church of the Bible or not! We must worship by God's standard!

#17 The Lord's Church Still Exists Today

The church of the New Testament was vitally important and incomparably valuable to Jesus! He had planned for it before the Creation (Eph. 3:10-11). He came to this earth and promised to build it Himself (Matt. 16:18). He ensured its coming by purchasing it with His own blood (Acts 20:28). He sent the Holy Spirit to establish it in Acts 2 (2:32-47). He is both the head of the church and the Savior of it (Eph. 5:23). The church that He started in Jerusalem on Pentecost nearly 2,000 years ago is still in existence on this earth today. Some have questioned whether that "original" church could still be around today, but what we will see in the Bible is that God had no other plan for His church than perpetual existence until the final return of Christ.

First, the prophecy of Daniel proves the Lord's church still exists today. In about 600 B.C., Daniel prophesied of the church. "In the days of these kings the God of heaven will set up a kingdom which shall never be destroyed; and the kingdom shall not be left to other people; it shall break in pieces and consume all these kingdoms, and it shall stand forever" (Dan. 2:44). It "shall never be destroyed." "It shall stand forever." It is still here today!

Second, the promise of Jesus proves the Lord's church still exists today. When Jesus promised, "I will build My church," He went on to say, "and the gates of Hades shall not prevail against it" (Matt. 16:18). Jesus was emphasizing that nothing would be able to overpower His church. It is still here today!

Third, the continual saving of sinners proves the Lord's church still exists today. The church began in Acts 2, when the first people responded to the full message of the gospel and were baptized "for the remission of sins" (2:38, 41). Those who were "saved" were added to the church (2:41), and God was adding to the church "daily those who were being saved" (2:47). As long as God is saving people, He is adding them to His church. It is still here today!

Fourth, the continual presence of the Bible proves the Lord's church still exists today. In the parable of the soils, Jesus called the gospel, "the word of the kingdom" (Matt. 13:19), and said it was "the seed" (Luke 8:11). Think about the nature of a seed. Wherever and whenever the seed of the kingdom (i.e., the gospel) is planted, it produces a kingdom identical in every respect to the kingdom that was established in the first century. It is still here today!

Fifth, the ultimate delivery of His church to heaven proves the Lord's church still exists today. When Jesus returns at the end of time, He is going to deliver "the kingdom to God the Father" (1 Cor. 15:24). Jesus cannot deliver the church to God if it does not still exist. It is still here today!

The Lord only has one church (Eph. 4:4). Since we have the pattern for the Lord's church in His Word, and know exactly what His church looks like, let us find His church today and restore it precisely as He wanted it to be.

#18 Sin Separates Man from God

When God first created mankind in the Garden of Eden, they enjoyed a perfect relationship with God, dwelling together with Him without any barriers. Adam and Eve "heard the sound of the Lord God walking in the garden in the cool of the day" (Gen. 3:8). But something happened. Man did something (called "sin") that changed that intimate relationship. And ever since that day, man's greatest need has been to get back into that perfect union with God. What is sin? Why is it so important for us to know about it?

First, sin is the result of violating the will of God. In the Garden, God told man not to eat of "the tree of knowledge of good and evil" (Gen. 2:17). But, with his free will to make his own decisions, man chose to violate the will of God and "ate" of the fruit (Gen. 3:6). The Bible calls this very first act of violating God's will, "sin" (1 Tim. 2:14). Sin is breaking the "law" of God and acting in an "unrighteous" manner (1 John 3:4; 5:17). That's serious!

Second, sin is a personal choice. As free moral agents, Adam and Eve made a choice and they sinned against God. Sin occurs when a person "is drawn away by his own desires" (Jas. 1:14-15) and "commits lawlessness" (1 John 3:4). Sin is personally choosing to disobey God's law (Ezek. 18:20). No one, including the devil, can make another person sin.

Third, sin is not inherited. As sin is a choice to "transgress" God's law (1 John 3:4) or to refuse to "do" God's law (Jas. 4:17), it is obvious that this is not something that is or can be inherited. Scripture teaches that the "son shall not bear the guilt of the father, nor the father bear the guilt of the son" (Ezek. 18:20). Each person is responsible to God for his own sin.

Fourth, sin results in separation from God. Each of the previous points may seem academic until one considers the devastating consequences of sin. God warned of sin's consequences in the beginning—"you shall surely die" (Gen. 2:17). This was not physical death, but spiritual death. When Adam and Eve sinned, they were driven from the presence of God (Gen. 3:24), thus teaching us that spiritual death is a separation of man from God. Paul wrote, "The wages of sin is death" (Rom. 6:23). Scripture teaches, "Your iniquities have separated you from your God; and your sins have hidden His face from you, so that He will not hear" (Isa. 59:1-2). But these consequences of sin are not limited only to life on this earth. If man does nothing to address and correct this separation from God caused by his sins, he "shall be punished with everlasting destruction from the presence of the Lord and from the glory of His power" (2 Thess. 1:8-9). There is nothing more serious than that!

It is essential that we understand the true nature and gravity of sin, so that we can understand the desperate need that we have to be saved from our sins. Only the Bible can tell us how to be saved and to be right with God!

#19 God Wants All People to Be Saved

You will not find two things that are more polar opposite than "God" and "sin." Sin is the most devastating disease on the face of the earth, because of who it afflicts and because of its eternal consequences. "Sin" separates man from his "God," because sin is contrary to the holy nature of God (Hab. 1:13). Yet, even though man sins by disregarding and violating the will of God, there is an abundance of love, grace and patience that God has for man that is hard to truly fathom. Consider how strongly God wants all people to be saved.

First, the Bible teaches that all are lost in their sins. "All have sinned and fall short of the glory of God" (Rom. 3:23). But the Bible does not teach that those who are lost cannot be saved from their sins.

Second, the Bible teaches that all will be judged. "For we must all appear before the judgment seat of Christ, that each one may receive the things done in the body, according to what he has done..." (2 Cor. 5:10). But the Bible does not teach that we cannot be prepared for judgment.

Third, the Bible teaches that God wants all to be saved. God "desires all men to be saved and to come to the knowledge of the truth" (1 Tim. 2:4). "The Lord is...not willing that any should perish but that all should come to repentance" (2 Pet. 3:9). Thus, all have the opportunity to be saved.

Fourth, the Bible teaches that Jesus died for all. Jesus came to this earth that "He might taste death for everyone" (Heb. 2:9; cf. 2 Cor. 5:14-15). His blood "redeemed [people] out of every tribe and tongue and people and nation" (Rev. 5:9). Jesus shed His blood so that all could be saved!

Fifth, the Bible teaches that Jesus commissioned His disciples to take the saving power of the gospel to all people. "Go into all the world and preach the gospel to every creature" (Mark 16:15), "warning every man and teaching every man" (Col. 1:28). Sending the gospel out to all peoples emphasizes that God wants all to be saved and that all men can be saved.

Sixth, the Bible teaches that God is no respecter of persons when it comes to salvation. He invites all to come to Christ and be saved (Matt. 11:28; Tit. 2:11). "God shows no partiality. But in every nation whoever fears Him and works righteousness is accepted by Him" (Acts 10:34-35).

Seventh, the Bible teaches that salvation is the gift of God. Everyone needs to be saved from their sins! The great thing is that no one has to be lost! Being saved "is the gift of God" (Eph. 2:8). "God so loved the world that He gave His only begotten Son" (John 3:16), in order that everyone in the world might have the opportunity to be saved.

There is no reason for anyone (including you) to not be saved! The loving God of heaven wants you to be saved! He has done everything He can to make that possible! Are you saved? The Bible alone tells us how to be saved!

#20 One Must Be Saved As Authorized in Scripture

There is no Bible doctrine more important than salvation, for this concerns one's spiritual condition, the state of one's relationship with God and the eternal destiny of one's soul. This is not a matter that can be taken lightly, nor should we just assume that what others have told us is Biblically accurate. There is only one place that we can turn to learn all there is to know about salvation and how we can be saved from sin!

First, the Bible teaches that Christ has all authority in the matter of salvation. In the Great Commission, Jesus told His disciples that "all authority" had been given to Him, and then He told them what they needed to preach so that people could be saved (Matt. 28:18-20). His all-authoritative Word (in the Bible) is the only source we have today to know everything that God expects of us in order to be saved. Jesus is truly "the author of eternal salvation" (Heb. 5:9). Preachers, friends, family members and even our own feelings are not the authority when it comes to salvation.

Second, the Bible teaches that one is only saved by the grace of God. We must ever be mindful that it is truly God's grace that saves us (Eph. 2:5, 8), and it was "according to the riches of His grace" that He sent Jesus to die for us, so that we could be saved "through His blood" (Eph. 1:7). His grace is available to all (Tit. 2:11), but salvation is not by grace alone. We only have "access" to His grace by a proper response to His Word (Rom. 5:1-2).

Third, the Bible teaches that one can only be saved by God's grace through obedience to His will. Jesus is "the author of eternal salvation," and the verse goes on to say, "to all who obey Him" (Heb. 5:9). When we "keep His commandments" and "do whatever" He tells us to do, we demonstrate our love for Him (John 14:15; 15:14). Jesus issued a very clear warning, "Not everyone who says to Me, 'Lord, Lord,' shall enter the kingdom of heaven, but he who does the will of My Father in heaven" (Matt. 7:21). Our entrance into heaven is dependent upon doing God's will!

The salvation of your soul is so very important! There is nothing more crucial than knowing for absolute Biblical certainty (and not just a feeling that you have) that you have followed God's plan precisely as He has revealed it in His Word. Take a moment, and for your own benefit, answer these questions.

Are you saved? ❏ Yes   ❏ No   ❏ I don't know

If yes, how were you saved? _____

_____

Have you ever been baptized? ❏ Yes   ❏ No

If yes, for what reason(s) were you baptized? _____

_____

#21 | One Must Believe Jesus Is God's Son to Be Saved

From the moment that Adam and Eve sinned in the beginning, God began to reveal His plan to save man from his sins. His plan centered around the sending of His Son to pay the ultimate price, by sacrificing Himself on the cross in our place and bearing all of our sins upon Himself (John 3:16; Eph. 5:2; 1 Pet. 2:24). God wants you to be saved, and He has told you in His Word exactly what He expects of you in order to be saved.

First, the Bible teaches that we must believe in order to be saved. When the jailer in Philippi asked—"What must I do to be saved?"—he was told, "Believe on the Lord Jesus Christ, and you will be saved" (Acts 16:31). That faith is produced in man's heart today by hearing God's Word (Rom. 10:17). We must learn from the Bible what Jesus did for us and why He did it, in order to have a "faith" that can "please Him" and save us (Heb. 11:6).

Second, the Bible teaches what we must believe in order to be saved. "...These are written that you may believe that Jesus is the Christ, the Son of God, and that believing you may have life in His name" (John 20:30-31). To be saved, one must believe that Jesus came down from heaven (John 6:38), that He performed many miracles (John 3:2), that He lived a sinless life (Heb. 4:15), that He died on the cross with all of our sins laid upon Him (Isa. 53:6), that His lifeless body was buried (1 Cor. 15:3), that He was raised from the dead on the third day (Acts 2:24-32), and that He is now back in heaven at the right hand of God (Acts 2:33-36). The evidence for His deity is overwhelming!

Third, the Bible teaches what will happen if we do not believe that Jesus is God's Son. Since the Bible makes it clear that we must believe in order to be saved, what will happen to those who do not believe? Jesus said, "If you do not believe that I am He, you will die in your sins" (John 8:24). Your sins will not be forgiven and you will continue to be separated from God. In fact, Jesus later said, "He who does not believe will be condemned" (Mark 16:16).

Fourth, the Bible teaches that faith alone is not all that is needed for salvation. So, if a person believes in Jesus, does that mean that they are saved right then, and that nothing else is needed in order to be saved? The Bible answers that emphatically when it states, "Faith by itself...is dead...You see then that a man is justified...not by faith only" (Jas. 2:17, 24). Faith alone does not save, otherwise "the demons," who "believe and tremble," would be saved (Jas. 2:19).

The Bible says "those who believe" in Jesus have been given "the right to become children of God" (John 1:12). To exercise that right, they must look to God's Word to find all that is required in order to be saved. What a wonderful gift that God has given us in salvation! We don't deserve it, but He offers it anyway! *Is there any reason you should not believe right now?*

#22 One Must Repent of His Sins to Be Saved

The pursuit of salvation from sins ought to be the most important undertaking in any person's life. But salvation does not come by following a strategy devised by a religious leader or some church. Salvation is only obtained by finding and following the plan designed by the God of heaven. In order to be saved from sins, one must believe that Jesus is God's Son (Acts 16:31; John 20:30-31; 8:24). But that is not all one must do!

First, the Bible teaches that we must repent in order to be saved. "God...now commands all men everywhere to repent, because He has appointed a day on which He will judge the world" (Acts 17:30-31). The Lord is longing that "all should come to repentance" (2 Pet. 3:9), in order that they might obtain "the remission of sins" (Acts 2:38).

Second, the Bible teaches what it means to repent. Repenting of sin is an active response to the gospel of Christ (Acts 17:30), but what is repentance? Jesus told of a father who instructed his son, "Go, work today in my vineyard." The son "answered and said, 'I will not,' but afterward he regretted it and went" (Matt. 21:28-29). Another translation says that "afterward he changed his mind and went." Repentance is a change of mind that leads to a change of life, in which one decides to turn away from sin and "turn to God" (Acts 26:20). It is not merely being sorrowful for having done wrong and asking for forgiveness. The report of the jailer, when he took Paul and Silas and "washed their wounds" (Acts 16:33), is a visual illustration of one who turned from wrong and started to try to make it right.

Third, the Bible teaches what should bring about repentance. What is it that ought to bring about repentance in one's heart? There are a number of motivators that can lead one to repent: (1) the command by God (Acts 17:30); (2) the goodness of God (Rom. 2:4); (3) awareness of the gravity of sin (Acts 2:37-38); (4) godly sorrow for sin (2 Cor. 7:10); (5) fear of judgment (Acts 17:30-31); (6) desire to be forgiven of sin (Luke 24:47).

Fourth, the Bible teaches what will happen if we do not repent of our sins. Since the Bible makes it clear that we must repent in order to be saved, what will happen to those who do not repent? Jesus said, "I tell you, no; but unless you repent you will all likewise perish" (Luke 13:3). Before one repents, there is no concern, regret or determination at all to do anything about one's sins. Such will cause one to "perish," if he does not turn.

The Bible says that true "repentance leads to life" (Acts 11:18). One is not granted a new life in Christ at the moment of repentance, for there is more that he must do based upon his turn from sin. But one is on the path to be granted a life from free sin when he makes up his mind to repent. *Is there any reason that you should not repent right now?*

When one begins to walk down a path, the ultimate goal is to reach the destination. There will be things to see and do along the way, but the true objective is to take each of the necessary steps in order to reach the goal. The path that leads to salvation from sin is very similar to that. The ultimate objective is being freed from the sins that separate one from God. In order to reach that destination, there are steps that are required by God. One must believe that Jesus is God's Son (John 3:16). One must repent of his sins (Acts 17:30). But that is not all that one must do!

First, the Bible teaches that we must confess in order to be saved. The apostle Paul wrote, "For with the heart one believes unto righteousness, and with the mouth confession is made unto salvation" (Rom. 10:10). Confession is an obvious prerequisite to salvation in this passage. This confession is to be done "before men" (Matt. 10:32), "in the presence of many witnesses" (1 Tim. 6:12). Therefore, this is a public act that takes place prior to salvation.

Second, the Bible teaches what we must confess. It is vital that we understand what God is asking us to confess in order to be saved. What one will not find in the New Testament is the Lord calling upon non-Christians to confess their sins before men, in order to be saved. Nor will one find God asking for individuals to speak their personal testimony as an act of confession. Rather, "the good confession" (1 Tim. 6:12) is a verbal acknowledgement of the faith that is in one's heart. Specifically, you are to "confess with your mouth the Lord Jesus," expressing that you "believe in your heart that God has raised Him from the dead" (Rom. 10:9). God longs "that every tongue should confess that Jesus Christ is Lord" (Phil. 2:11). In order to be saved, the Ethiopian in Acts 8 confessed, "I believe that Jesus Christ is the Son of God" (8:37). One cannot be saved from his sins without confessing his faith in Jesus Christ.

Third, the Bible teaches what will happen if we do not confess our faith in Jesus. The promise of Jesus is that "whoever confesses Me before men, him I will also confess before My Father who is in heaven" (Matt. 10:32). However, choosing to not confess Jesus is equivalent to denying Him, and Jesus warned, "But whoever denies Me before men, him I will also deny before My Father who is in heaven" (10:33). As with each step in God's plan of salvation, drastic consequences await when individuals choose to not take the necessary step outlined in Scripture.

To be saved according to God's plan (which is the only plan that can lead us to our final destination of salvation from sin), a person must be willing to publicly acknowledge his faith in Jesus. This is simply saying the same thing that God says about Jesus—that He is the Son of God. *Do you believe that with all of your heart? Is there any reason you should not confess your faith in Jesus right now?*

#24 One Must Be Immersed into Christ to Be Saved

The subject of baptism is one of the most thrilling in all of the Bible, and yet it is one of the most widely disputed in the religious world. Does baptism have anything to do with our salvation? Must one be baptized in order to be saved and to go to heaven? Let us not look to man or a church for this answer, but let us look to God and to His Word for His authoritative answer.

First, the Bible teaches who a Scriptural candidate for baptism is. In the New Testament, only persons who met certain conditions were baptized. To be Scripturally baptized, one must first be taught the gospel (Mark 16:15-16), believe the gospel (Acts 8:12), be convicted of sins (Acts 2:37), repent of sins (Acts 2:38), confess faith in Jesus Christ (Acts 8:36-38) and arise of his own free will (Acts 22:16) to fulfill the purpose of baptism as specified in Scripture.

Second, the Bible teaches what the Scriptural method for baptism is. The Bible very plainly describes that in Bible baptism "much water" is required (John 3:5), for the person being baptized must come "to" the water (Matt. 3:11), go "down into the water" (Acts 8:36), be "buried...in baptism" (Col. 2:12), be "raised" from the water (Rom. 6:4) and come "up out of the water" (Acts 8:39). The Bible makes it very clear that baptism is an immersion of the body (i.e., a burial, Col. 2:12) into water.

Third, the Bible teaches what the Scriptural purpose of baptism is. If we allow only God's Word to teach us (without addition or subtraction), the Lord makes it abundantly clear that baptism is absolutely essential to our salvation. In Bible baptism, one is "saved" from past sins (Mark 16:16; 1 Pet. 3:21), obtains "the remission of sins" (Acts 2:38), has sins "washed away" (Acts 22:16), is "freed from sin" (Rom. 6:3-7), is "born again" (John 3:3-7), "enters the kingdom of God" (John 3:5), enters the "one body" of Christ (1 Cor. 12:13), becomes a "child of God" (Gal. 3:26-27), "puts on Christ" (Gal. 3:27), enters "into Christ" (Rom. 6:3), becomes a New Testament "Christian" (Matt. 28:19+Acts 11:26), and "appeals to God for a good conscience" (1 Pet. 3:21). There is no New Testament passage that places baptism after one's salvation.

Fourth, the Bible teaches what will happen if one is not baptized. Think again about all that the Bible says takes place when one is baptized, and realize that none of those things can be enjoyed by a person who is not baptized with Bible baptism. In fact, Jesus says, "Unless one is born of water and the Spirit, he cannot enter the kingdom of God" (John 3:5). Salvation is not his!

Baptism alone will not save. But when a believer in Jesus repents of his sins and confesses his faith, he must be immersed in water to obtain the forgiveness of sins. Jesus said, "He who believes and is baptized shall be saved" (Mark 16:16). *Have you done this? Is there any reason you should not be baptized right now? Make today "the day of salvation" (2 Cor. 6:2)!*

#25 One Must Be "In Christ" to Be Saved

There are some people who are very good at giving directions—they can tell you *where* something is and *how* to get there. Thankfully, we have a God who is "perfect in knowledge" (Job 37:16), for "His way is perfect" (Psa. 18:30). When He tells us *where* something is and *how* to get there (especially the most important directions of all, which concern the salvation of our souls), we can be confident that His Word will be precise and understandable. Let us observe just how clear God's directions are.

First, God tells us *where* we must be in order to saved! The Bible emphatically teaches that "all spiritual blessings are IN CHRIST" (Eph. 1:3). What are those "spiritual blessings"? Are they all that important? Consider a few:

- In Christ is "redemption" (Col. 1:13-14; Eph. 1:7).
- In Christ is "the forgiveness of sins" (Eph. 1:7).
- In Christ is "an inheritance" (Eph. 1:11).
- In Christ is "no condemnation" (Rom. 8:1).
- In Christ is "sanctification" (1 Cor. 1:2).
- In Christ is "hope" (1 Cor. 15:19).
- In Christ are "all the promises of God" (2 Cor. 1:20).
- In Christ is "a new creation" (2 Cor. 5:17).
- In Christ is "grace" (2 Tim. 2:1).
- In Christ is "eternal life" (1 John 5:11).
- In Christ is "salvation" (2 Tim. 2:10).

Think about that list. Realize that it is not even all of the spiritual blessings found in Scripture. Ask yourself, "Do I need to be 'in Christ'?"

Second, God tells us what is *not* "in Christ." By implication, we can know that those who are outside of Christ have NO redemption, forgiveness of sins, inheritance, sanctification, hope, promises of God, grace, eternal life or salvation. In fact, they have all condemnation, for they are not a new creation in Christ. Think about that list now from this perspective. Ask yourself again, "Do I need to be 'in Christ'?" Absolutely! But, *how?*

Third, God tells us *how* to get "into Christ." Thankfully, God's directions are precise and understandable. "For as many of you as were *baptized into Christ* have put on Christ" (Gal. 3:27; see also Rom. 6:3). Those two verses emphatically teach that baptism is the only one way INTO CHRIST. Before baptism, one is outside of Christ and deficient of EVERY spiritual blessing. Only when a penitent believer is baptized does he move from being outside of Christ to now being "in Christ," wherein are all spiritual blessings, including salvation. *Ask yourself, "Am I 'in Christ'?" If not, today can be that day!*

#26 A Christian Must Live a Faithful Life to God

When one is baptized into Christ and becomes a Christian, he begins a new life (Rom. 6:4), in which he is to set aside his old way of life (2 Cor. 5:17; Eph. 4:22) and excitedly pursue his new life in Christ and his new relationship with his Savior and Lord. Jesus summarized His expectations and made this promise, "Be faithful unto death, and I will give you the crown of life" (Rev. 2:10). What is involved in being faithful? Consider these ten things.

Grow. The Lord wants us to increase our knowledge, our faith and our trust in Him (2 Pet. 1:5-11; 3:18), which we are able to do by regularly studying His Word (2 Tim. 2:15) and praying (Col. 4:2).

Worship. The Lord wants us to long to worship Him (John 4:24; Matt. 4:10) and praise Him from our hearts (Heb. 13:15; Eph. 5:19), especially on the first day of each week (Acts 20:7; Heb. 10:25).

Serve. The Lord wants us to look beyond ourselves (Phil. 2:3-4) and to find opportunities to serve others (Gal. 5:13) and do good to them (Gal. 6:10).

Teach. The Lord wants us to show others the way to heaven by teaching the gospel (Mark 16:15), living a Christian life (Matt. 5:16) and answering their questions (1 Pet. 3:15).

Obey. The Lord wants us to conform our lives to His will by submitting to Him (Jas. 4:7) and obeying His commands (Heb. 5:9; Matt. 7:21; 1 John 1:7).

Prioritize. The Lord wants us to put Christ (Col. 1:18) and His church (Matt. 6:33) first in our lives, especially in how we spend our time (Eph. 5:16).

Work. The Lord wants us to be busy in His kingdom (1 Cor. 3:9), being "steadfast, immovable, always abounding in the work of the Lord" (1 Cor. 15:58).

Separate. The Lord wants us to set ourselves apart from the ways of the world (Rom. 12:2; 1 Pet. 2:11), to keep ourselves pure (1 Pet. 1:15-16; 1 John 2:15-17) and to live godly lives (Tit. 2:11-12).

Endure. The Lord wants us to persevere through difficult times as a Christian (2 Tim. 2:3), looking to Jesus as our example for strength (Heb. 12:1-3) and ever pressing on to the eternal goal of heaven (Phil. 3:14).

Aim. The Lord wants us to set our sights on the glorious reward of heaven (Matt. 6:20; Col. 3:1-4) and live every day in eager anticipation of Jesus' return to take the children of God home with Him (Phil. 3:20-21; Tit. 2:13).

Faithfulness is essential. If we fail to remain faithful to the Lord, the Bible teaches that we can be lost (2 Pet. 2:20-22; Jas. 5:19-20; Gal. 5:4). Let us determine to stay true to God, to His word, to His church, and diligently seek to please Him above all else! What a wonderful blessing it is to be a Christian!

#27 One Day Jesus Will Return from Heaven

There is a tremendously thrilling event that is still to take place in the future. The day is going to come when Jesus Himself will return from heaven. What does the Bible have to say about that final day?

First, the Bible teaches that the second coming of Jesus Christ is certain. Jesus Himself promised, "I will come again" (John 14:1-3). The angels announced, "This Jesus...will come" (Acts 1:11). The Bible guarantees it.

Second, the Bible teaches that the exact timing of the second coming of Christ is unknown. Jesus taught that "no one knows" the "day and hour" of His return, "but My Father only" (Mark 13:32). He said that the day would come as unexpected as a thief in the night (Matt. 24:42-44; cf. 1 Thess. 5:2).

Third, the Bible teaches that the coming of Christ will be overwhelmingly spectacular. "The Lord Himself will descend from heaven with a shout, with the voice of an archangel, and with the trumpet of God" (1 Thess. 4:16), and with "all the holy angels" (Matt. 25:31). "Every eye will see Him" (Rev. 1:7). "All who are in the graves will hear His voice and come forth" (John 5:28-29). Then, "the earth and its works will be burned up" (2 Pet. 3:10).

Fourth, the Bible teaches that there is life after death. Jesus' account of a rich man and a beggar in Luke 16:19-31 teaches this quite clearly. The resurrection of Christ guarantees our own resurrection from the dead (1 Cor. 15:20-23), after which we will live in another place forever (John 5:28-29).

Fifth, the Bible teaches that there is going to be a judgment. When Jesus returns at the end of the world, "we must all appear before the judgment seat of Christ, that each one may receive the things done in the body, according to what he has done, whether good or bad" (2 Cor. 5:10). At that time, our eternal sentence will be announced (Matt. 25:31-46).

Sixth, the Bible teaches that there are two (and only two) very real destinies in the eternal realm. There is an eternal realm called "heaven" (1 Pet. 1:4) and an eternal realm called "hell" (Matt. 10:28). Scripture makes it plain that both places will last forever and ever (Matt. 25:46), and there will be no passage or transference from one to the other (Luke 16:26).

Seventh, the Bible teaches that obtaining eternal life is conditional. Not everyone is going to go heaven; in fact, Jesus said that only a "few" are on the path that leads to eternal "life" (Matt. 7:13-14). Jesus went on to say that only a person "who does the will of My Father in heaven" will "enter" into heaven (7:21). Therefore, one who does not do the Father's will is promised an eternal separation from Him (7:23; 2 Thess. 1:9).

One day Jesus is going to return and take God's children to heaven with Him! Are you ready for that day? We must be ready (Matt. 24:44)!

We have covered a lot of ground in this series of studies. In our quest to understand life and what it's all about, we have not sought the wisdom of man or the wisdom of the world. Such wisdom is too varied, too limited and, truthfully, has no authority in providing the absolute truth that is so vitally needed. The only source of Divine wisdom and absolute truth on this earth is found in one place—the Bible! Therefore, to the Bible alone we must go to find the answers to life's most foundational (and essential) questions, which we introduced in the very first lesson in this series.

First, how do you answer, "Where am I from?" *What does the Bible say?* Like everything else on this earth, I am the result of the creative power of the Almighty God. "In the beginning God created the heavens and the earth" (Gen. 1:1). At that time, "God said, 'Let Us make man in Our image, according to Our likeness...'" (Gen. 1:26-27). In His likeness, God gave to each person an eternal soul that is distinct from and infinitely more valuable than his earthly body (Matt. 10:28; Jas. 2:26). *"Where am I from?" God made me!*

Second, how do you answer, "Why am I here?" *What does the Bible say?* This question cannot be disassociated from the first question. A person's *purpose* in this life is directly tied to their *origin!* God Himself ties these two essentials together: "Everyone who is called by My name, Whom I have created for My glory; I have formed him, yes, I have made him" (Isa. 43:7). God made us! For what purpose? For His glory! Our purpose on this earth is to glorify God (1 Cor. 10:31). We glorify God by obeying Him (1 Cor. 6:19-20), doing His "work" (John 17:4; 1 Pet. 2:12) and "bearing much fruit" for Him (John 15:8; Phil. 1:11). In fact, to "fear God and keep His commandments...is man's all" (Ecc. 12:13). *"Why am I here?" To glorify God through my life!*

Third, how do you answer, "Where am I going?" *What does the Bible say?* Again, this question cannot be disassociated from the previous question. A person's *destiny* is directly tied to how he fulfills his God-given *purpose* in life! There is life after death! Where I am going at that point depends entirely upon how I live my life on this earth. "For we must all appear before the judgment seat of Christ, that each one may receive the things done in the body, according to what he has done, whether good or bad" (2 Cor. 5:10). *"Where am I going?"* Whether I go to heaven or whether I go to hell for eternity will be determined by the Judge, as He compares my life with what He has commanded me to do in His Word (John 12:48; Rev. 20:12; Matt. 7:21).

How do YOU answer these questions? Are you fulfilling your God-given purpose in this life? Are you ready to stand before Jesus on the day of judgment? Have you been baptized for the forgiveness of your sins? Are you living faithfully to the will of God? Let's go back to the Bible and use it as our only guide to an eternal home with God in heaven!

Walking Daily with My Lord

NOVEMBER:

28 DAYS
To Become More Thankful

"Giving thanks always
for all things to God the Father
in the name of our Lord Jesus Christ"
(Ephesians 5:20).

🔢DAYS To Become More Thankful

Above Everyone Else on Earth,
Christians Have So Much for Which to Be Thankful!

The account of Jesus healing ten lepers in Luke 17 teaches that I must:

1. **Open My Mind**...to Know What God Expects of Me (17:17-18).

2. **Open My Eyes**...to See What God Has Done for Me (17:12-14).

3. **Open My Mouth**...to Express My Humble Gratitude (17:15-16).

As Christians blessed over-abundantly by a overly-gracious God, we must learn to see God's blessings and give Him thanks continually!

Use the following pages over the next 28 days to:

1. Intentionally find things for which to be thankful.

2. Make a list every day for which to give thanks.

3. Include the special category of thanks for each day.

4. Pray a special prayer of thanksgiving every day.

5. Develop a habit of saying, "Thank you, God!" throughout your day.

Let's become more thankful over the next 28 days...

☐ Day 1	☐ Day 8	☐ Day 15	☐ Day 22
☐ Day 2	☐ Day 9	☐ Day 16	☐ Day 23
☐ Day 3	☐ Day 10	☐ Day 17	☐ Day 24
☐ Day 4	☐ Day 11	☐ Day 18	☐ Day 25
☐ Day 5	☐ Day 12	☐ Day 19	☐ Day 26
☐ Day 6	☐ Day 13	☐ Day 20	☐ Day 27
☐ Day 7	☐ Day 14	☐ Day 21	☐ Day 28

Day #1 to Become More Thankful

*"Giving thanks always for all things to God the Father
in the name of our Lord Jesus Christ" (Eph. 5:20).*

Take time to fill in your "Thankful List/Journal" for today.

Then, give thanks to God.

Today, I am thankful for:

_____

_____

_____

_____

_____

_____

_____

_____

_____

_____

_____

_____

Special Thanksgiving for Day #1:

Give a special thanks to God today for
God's Unconditional, Enduring Love
(John 3:16; Rom. 8:38-39; 1 John 4:7-16; Psa. 136:1).

Day #2 to Become More Thankful

*"Giving thanks always for all things to God the Father
in the name of our Lord Jesus Christ" (Eph. 5:20).*

Take time to fill in your "Thankful List/Journal" for today.

Then, give thanks to God.

Today, I am thankful for:

_____

_____

_____

_____

_____

_____

_____

_____

_____

_____

_____

Special Thanksgiving for Day #2:

Give a special thanks to God today for
The Death of Jesus on the Cross
(Rom. 5:6-11; 2 Cor. 9:15; 1 Pet. 2:21-24; Isa. 53:1-12).

Day #3 to Become More Thankful

*"Giving thanks always for all things to God the Father
in the name of our Lord Jesus Christ" (Eph. 5:20).*

Take time to fill in your "Thankful List/Journal" for today.

Then, give thanks to God.

Today, I am thankful for:

Special Thanksgiving for Day #3:

Give a special thanks to God today for
Complete Forgiveness of Sins
(Psa. 103:12; Heb. 8:12; Rom. 8:1; 1 John 1:7).

Day #4 to Become More Thankful

"Giving thanks always for all things to God the Father
in the name of our Lord Jesus Christ" (Eph. 5:20).

Take time to fill in your "Thankful List/Journal" for today.

Then, give thanks to God.

Today, I am thankful for:

_____

_____

_____

_____

_____

_____

_____

_____

_____

_____

_____

_____

Special Thanksgiving for Day #4:

Give a special thanks to God today for
Abundant Grace
(1 Tim. 1:12-15; Rom. 5:20-21; 1 Cor. 15:10; Tit. 2:11; 3:4-7).

Day #5 to Become More Thankful

*"Giving thanks always for all things to God the Father
in the name of our Lord Jesus Christ" (Eph. 5:20).*

Take time to fill in your "Thankful List/Journal" for today.

Then, give thanks to God.

Today, I am thankful for:

_____

_____

_____

_____

_____

_____

_____

_____

_____

_____

_____

Special Thanksgiving for Day #5:

Give a special thanks to God today for
The Bible
(Psa. 119:47, 97; Heb. 4:12; Rom. 1:16; 1 Pet. 1:23).

Day #6 to Become More Thankful

"Giving thanks always for all things to God the Father in the name of our Lord Jesus Christ" (Eph. 5:20).

Take time to fill in your "Thankful List/Journal" for today.

Then, give thanks to God.

Today, I am thankful for:

_____

_____

_____

_____

_____

_____

_____

_____

_____

_____

_____

_____

Special Thanksgiving for Day #6:

Give a special thanks to God today for
The Privilege of and Confidence in Prayer
(Psa. 4:3; Phil. 4:6-7; 1 John 5:14-15; 1 Pet. 3:12).

Day #7 to Become More Thankful

"Giving thanks always for all things to God the Father
in the name of our Lord Jesus Christ" (Eph. 5:20).

Take time to fill in your "Thankful List/Journal" for today.

Then, give thanks to God.

Today, I am thankful for:

_____

_____

_____

_____

_____

_____

_____

_____

_____

_____

_____

_____

Special Thanksgiving for Day #7:

Give a special thanks to God today for
God's Faithfulness to His Promises
(Heb. 6:18; Tit. 1:2; 1 Cor. 1:9; 10:13; 1 John 1:9; 2 Pet. 1:4).

Day #8 to Become More Thankful

"Giving thanks always for all things to God the Father
in the name of our Lord Jesus Christ" (Eph. 5:20).

Take time to fill in your "Thankful List/Journal" for today.

Then, give thanks to God.

Today, I am thankful for:

_____

_____

_____

_____

_____

_____

_____

_____

_____

_____

_____

_____

Special Thanksgiving for Day #8:

Give a special thanks to God today for
The Privilege to Be Called a Child of God
(1 John 3:1; Rom. 8:14-17; Gal. 3:26-27; Matt. 7:7-11).

Day #9 to Become More Thankful

*"Giving thanks always for all things to God the Father
in the name of our Lord Jesus Christ" (Eph. 5:20).*

Take time to fill in your "Thankful List/Journal" for today.

Then, give thanks to God.

Today, I am thankful for:

Day #10 to Become More Thankful

*"Giving thanks always for all things to God the Father
in the name of our Lord Jesus Christ" (Eph. 5:20).*

Take time to fill in your "Thankful List/Journal" for today.

Then, give thanks to God.

Today, I am thankful for:

_____

_____

_____

_____

_____

_____

_____

_____

_____

_____

_____

_____

Special Thanksgiving for Day #10:

Give a special thanks to God today for
The Abundance of Spiritual Blessings from God
(Eph. 1:3; John 10:10; Jas. 1:17; Prov. 10:22).

Day #11 to Become More Thankful

"Giving thanks always for all things to God the Father
in the name of our Lord Jesus Christ" (Eph. 5:20).

Take time to fill in your "Thankful List/Journal" for today.

Then, give thanks to God.

Today, I am thankful for:

_____

_____

_____

_____

_____

_____

_____

_____

_____

_____

_____

_____

Special Thanksgiving for Day #11:

Give a special thanks to God today for
The Burdens That God Bears for You
(Psa. 55:22; 1 Pet. 5:6-7; Matt. 6:8; 7:7-11; 11:28-30).

Day #12 to Become More Thankful

*"Giving thanks always for all things to God the Father
in the name of our Lord Jesus Christ" (Eph. 5:20).*

Take time to fill in your "Thankful List/Journal" for today.

Then, give thanks to God.

Today, I am thankful for:

Day #13 to Become More Thankful

*"Giving thanks always for all things to God the Father
in the name of our Lord Jesus Christ" (Eph. 5:20).*

Take time to fill in your "Thankful List/Journal" for today.

Then, give thanks to God.

Today, I am thankful for:

_____

_____

_____

_____

_____

_____

_____

_____

_____

_____

_____

_____

Special Thanksgiving for Day #13:

Give a special thanks to God today for
Deliverance from Temptation
(Matt. 6:13; 26:41; 1 Cor. 10:13; 2 Pet. 2:9).

Day #14 to Become More Thankful

"Giving thanks always for all things to God the Father in the name of our Lord Jesus Christ" (Eph. 5:20).

Take time to fill in your "Thankful List/Journal" for today.

Then, give thanks to God.

Today, I am thankful for:

_____

_____

_____

_____

_____

_____

_____

_____

_____

_____

_____

_____

Special Thanksgiving for Day #14:

Give a special thanks to God today for
Daily Provisions Supplied By God
(Matt. 6:11, 25-34; Phil. 4:19; Psa. 23:1).

Day #15 to Become More Thankful

*"Giving thanks always for all things to God the Father
in the name of our Lord Jesus Christ" (Eph. 5:20).*

Take time to fill in your "Thankful List/Journal" for today.

Then, give thanks to God.

Today, I am thankful for:

Special Thanksgiving for Day #15:

Give a special thanks to God today for
The Peace of God Which Surpasses Understanding
(Phil. 4:6-7; John 16:33; Rom. 5:1; Col. 3:15).

Day #16 to Become More Thankful

*"Giving thanks always for all things to God the Father
in the name of our Lord Jesus Christ" (Eph. 5:20).*

Take time to fill in your "Thankful List/Journal" for today.

Then, give thanks to God.

Today, I am thankful for:

_____

_____

_____

_____

_____

_____

_____

_____

_____

_____

_____

_____

_____

Special Thanksgiving for Day #16:

Give a special thanks to God today for
The Church That Belongs to Christ
(Matt. 16:18; Acts 20:28; Eph. 1:22-23; 3:10-11, 21).

Day #17 to Become More Thankful

*"Giving thanks always for all things to God the Father
in the name of our Lord Jesus Christ" (Eph. 5:20).*

Take time to fill in your "Thankful List/Journal" for today.

Then, give thanks to God.

Today, I am thankful for:

Day #18 to Become More Thankful

*"Giving thanks always for all things to God the Father
in the name of our Lord Jesus Christ" (Eph. 5:20).*

Take time to fill in your "Thankful List/Journal" for today.

Then, give thanks to God.

Today, I am thankful for:

_____

_____

_____

_____

_____

_____

_____

_____

_____

_____

_____

Special Thanksgiving for Day #18:

Give a special thanks to God today for
Faithful Leaders of the Lord's Church
(1 Thess. 5:11-13; 1 Tim. 5:17; Heb. 13:17-18).

Day #19 to Become More Thankful

"Giving thanks always for all things to God the Father in the name of our Lord Jesus Christ" (Eph. 5:20).

Take time to fill in your "Thankful List/Journal" for today.

Then, give thanks to God.

Today, I am thankful for:

Day #20 to Become More Thankful

*"Giving thanks always for all things to God the Father
in the name of our Lord Jesus Christ" (Eph. 5:20).*

Take time to fill in your "Thankful List/Journal" for today.

Then, give thanks to God.

Today, I am thankful for:

Special Thanksgiving for Day #20:

Give a special thanks to God today for
Your Family
(Eph. 5:22-6:4; Psa. 127:1-5; 1 Tim. 5:4; Prov. 31:10-31; 18:22).

Day #21 to Become More Thankful

*"Giving thanks always for all things to God the Father
in the name of our Lord Jesus Christ" (Eph. 5:20).*

Take time to fill in your "Thankful List/Journal" for today.

Then, give thanks to God.

Today, I am thankful for:

_____

_____

_____

_____

_____

_____

_____

_____

_____

_____

_____

_____

Special Thanksgiving for Day #21:

Give a special thanks to God today for
The Privilege of Telling Others about Jesus Christ
(Mark 16:15; Matt. 28:19-20; Col. 1:28).

Day #22 to Become More Thankful

*"Giving thanks always for all things to God the Father
in the name of our Lord Jesus Christ" (Eph. 5:20).*

Take time to fill in your "Thankful List/Journal" for today.

Then, give thanks to God.

Today, I am thankful for:

_____

_____

_____

_____

_____

_____

_____

_____

_____

_____

_____

_____

Special Thanksgiving for Day #22:

Give a special thanks to God today for
The Opportunity to Give to God
(2 Cor. 9:7-8; Matt. 6:19-21; Acts 20:35; Luke 6:38).

Day #23 to Become More Thankful

*"Giving thanks always for all things to God the Father
in the name of our Lord Jesus Christ" (Eph. 5:20).*

Take time to fill in your "Thankful List/Journal" for today.

Then, give thanks to God.

Today, I am thankful for:

Day #24 to Become More Thankful

"Giving thanks always for all things to God the Father
in the name of our Lord Jesus Christ" (Eph. 5:20).

Take time to fill in your "Thankful List/Journal" for today.

Then, give thanks to God.

Today, I am thankful for:

Special Thanksgiving for Day #24:

Give a special thanks to God today for
The Privilege of Worship
(Psa. 122:1; John 4:23-24; Col. 3:16; Heb. 10:24-25).

Day #25 to Become More Thankful

*"Giving thanks always for all things to God the Father
in the name of our Lord Jesus Christ" (Eph. 5:20).*

Take time to fill in your "Thankful List/Journal" for today.

Then, give thanks to God.

Today, I am thankful for:

Special Thanksgiving for Day #25:

Give a special thanks to God today for
The Continual Presence of God in Your Life
(Matt. 28:20; Heb. 13:5; Psa. 139:1-24; Josh. 1:5, 9).

Day #26 to Become More Thankful

*"Giving thanks always for all things to God the Father
in the name of our Lord Jesus Christ" (Eph. 5:20).*

Take time to fill in your "Thankful List/Journal" for today.

Then, give thanks to God.

Today, I am thankful for:

Day #27 to Become More Thankful

*"Giving thanks always for all things to God the Father
in the name of our Lord Jesus Christ" (Eph. 5:20).*

Take time to fill in your "Thankful List/Journal" for today.

Then, give thanks to God.

Today, I am thankful for:

Day #28 to Become More Thankful

*"Giving thanks always for all things to God the Father
in the name of our Lord Jesus Christ" (Eph. 5:20).*

Take time to fill in your "Thankful List/Journal" for today.

Then, give thanks to God.

Today, I am thankful for:

_____

_____

_____

_____

_____

_____

_____

_____

_____

_____

_____

_____

Special Thanksgiving for Day #28:

Give a special thanks to God today for
God Is Able and in Control
(Eph. 3:20-21; Prov. 19:21; Mark 10:27; Psa. 37:23-25).

Walking Daily with My Lord

DECEMBER:

2|8 DAYS

To Encourage One Another

"Therefore encourage one another
and build up one another,
just as you also are doing"
(1 Thessalonians 5:11).

28DAYS To Encourage One Another

Every Christian (Without Exception) Needs Encouragement!

It Is the Responsibility of Every Christian (Without Exception) to Encourage Fellow Christians!

The work of effective encouragement of others requires:

1. **Observation**

   - Put Our Eyes on Each Other (Acts 11:23, 25; Matt. 9:36).

   - Put Our Minds on Each Other (Heb. 10:24).

2. **Operation**

   - Our Purpose: Call alongside and build up (1 Thess. 5:11).

   - Our Procedure: In word and in deed (1 John 3:18).

   - Our Persistence: Daily and without delay (Heb. 3:13).

Use the following pages over the next 28 days to:

1. Identify people in the church to encourage.

2. Identify ways to effectively encourage brethren.

3. Use the special category of encouragement each day.

4. Consider ways that you have been encouraged.

5. Ask God to help you to be a better encourager.

Let's encourage one another over the next 28 days...

☐ Day 1	☐ Day 8	☐ Day 15	☐ Day 22
☐ Day 2	☐ Day 9	☐ Day 16	☐ Day 23
☐ Day 3	☐ Day 10	☐ Day 17	☐ Day 24
☐ Day 4	☐ Day 11	☐ Day 18	☐ Day 25
☐ Day 5	☐ Day 12	☐ Day 19	☐ Day 26
☐ Day 6	☐ Day 13	☐ Day 20	☐ Day 27
☐ Day 7	☐ Day 14	☐ Day 21	☐ Day 28

Day #1 to Encourage One Another

*"Therefore encourage one another and build up one another,
just as you also are doing" (1 Thess. 5:11).*

Take time to fill in your "Encouragement Journal" for today.

Pray and ask God to help you to be an encourager today.

Someone I tried to encourage today:

_____

_____

How I tried to encourage someone today:

_____

_____

_____

Someone who encouraged me today:

_____

_____

How I was encouraged today:

_____

_____

_____

Special Way to Encourage Someone Today #1:

**Send a note:
"I'm glad that you're my brother/sister in Christ!"**
(Phil. 1:3-5).

Day #2 to Encourage One Another

"Therefore encourage one another and build up one another,
just as you also are doing" (1 Thess. 5:11).

Take time to fill in your "Encouragement Journal" for today.

Pray and ask God to help you to be an encourager today.

Someone I tried to encourage today:

_____

_____

How I tried to encourage someone today:

_____

_____

_____

Someone who encouraged me today:

_____

_____

How I was encouraged today:

_____

_____

_____

Special Way to Encourage Someone Today #2:

Seek to build someone up
who is discouraged or overwhelmed
(1 Thess. 5:14).

Day #3 to Encourage One Another

"Therefore encourage one another and build up one another,
just as you also are doing" (1 Thess. 5:11).

Take time to fill in your "Encouragement Journal" for today.

Pray and ask God to help you to be an encourager today.

Someone I tried to encourage today:

_____

_____

How I tried to encourage someone today:

_____

_____

_____

Someone who encouraged me today:

_____

_____

How I was encouraged today:

_____

_____

_____

Special Way to Encourage Someone Today #3:

**Express appreciation
to an elder for his labors**
(1 Thess. 5:12-13).

Day #4 to Encourage One Another

*"Therefore encourage one another and build up one another,
just as you also are doing" (1 Thess. 5:11).*

Take time to fill in your "Encouragement Journal" for today.

Pray and ask God to help you to be an encourager today.

Someone I tried to encourage today:

How I tried to encourage someone today:

Someone who encouraged me today:

How I was encouraged today:

Special Way to Encourage Someone Today #4:

**Visit a widow or shut-in
or elderly member in their home**
(Jas. 1:27).

Day #5 to Encourage One Another

"Therefore encourage one another and build up one another,
just as you also are doing" (1 Thess. 5:11).

Take time to fill in your "Encouragement Journal" for today.

Pray and ask God to help you to be an encourager today.

Someone I tried to encourage today:

How I tried to encourage someone today:

Someone who encouraged me today:

How I was encouraged today:

Special Way to Encourage Someone Today #5:

Plan to be at worship and church services
every time you can
(Heb. 10:25).

Day #6 to Encourage One Another

"Therefore encourage one another and build up one another,
just as you also are doing" (1 Thess. 5:11).

Take time to fill in your "Encouragement Journal" for today.

Pray and ask God to help you to be an encourager today.

Someone I tried to encourage today:

_____

_____

How I tried to encourage someone today:

_____

_____

_____

Someone who encouraged me today:

_____

_____

How I was encouraged today:

_____

_____

_____

Special Way to Encourage Someone Today #6:

Make a call:
"I just wanted to see how you're doing today"
(1 Cor. 12:25).

Day #7 to Encourage One Another

"Therefore encourage one another and build up one another,
just as you also are doing" (1 Thess. 5:11).

Take time to fill in your "Encouragement Journal" for today.

Pray and ask God to help you to be an encourager today.

Someone I tried to encourage today:

_____

_____

How I tried to encourage someone today:

_____

_____

_____

Someone who encouraged me today:

_____

_____

How I was encouraged today:

_____

_____

_____

Special Way to Encourage Someone Today #7:

Compliment someone
who recently did a good job in the church
(Mark 14:6-9).

Day #8 to Encourage One Another

*"Therefore encourage one another and build up one another,
just as you also are doing" (1 Thess. 5:11).*

Take time to fill in your "Encouragement Journal" for today.

Pray and ask God to help you to be an encourager today.

Someone I tried to encourage today:

_____

_____

How I tried to encourage someone today:

_____

_____

_____

Someone who encouraged me today:

_____

_____

How I was encouraged today:

_____

_____

_____

Special Way to Encourage Someone Today #8:

**Invite someone
to have lunch or coffee together**
(Acts 2:46).

Day #9 to Encourage One Another

"Therefore encourage one another and build up one another,
just as you also are doing" (1 Thess. 5:11).

Take time to fill in your "Encouragement Journal" for today.

Pray and ask God to help you to be an encourager today.

Someone I tried to encourage today:

How I tried to encourage someone today:

Someone who encouraged me today:

How I was encouraged today:

Special Way to Encourage Someone Today #9:

**Lend a helping hand
to someone in the church**
(Gal. 5:13).

Day #10 to Encourage One Another

*"Therefore encourage one another and build up one another,
just as you also are doing" (1 Thess. 5:11).*

Take time to fill in your "Encouragement Journal" for today.

Pray and ask God to help you to be an encourager today.

Someone I tried to encourage today:

_____

_____

How I tried to encourage someone today:

_____

_____

_____

Someone who encouraged me today:

_____

_____

How I was encouraged today:

_____

_____

_____

Special Way to Encourage Someone Today #10:

**Send a note:
"I prayed for you today! May God bless you!"**
(Eph. 1:15-16).

Day #11 to Encourage One Another

"Therefore encourage one another and build up one another,
just as you also are doing" (1 Thess. 5:11).

Take time to fill in your "Encouragement Journal" for today.

Pray and ask God to help you to be an encourager today.

Someone I tried to encourage today:

How I tried to encourage someone today:

Someone who encouraged me today:

How I was encouraged today:

Special Way to Encourage Someone Today #11:

Smile and give a warm hug
to someone who has struggled lately
(Phil. 2:28-30).

Day #12 to Encourage One Another

*"Therefore encourage one another and build up one another,
just as you also are doing" (1 Thess. 5:11).*

Take time to fill in your "Encouragement Journal" for today.

Pray and ask God to help you to be an encourager today.

Someone I tried to encourage today:

_____

_____

How I tried to encourage someone today:

_____

_____

_____

Someone who encouraged me today:

_____

_____

How I was encouraged today:

_____

_____

_____

Special Way to Encourage Someone Today #12:

**Express appreciation
to someone who may rarely receive any**
(Col. 4:12-13).

Day #13 to Encourage One Another

"Therefore encourage one another and build up one another,
just as you also are doing" (1 Thess. 5:11).

Take time to fill in your "Encouragement Journal" for today.

Pray and ask God to help you to be an encourager today.

Someone I tried to encourage today:

_____

_____

How I tried to encourage someone today:

_____

_____

_____

Someone who encouraged me today:

_____

_____

How I was encouraged today:

_____

_____

_____

Special Way to Encourage Someone Today #13:

Share a Bible verse
that means a lot to you and has helped you
(Acts 20:32).

Day #14 to Encourage One Another

"Therefore encourage one another and build up one another,
just as you also are doing" (1 Thess. 5:11).

Take time to fill in your "Encouragement Journal" for today.

Pray and ask God to help you to be an encourager today.

Someone I tried to encourage today:

_____

_____

How I tried to encourage someone today:

_____

_____

_____

Someone who encouraged me today:

_____

_____

How I was encouraged today:

_____

_____

_____

Special Way to Encourage Someone Today #14:

Celebrate and congratulate
an accomplishment someone enjoyed
(1 Cor. 12:26b).

Day #15 to Encourage One Another

*"Therefore encourage one another and build up one another,
just as you also are doing" (1 Thess. 5:11).*

Take time to fill in your "Encouragement Journal" for today.

Pray and ask God to help you to be an encourager today.

Someone I tried to encourage today:

How I tried to encourage someone today:

Someone who encouraged me today:

How I was encouraged today:

Special Way to Encourage Someone Today #15:

**Extend comfort or sympathy
to someone suffering or lonely**
(2 Cor. 1:3-6).

Day #16 to Encourage One Another

"Therefore encourage one another and build up one another,
just as you also are doing" (1 Thess. 5:11).

Take time to fill in your "Encouragement Journal" for today.

Pray and ask God to help you to be an encourager today.

Someone I tried to encourage today:

_____

_____

How I tried to encourage someone today:

_____

_____

_____

Someone who encouraged me today:

_____

_____

How I was encouraged today:

_____

_____

_____

Special Way to Encourage Someone Today #16:

Send a note:
"I'm glad that we are part of the same church!"
(Col. 1:3-4).

Day #17 to Encourage One Another

"Therefore encourage one another and build up one another,
just as you also are doing" (1 Thess. 5:11).

Take time to fill in your "Encouragement Journal" for today.

Pray and ask God to help you to be an encourager today.

Someone I tried to encourage today:

How I tried to encourage someone today:

Someone who encouraged me today:

How I was encouraged today:

Special Way to Encourage Someone Today #17:

Arrive early or stay late at worship
to meet, greet and visit
(3 John 14).

Day #18 to Encourage One Another

"Therefore encourage one another and build up one another,
just as you also are doing" (1 Thess. 5:11).

Take time to fill in your "Encouragement Journal" for today.

Pray and ask God to help you to be an encourager today.

Someone I tried to encourage today:

_____

_____

How I tried to encourage someone today:

_____

_____

_____

Someone who encouraged me today:

_____

_____

How I was encouraged today:

_____

_____

_____

Special Way to Encourage Someone Today #18:

Take a meal to someone
who has been having a hard time
(Acts 20:35).

Day #19 to Encourage One Another

*"Therefore encourage one another and build up one another,
just as you also are doing" (1 Thess. 5:11).*

Take time to fill in your "Encouragement Journal" for today.

Pray and ask God to help you to be an encourager today.

Someone I tried to encourage today:

How I tried to encourage someone today:

Someone who encouraged me today:

How I was encouraged today:

Special Way to Encourage Someone Today #19:

**Express appreciation
to someone who works for the church**
(1 Cor. 15:58).

Day #20 to Encourage One Another

*"Therefore encourage one another and build up one another,
just as you also are doing" (1 Thess. 5:11).*

Take time to fill in your "Encouragement Journal" for today.

Pray and ask God to help you to be an encourager today.

Someone I tried to encourage today:

_____

_____

How I tried to encourage someone today:

_____

_____

_____

Someone who encouraged me today:

_____

_____

How I was encouraged today:

_____

_____

_____

Special Way to Encourage Someone Today #20:

**Send a note of praise
to a young person in the church**
(2 Tim. 1:3-4).

Day #21 to Encourage One Another

*"Therefore encourage one another and build up one another,
just as you also are doing" (1 Thess. 5:11).*

Take time to fill in your "Encouragement Journal" for today.

Pray and ask God to help you to be an encourager today.

Someone I tried to encourage today:

How I tried to encourage someone today:

Someone who encouraged me today:

How I was encouraged today:

Special Way to Encourage Someone Today #21:

**Invite someone
to hang out or go somewhere together**
(2 Tim. 4:9).

Day #22 to Encourage One Another

"Therefore encourage one another and build up one another,
just as you also are doing" (1 Thess. 5:11).

Take time to fill in your "Encouragement Journal" for today.

Pray and ask God to help you to be an encourager today.

Someone I tried to encourage today:

_____

_____

How I tried to encourage someone today:

_____

_____

_____

Someone who encouraged me today:

_____

_____

How I was encouraged today:

_____

_____

_____

Special Way to Encourage Someone Today #22:

Reach out to someone
who always seems to reach out to others
(3 John 1-4).

Day #23 to Encourage One Another

"Therefore encourage one another and build up one another,
just as you also are doing" (1 Thess. 5:11).

Take time to fill in your "Encouragement Journal" for today.

Pray and ask God to help you to be an encourager today.

Someone I tried to encourage today:

How I tried to encourage someone today:

Someone who encouraged me today:

How I was encouraged today:

Special Way to Encourage Someone Today #23:

Make a call:
"I was thinking about you and praying for you today"
(Phil. 1:7-11).

Day #24 to Encourage One Another

*"Therefore encourage one another and build up one another,
just as you also are doing" (1 Thess. 5:11).*

Take time to fill in your "Encouragement Journal" for today.

Pray and ask God to help you to be an encourager today.

Someone I tried to encourage today:

_____

_____

How I tried to encourage someone today:

_____

_____

_____

Someone who encouraged me today:

_____

_____

How I was encouraged today:

_____

_____

_____

Special Way to Encourage Someone Today #24:

**Express appreciation
for a kind act of service done to another**
(3 John 5-6).

Day #25 to Encourage One Another

*"Therefore encourage one another and build up one another,
just as you also are doing" (1 Thess. 5:11).*

Take time to fill in your "Encouragement Journal" for today.

Pray and ask God to help you to be an encourager today.

Someone I tried to encourage today:

_____

_____

How I tried to encourage someone today:

_____

_____

_____

Someone who encouraged me today:

_____

_____

How I was encouraged today:

_____

_____

_____

Special Way to Encourage Someone Today #25:

**Let someone who is missing worship
know he/she is missed**
(Heb. 10:24).

Day #26 to Encourage One Another

*"Therefore encourage one another and build up one another,
just as you also are doing" (1 Thess. 5:11).*

Take time to fill in your "Encouragement Journal" for today.

Pray and ask God to help you to be an encourager today.

Someone I tried to encourage today:

How I tried to encourage someone today:

Someone who encouraged me today:

How I was encouraged today:

Special Way to Encourage Someone Today #26:

**Invite others
into your home for fellowship**
(1 Pet. 4:9).

Day #27 to Encourage One Another

*"Therefore encourage one another and build up one another,
just as you also are doing" (1 Thess. 5:11).*

Take time to fill in your "Encouragement Journal" for today.

Pray and ask God to help you to be an encourager today.

Someone I tried to encourage today:

_____

_____

How I tried to encourage someone today:

_____

_____

_____

Someone who encouraged me today:

_____

_____

How I was encouraged today:

_____

_____

_____

Special Way to Encourage Someone Today #27:

**Send a note of praise
to a young parent in the church**
(1 Sam. 1:26-28).

Day #28 to Encourage One Another

"Therefore encourage one another and build up one another,
just as you also are doing" (1 Thess. 5:11).

Take time to fill in your "Encouragement Journal" for today.

Pray and ask God to help you to be an encourager today.

Someone I tried to encourage today:

How I tried to encourage someone today:

Someone who encouraged me today:

How I was encouraged today:

Special Way to Encourage Someone Today #28:

**Do a random (even little) act of kindness
for a church member**
(Gal. 6:10).

Made in the USA
Columbia, SC
29 December 2018